"When this anthology knocks at your door, open it and join the dance. Combining the canonic and the unexpected, Paola S. Hernández and Analola Santana have assembled here an impressive team of collaborators in order to embrace and interrogate the full performatic complexity of our Latinx histories. The book will foster many critical re-examinations and controversies in the years to come. This is an indispensable contribution to our field."

Leo Cabranes-Grant, University of California, Santa Bárbara/Changó

"Editors Paola S. Hernández and Analola Santana have curated an eminently useful collection of concise but meaty introductions to fifty of the Latinx Americas' greatest theatre and performance artists and groups. Ranging from Aguirre to Yuyachkani, their collective activity spans the last seven decades and the entire hemisphere; and the essays, written by some of today's leading theatre and performance studies scholars, will leave the reader eager for more volumes."

Jean Graham-Jones, Lucille Lortel Professor of Theatre, CUNY, New York

FIFTY KEY FIGURES IN LATINX AND LATIN AMERICAN THEATRE

Fifty Key Figures in Latinx and Latin American Theatre is a critical introduction to the most influential and innovative theatre practitioners in the Americas, all of whom have been pioneers in changing the field. The chosen artists work through political, racial, gender, class, and geographical divides to expand our understanding of Latin American and Latinx theatre while at the same time offering a space to discuss contested nationalities and histories. Each entry considers the artist's or collective's body of work in its historical, cultural, and political context and provides a brief biography and suggestions for further reading. The volume covers artists from the present day to the 1960s—the emergence of a modern theatre that was concerned with Latinx and Latin American themes distancing themselves from an European approach.

A deep and enriching resource for the classroom and individual study, this is the first book that any student of Latinx and Latin American theatre should read.

Paola S. Hernández is Professor of Spanish & Interdisciplinary Theatre Studies at the University of Wisconsin-Madison.

Analola Santana is Associate Professor of Latin American Theatre at Dartmouth College.

ROUTLEDGE KEY GUIDES

Fifty Key Theatre Directors
Shomit Mitter and Maria Shevtsova

Fifty Key Contemporary Thinkers
John Lechte

Art History
The Key Concepts
Jonathan Harris

Fifty Contemporary Choreographers
Jo Butterworth and Lorna Sanders

Fifty Key Figures in Latinx and Latin American Theatre
Edited by Paola S. Hernández and Analola Santana

For a full list of titles in this series, please visit: https://www.routledge.com/Routledge-Key-Guides/book-series/RKG

FIFTY KEY FIGURES IN LATINX AND LATIN AMERICAN THEATRE

Edited by
Paola S. Hernández and Analola Santana

LONDON AND NEW YORK

Cover image: © Lightspring | Shutterstock

Published 2022
by Routledge
4 Park Square, Milton Park, Abingdon, Oxon, OX14 4RN

and by Routledge
52 Vanderbilt Avenue, New York, NY 10017

Routledge is an imprint of the Taylor & Francis Group, an informa business

© 2022 selection and editorial matter, Paola S. Hernández and Analola Santana; individual chapters, the contributors

The right of Paola S. Hernández and Analola Santana to be identified as the authors of the editorial material, and of the authors for their individual chapters, has been asserted in accordance with sections 77 and 78 of the Copyright, Designs and Patents Act 1988.

All rights reserved. No part of this book may be reprinted or reproduced or utilised in any form or by any electronic, mechanical, or other means, now known or hereafter invented, including photocopying and recording, or in any information storage or retrieval system, without permission in writing from the publishers.

Trademark notice: Product or corporate names may be trademarks or registered trademarks, and are used only for identification and explanation without intent to infringe.

British Library Cataloguing-in-Publication Data
A catalogue record for this book is available from the British Library

Library of Congress Cataloging-in-Publication Data
A catalog record has been requested for this book

ISBN: 978-0-367-70131-4 (hbk)
ISBN: 978-0-367-70127-7 (pbk)
ISBN: 978-1-003-14470-0 (ebk)

DOI: 10.4324/9781003144700

Typeset in Bembo
by Newgen Publishing UK

In loving memory of Laurietz Seda, who left us too soon, but whose contributions to the field of Latin American theatre will always be remembered.

CONTENTS

Alphabetical list of contents   x
Notes on contributors   xiv

Introduction   1
PAOLA S. HERNÁNDEZ AND ANALOLA SANTANA

Fifty Key Figures in Latinx and Latin American Theatre   19

ALPHABETICAL LIST OF CONTENTS

Carmen Aguirre (1967–)	21
MARTHA HERRERA-LASSO GONZÁLEZ	
Luis Alfaro (1963–)	24
DAVID ROMÁN	
Lola Arias (1976–)	28
CECILIA SOSA	
Quique Avilés (1965–)	33
ELAINE M. MILLER	
Josefina Báez (1960–)	37
MEGAN BAILON	
Sabina Berman (1955–)	41
STUART A. DAY	
Augusto Boal (1931–2009)	45
GINA SANDÍ-DÍAZ	
Guillermo Calderón (1971–)	49
JENNIFER JOAN THOMPSON	
El Ciervo Encantado (1996–)	53
BRETTON WHITE	
Migdalia Cruz (1958–)	57
LILLIAN MANZOR	
Nilo Cruz (1961–)	61
DEBRA A. CASTILLO	

ALPHABETICAL LIST OF CONTENTS

Cuatrotablas (1971–) and Mario Delgado (1947–2016) LETICIA ROBLES-MORENO	65
María Irene Fornés (1930–2018) ANNE GARCÍA-ROMERO	69
Griselda Gambaro (1928–) BRENDA WERTH	73
Guillermo Gómez-Peña (1955–) PAOLA MARÍN	78
Quiara Alegría Hudes (1977–) JASON RAMÍREZ	83
Manuela Infante (1980–) CARLOS A. ORTIZ	87
Sara Joffré (1935–2014) LAURIETZ SEDA	90
KIMVN Teatro (2008–) and Paula González Seguel (1983–) JIMMY A. NORIEGA	94
Lagartijas Tiradas al Sol (2003–) JULIE ANN WARD	98
John Leguizamo (1964–) JIMMY A. NORIEGA	101
Conchi León (1973–) CHRISTINA BAKER	105
Josefina López (1969–) MICHELLE WARREN	109
Eduardo Machado (1953–) ERIC MAYER-GARCÍA	112
Rosa Luisa Márquez (1947–) KIMBERLY DEL BUSTO RAMÍREZ	116
Lin-Manuel Miranda (1980–) PATRICIA HERRERA	121

ALPHABETICAL LIST OF CONTENTS

Cherríe Moraga (1952–)	125
MELISSA HUERTA	
Gustavo Ott (1963–)	130
ANGELA MARINO	
Dolores Prida (1943–2013)	133
ISRAEL REYES	
Juan Radrigán (1937–2016)	137
ANA ELENA PUGA	
Jesusa Rodríguez (1955–)	142
GASTÓN A. ALZATE	
Marco Antonio Rodríguez (1971–)	147
CAMILLA STEVENS	
Hugo Salcedo (1964–)	150
IANI MORENO	
Luis Rafael Sánchez (1936–)	154
ERIC MAYER-GARCÍA	
Octavio Solis (1958–)	158
CARLA DELLA GATTA	
Rafael Spregelburd (1970–)	162
GAIL A. BULMAN	
Caridad Svich (1963–)	167
TREVOR BOFFONE	
Teatro de los Andes (1991–)	171
BEATRIZ J. RIZK	
El Teatro Campesino (1965–) and Luis Valdez (1940–)	176
JORGE A. HUERTA	
Teatro La Candelaria (1966–) and Santiago García (1928–2020)	181
LAISSA M. RODRÍGUEZ MORENO	
Teatro de Ciertos Habitantes (1997–) and Claudio Valdés Kuri (1965–)	185
ANALOLA SANTANA	

ALPHABETICAL LIST OF CONTENTS

Teatro La Fragua (1979–) LISA JACKSON-SCHEBETTA	189
Teatro El Galpón (1949–) SARAH M. MISEMER	193
Teatro Línea de Sombra (1993–) PAOLA S. HERNÁNDEZ	198
Teatro Malayerba (1979–) and Arístides Vargas (1954–) LOLA PROAÑO GÓMEZ	202
Teatro da Vertigem (1992–) CARLOS CORTEZ MINCHILLO	206
Vivi Tellas (1955–) PAMELA BROWNELL	209
Timbre 4 (1999–) and Claudio Tolcachir (1975–) ANNA WHITE-NOCKLEBY	213
Cándido Tirado (1955–) JASON RAMÍREZ	217
Grupo Cultural Yuyachkani (1971–) KATHERINE JEAN NIGH	221

NOTES ON CONTRIBUTORS

Gastón A. Alzate is Professor of Latin American Theater at California State University, Los Angeles. He obtained the National Essay Award in 1993 (Colombian Ministry of Culture). In 2011 he was Resident Researcher at the Freie Universität in Berlin. In 2017 he received the Woodyard Professorship (Latin American Theatre Review). He is well known for his work on Mexican cabaret, is editor of *Editorial KARPA* (2008–present), and has published in the United States, Mexico, Brazil, Colombia, Turkey, Spain, Germany, and France.

Megan Bailon recently completed her PhD in the Department of Spanish and Portuguese at the University of Wisconsin-Madison where she currently is Lecturer in Chican@ and Latin@ Studies. Her current research interests include embodied explorations of labor in migration in contemporary Caribbean theatre and performance art and the politics of care in performance.

Christina Baker is Assistant Professor of Latin/x American Theatre at Temple University. Focusing on twenty-first-century Mexican theatre and performance, her work explores how sound design, musical choices, and other sonic stimuli relate dissident socio-political critiques and create possibilities for articulating new definitions of belonging. She has published numerous scholarly articles and reviews in journals such as *Chasqui*, *Romance Notes*, *Revista de Estudios Hispánicos*, and *Latin American Theatre Review*.

Trevor Boffone is Lecturer in the Women's, Gender & Sexuality Studies Program at the University of Houston. He is the author of *Renegades: Digital Dance Cultures from Dubsmash to TikTok* (Oxford University Press, 2021). He is the co-editor of various volumes: *Encuentro: Latinx Performance for the New American Theater*; *Nerds, Goths,*

Geeks, and Freaks: Outsiders in Chicanx and Latinx Young Adult Literature; *Shakespeare and Latinidad*; and *Seeking Common Ground: Latinx and Latin American Theatre and Performance*.

Pamela Brownell is Assistant Professor in Theatre Theory and Criticism at the University of Buenos Aires and a postdoctoral fellow of the National Research and Technical Research Council (CONICET) at the National University of the Arts. She holds a PhD in Art History and Theory (UBA) and graduate degrees in Arts (UBA) and Journalism (UNLZ). Her current research focuses on documentary and biographical practices in contemporary Latin American theatre.

Gail A. Bulman is Associate Professor of Spanish and Director of the Program on Latin America and the Caribbean at Syracuse University, where she teaches Latin American theatre and narrative. She is the author of *Staging Words, Performing Worlds: Intertextuality and Nation in Contemporary Latin American Theater* (Bucknell University Press, 2007) and *Feeling the Gaze: Image and Affect in Contemporary Argentine and Chilean Performance* (University of North Carolina Press, 2022) and several published articles and book chapters.

Debra A. Castillo is Stephen H. Weiss Presidential Fellow, Emerson Hinchliff Professor of Hispanic Studies, and Professor of Comparative Literature at Cornell University. Her most recent books include *Mexican Public Intellectuals* (Palgrave Macmillan, 2014 with Stuart Day), *South of the Future: Speculative Biotechnologies and Care Markets in South Asia and Latin America* (SUNY-Albany University Press, 2020 with Anindita Banerjee) and *The Scholar as Human* (Cornell University Press, 2021 with Anna Sims Bartel).

Carlos Cortez Minchillo is Associate Professor in the Department of Spanish and Portuguese at Dartmouth College. He specializes in modern and contemporary Brazilian literature and inter-American cultural exchanges in the twentieth century. He is the author of *Erico Verissimo, escritor do mundo* (Edusp, 2016) [Erico Verissimo, World Writer], awarded with the 2018 Casa de las Américas Prize. Minchillo is currently working on fictional representations of dissidence and insurgency in Brazilian literature, theatre, cinema, and popular music.

Stuart A. Day is Professor of Spanish at the University of Kansas. A graduate of Northern Arizona University, the University of Arizona, and Cornell University, his recent books and editions include *Outside Theater: Alliances That Shape Mexico* (University of Arizona Press, 2017), *Modern Mexican Culture* (University of Arizona Press, 2017), *Mexican Public Intellectuals* (with Debra A. Castillo, Palgrave Macmillan, 2014), and *Performances that Change the Americas* (Routledge, 2021). Day is Managing Editor of the *Latin American Theatre Review*.

Kimberly del Busto Ramírez is Professor of English at LaGuardia-CUNY. Her specializations include drama and performance related to the unaccompanied children's exodus *Operation Pedro Pan* that transported her mother, aunt, uncle, and 14,045 other Cuban children to the United States. Kim's academic and creative work has been featured in volumes, theatres, and conferences worldwide. She holds a PhD in Theatre from The Graduate Center-CUNY, and an MFA in Playwriting from the University of Georgia.

Carla Della Gatta is Assistant Professor of English at Florida State University. She is a theatre historian and performance theorist who examines ethnic and bilingual theatre through dramaturgy and aurality. She is author of *Latinx Shakespeares: Staging U.S. Intracultural Theater* (forthcoming from Michigan University Press, 2022) and co-editor with Trevor Boffone of *Shakespeare and Latinidad* (Edinburgh University Press, 2021). She has received awards and fellowships from the Woodrow Wilson Foundation, New York Public Library, Folger Shakespeare Library, and ASTR.

Anne García-Romero is Associate Professor in the Department of Film, Television, and Theatre at the University of Notre Dame. Her book *The Fornes Frame: Contemporary Latina Playwrights and the Legacy of Maria Irene Fornes* (University of Arizona Press, 2016) explores works by six award-winning Latina playwrights. As a playwright, her plays have been developed and produced at the Public Theater, Goodman Theatre, Mark Taper Forum, Los Angeles Theatre Center, and South Coast Repertory. She is a founding member of The Fornés Institute.

Paola S. Hernández is Professor of Spanish and Interdisciplinary Theatre Studies, and Director of the Center for Visual Cultures at the University of Wisconsin-Madison. She is the author of *Staging Lives in Latin America: Bodies-Objects-Archives* (Northwestern University Press, 2021) and *El teatro de Argentina y Chile: Globalización, resistencia y desencanto* (Corregidor, 2009). She is co-editor (with Pamela Brownell) of *Biodrama/Proyecto Archivos: seis documentales escénicos* by *Vivi Tellas* (Papeles Teatrales, Universidad de Córdoba, 2017), as well as of *Imagining Human Rights in Twenty-First-Century Theater: Global Perspectives* (with Brenda Werth and Florian Becker, Palgrave Macmillan, 2013).

Patricia Herrera is Associate Professor of Theater affiliated with American Studies and Women, Gender, and Sexualities Studies programs at the University of Richmond. As a community-engaged educator, scholar, and artist, she uses the arts, theatre, and performance to collectively practice justice. Her most recent book is *Nuyorican Feminist Performance* (University of Michigan Press, 2020). Since 2011 she worked on a public humanities project entitled *Civil Rights and Education in Richmond, Virginia: A Documentary Theater Project*, which has led to the creation of a digital archive The Fight for Knowledge, as well as three community exhibitions at The Valentine Museum and a series of seven docudramas about gentrification, educational disparities, HIV/AIDS, segregation, and Latinos in Richmond.

Martha Herrera-Lasso González is an independent scholar, dramaturg and playwright based in Mexico City. She holds a PhD in Performance Studies from UC Berkeley, an MA in Theatre Studies from UBC Vancouver, and a BA in Dramatic Literature and Theatre from UNAM in Mexico City.

Jorge A. Huerta holds the Chancellor's Associate's Endowed Chair III from the University of California, San Diego. He is a leading authority on contemporary Chicana/o and US Latina/o Theatre as well as a professional director. He has published several articles, edited three anthologies of plays, and written the landmark books: *Chicano Theatre: Themes and Forms* (Bilingual Press, 1982) and *Chicano Drama: Performance, Society, and Myth* (Cambridge 2000). Huerta has also directed in theatres across the country, including the San Diego Repertory, Seattle's Group Theatre, Washington, DC's Gala Hispanic Theatre, La Compañía de Teatro de Albuquerque and New York's Puerto Rican Traveling Theatre.

Melissa Huerta is Associate Professor of Spanish at Denison University, where she teaches Spanish language and courses in Latin American and Latinx literature, culture, and history. Her research focuses on Latinx theatre and performance. Huerta's current research focuses on the representation of Latinx reproductive decision-making in popular culture, such as theatre and television.

NOTES ON CONTRIBUTORS

Lisa Jackson-Schebetta is Associate Professor of Theater at Skidmore College. She has been published in *Theatre Survey*, *Theatre History Studies*, *Modern Drama*, *The Journal of American Drama and Theatre*, and others. Her first book is *Traveler, there is no road: Theatre, the Spanish Civil War and the Decolonial Imagination in the Americas* (University of Iowa Press, 2017). Her current project examines performance and peacemaking in the hemispheric Americas. She is a director, dramaturg, and devisor.

Lillian Manzor is Associate Professor of Modern Languages and Literatures, Hemispheric Caribbean Studies, and Founding Director of the Cuban Theater Digital Archive (www.cubantheater.org) at the University of Miami. She is co-editor of the book series Sualos, published jointly by Havana's Editorial Alarcos and Miami's CTDA Press. She is widely published in the field of Latin American and Latinx theatre and performance studies. As a community engaged scholar, she has developed US–Cuba cultural dialogues through theatre and performance.

Paola Marin is Associate Professor of Spanish at Cal State LA. She has published numerous articles and reviews on Spanish American and US Latinx artists in peer-reviewed journals in Latin America, the UK, and the US. Her translation into Spanish of Rustom Bharucha's *Performance and Terror* was released in 2017. She has co-edited several volumes on Latin American theatre and performance with Gastón Alzate (Ediciones Karpa, Cal State LA).

Angela Marino is Associate Professor in the Department of Theater, Dance, and Performance Studies of the University of California, Berkeley. She is the author of *Populism and Performance in the Bolivarian Revolution of Venezuela* (Northwestern University Press, 2018), which examines the role of popular performance in the political development of Venezuela's twenty-first-century socialism.

Eric Mayer-García is Assistant Professor of Theatre at Indiana University, Bloomington. He is currently working on his first book project, which draws on archival research to trace the transmission of theatre practices from Havana to different points in the Americas and back again, situating transnational movement as vital to the avant-garde. Mayer-García's research on Latinidad and histories of hemispheric exchange in experimental theatre has appeared in *Theatre History Studies*, *Chiricú Journal*, *Theatre Journal*, and various edited collections.

NOTES ON CONTRIBUTORS

Elaine M. Miller is Professor of Spanish at Christopher Newport University. A scholar of contemporary Central American and Mexican theatre and performance, she has published articles on Costa Rican and Mexican theatre and has co-edited *Diálogos dramatúrgicos: Costa Rica-México*, an anthology of Costa Rican and Mexican plays. She currently serves as contributing editor for Central American, Caribbean, and Mexican drama for the Library of Congress's *Handbook of Latin American Studies*.

Sarah M. Misemer is Professor in the Department of Hispanic Studies and Associate Director of undergraduate research in the LAUNCH office at Texas A&M University. She is the author of *Secular Saints: Performing Frida Kahlo, Carlos Gardel, Eva Perón, and Selena* (Tamesis, 2008), *Moving Forward, Looking Back: Trains, Literature, and the Arts in the River Plate* (Bucknell University Press, 2010), *Theatrical Topographies: Spatial Crises in Uruguayan Theater Post-2001* (Bucknell University Press, 2017) and co-editor of *The Trial That Never Ends: Hannah Arendt's Eichmann in Jerusalem in Retrospect* (Toronto University Press, 2017). She is the Editor for the Latin American Theatre Review Book series. Her main areas of research include contemporary Uruguayan and Argentine theatre, performance, and literature.

Iani Moreno is Associate Professor of Spanish at Suffolk University. Her interests include contemporary Latin American theatre, US–Mexico border studies, and contemporary Latin American cinema and music. She is the author of *Theatre of the Borderlands: Conflict, Violence, and Healing* (Lexington, 2017). She has directed university productions of contemporary Latin American plays and also translated numerous dramatic works written by Latin American dramatists.

Katherine Jean Nigh is Instructor in the Theater Arts Department at Pasadena City College. She is a performer, director, dramaturg, producer, and performance artist whose work deals with gender, queer identity, and the oppression of the female body (among other topics). Her research, pedagogy, and performance practices focus on theatre as a tool for social change/justice; performance of grief and mourning; national constructions of citizenship and belonging; and performance focused on race/gender and sexuality.

Jimmy A. Noriega is Associate Professor of Theatre at the College of Wooster. He is the co-editor of *Theatre and Cartographies of*

Power: Repositioning the Latina/o Americas (Southern Illinois University Press, 2018 with Analola Santana) and his research focuses on Latinx and Latin American theatre and performance. He has directed over fifty productions in English and Spanish, including invited performances at theatres and festivals in over a dozen countries. He is the current President of the American Society for Theatre Research (ASTR).

Carlos A. Ortiz is a PhD candidate at the University of Wisconsin-Madison specializing in contemporary Latin/x American theatre and performance. His current research examines contemporary performances that challenge the Western idea of the human. He incorporates theories from Queer Studies, New Media Studies, Cultural Studies, and New Materialisms into his research to argue that somatic and discursive explorations in performance can materialize more inclusive and sustainable conceptions of human beings.

Lola Proaño Gómez is Emeritus Professor at Pasadena City College. She has published *Poética, Política y Ruptura: Argentina 1966–73* (Atuel, Buenos Aires, 2002), *Poéticas de la globalización en el teatro latinoamericano* (Gestos, Irvine, 2007), *Estética comunitaria. Miradas desde la filosofía y la política* (Biblos, Buenos Aires, 2013); *Antología de teatro latinoamericano: 1950–2007* (Instituto Nacional de Teatro Argentino 2010). She has also published numerous articles and lectured across South America, the United States, England, Spain, and Germany. Currently she is Guest Researcher at the Gino Germani Institute for the Social Sciences at the University of Buenos Aires.

Ana Elena Puga is Associate Professor at The Ohio State University. She is the first author of *Performances of Suffering in Latin American Migration: Heroes, Martyrs, and Saints* (Palgrave Macmillan, 2020). She is also the author of *Memory, Allegory, and Testimony in South American Theatre: Upstaging Dictatorship* (Routledge, 2008) and the translator of an anthology of plays by Juan Rádrigan, *Finished From the Start and Other Plays* (Northwestern University Press, 2008).

Jason Ramírez is an award-winning actor, director, and playwright, holding memberships in the Actors' Equity Association, Society of Directors and Choreographers, and the Hispanic Organization of Latin Artists. As a playwright, he has been an award-winning member of María Irene Fornés's Hispanic Playwrights' in Residence Laboratory at INTAR, the Puerto Rican Traveling Theatre's Professional Playwrights' Unit, and the People's Theatre Playwrights' Project of

Washington Heights. He received his PhD from the CUNY Graduate Center and continues to investigate the intersection of Latino theatre and popular culture with an emphasis on commercial representations of Latinidad.

Israel Reyes is Associate Professor of Spanish and Portuguese at Dartmouth College. His publications include *Humor and the Eccentric Text in Puerto Rican Literature* (University Press of Florida, 2005), and scholarly articles on Judith Ortiz Cofer, Lalo Alcaraz, Nemesio Canales, Cristina García, and Manuel Ramos Otero. He is currently finishing a book manuscript titled *Embodied Economies: Diaspora and Transcultural Capital in Latinx Caribbean Fiction and Theater*.

Beatriz J. Rizk is the Educational Director of the International Hispanic Theatre Festival of Miami and a member of Teatro Avante. She has published numerous articles on Latina/o/x and Latin American theatre in specialized journals in the Americas and Europe. Her books include: *El Nuevo Teatro Latinoamericano: Una lectura histórica* (Prisma institute, 1987); *Posmodernismo y teatro en América Latina: Teorías y prácticas en el umbral del siglo XXI* (Iberoamericana, 2001); *Teatro y diáspora: Testimonios escénicos latinoamericanos* (Gestos, 2002); *El legado de Enrique Buenaventura* (Atuel, 2008); and *Imaginando un Continente: Utopía, democracia y neoliberalismo en el teatro latinoamericano* (two volumes) (LATR Books, 2010).

Leticia Robles-Moreno is Assistant Professor in the Department of Theatre & Dance at Muhlenberg College. Her research is focused on how theatre groups of "creación colectiva," as well as *artivist* collectives in the Americas, generate alternative political subjectivities, communities, and spaces of belonging in times of socio-political uprising. Her book project *Becoming Collective: Relational Cartographies of Resistance in the Americas* analyzes the political aesthetics of theatre, art, and activism, as modes of anti-neoliberal and intersectional bodily coexistence, from a combined perspective of Performance Studies, Critical Race Theory, and Affect Studies.

Laissa M. Rodríguez Moreno is Assistant Professor of Spanish at Coe College in Iowa. She obtained a doctorate in Hispanic Literature from the University of Wisconsin-Madison. Her research focuses on the intersections between Latin American literature, theatre, and performance studies. Other fields of interest are cultural studies, political philosophy, and historiography.

NOTES ON CONTRIBUTORS

David Román is Professor of English and American Studies at the University of Southern California. He has published several award-winning books on American theatre and performance, and he writes regularly on the literary, visual, and performing arts. He serves on the Board of Directors of Labyrinth Theater.

Gina Sandí-Díaz is Assistant Professor of Theatre at California State University, Fresno, where she specializes in Latinx and Latin American theatre, devised theatre, acting, and directing. Her scholarly and creative activity is centered on social change and culturally affirming practices. She currently serves as Vice-Chair of Representation, Equity, and Diversity for the Kennedy Center's American College Theatre Festival.

Analola Santana is Associate Professor of Theater at Dartmouth College. She is the author of *Teatro y Cultura de Masas: Encuentros y Debates* (Editorial Escenología, 2010) and *Freak Performances: Dissidence in Latin American Theatre* (University of Michigan Press, 2018). She is also the co-editor of *Theatre and Cartographies of Power: Repositioning the Latina/o Americas* (Southern Illinois University Press, 2018 with Jimmy Noriega). She works as a professional dramaturg and is a company member of Mexico's famed Teatro de Ciertos Habitantes.

Laurietz Seda is Professor of Spanish with an emphasis in Latin American Theatre and Caribbean Literature at the University of Connecticut- Storrs. Her books include *La Nueva Dramaturgia Puertorriqueña: Trans/acciones de la identidad* (Nuevos Cuadernos del Ateneo, 2018), *Teatro contra el olvido* (Universidad Científica del Sur, 2012), *Trans/Acting: Latin American and Latino Performance* (Bucknell University Press, 2009 with Jacqueline Bixler), and *Travesías trifrontes: Teatro peruano de vanguardia* (Universidad Mayor de San Marcos, 2009 with Rubén Quiróz).

Cecilia Sosa holds a PhD in Drama (Queen Mary, University of London) and currently works as a Senior Research Fellow at the Centre for the Study of post-conflict societies, University of Nottingham. She also works as an academic consultant for the project "Screening Violence: A Transnational Study of Post-Conflict Imaginaries" (University of Newcastle). Her first monograph is entitled *Queering Acts of Mourning in the Aftermath of Argentina's Dictatorship* (Tamesis Books, 2014) and has published extensively at the crossroads of memory, affect, and performance.

Camilla Stevens is Professor at Rutgers University, where she holds a joint appointment with Departments of Latino and Caribbean Studies and Spanish and Portuguese. She specializes in Latinx, Latin American, and Caribbean theatre and performance studies. Along with articles on race, migration, and cultural identity in Caribbean theatre, she has authored *Family and Identity in Contemporary Cuban and Puerto Rican Drama* (Florida University Press, 2004) and *Aquí and Allá: Transnational Dominican Theater and Performance* (University of Pittsburgh Press, 2019).

Jennifer Joan Thompson is a lecturer in theatre arts at the University of Pennsylvania. Her research examines the relationship between theatre and politics, with a focus on contemporary Latin American performance. Her current book project, *Dramaturgies of Democracy: Performance, Cultural Policy, and Citizenship in Chile (1980–2020)*, explores the dynamic between state politics, cultural policy, and theatrical aesthetics during the Chilean transition from dictatorship to democracy. Her research has been supported by Fulbright-Hays and Social Science Research Council grants.

Julie Ann Ward is Associate Professor of Twentieth- and Twenty-first-century Latin American Literatures and Cultures at the University of Oklahoma in Norman. She is the author of *A Shared Truth: The Theater of Lagartijas Tiradas al Sol* (University of Pittsburgh Press, 2019). Her research and writing appear in *InSight, Latin American Theatre Review, Los Angeles Review of Books, Paso de Gato, Quorum, Revista de Estudios Hispánicos, Revista de Literatura Mexicana Contemporánea, Theatre Journal,* and *TransModernity*.

Michelle Warren is Associate Professor of Spanish at the University of Nebraska at Kearney (UNK). Warren's research is focused on human rights and identity, including the intersections of ethnic, national, gender, and racial identities. Her current project centers on the collective work on oral histories dealing with Latinx immigration to the Central Plains of Nebraska for which she has received support from Humanities Nebraska and the Nebraska Cultural Endowment.

Brenda Werth is Associate Professor of Spanish and Latin American Studies at American University. She is author of the book *Theatre, Performance, and Memory Politics in Argentina* (Palgrave Macmillan, 2010) and co-editor (with Paola Hernández and Florian Becker) of *Imagining Human Rights in Twenty-First Century Theatre: Global Perspectives* (Palgrave Macmillan, 2013). She also co-translated and co-edited (with April Sweeney) the anthology, *Fauna and Other Plays by Romina Paula*, forthcoming with Seagull Press in 2022.

Bretton White is Assistant Professor of Spanish at Colby College, where she teaches courses on contemporary Caribbean cultural production, Latin American theatre and performance, and Spanish language. She is the author of *Staging Discomfort: Performance and Queerness in Contemporary Cuba* (University of Florida Press, 2020), which examines queer intimacies and affect in contemporary Cuban theatre. She has published articles on Cuban theatre, performance art, and visual culture in *Latin American Theatre Review*, *Gestos*, and *The Researcher: Caribbean Studies Across the Disciplines*.

Anna White-Nockleby is a Postdoctoral Fellow at Harvard University's Fellowships & Writing Center. Her research focuses on Latin American performance and visual media during periods of financial and political crisis, with particular emphasis on contemporary theatre in Argentina. Her articles, reviews, and essays have been published in *Revista Hispánica Moderna*, *Journal of Visual Culture*, *Theatre Journal*, *Modern Drama*, and the *Routledge Encyclopedia of Modernism*. She also works as a translator and editor.

INTRODUCTION

Paola S. Hernández and Analola Santana

It is perhaps uncommon to introduce an anthology where Latinx and Latin American playwrights and directors come together, as they are usually divided into two different categories that either separate them as two distinct groups or are piled together as one homogenous group without any differentiation.[1] To be clear, we understand Latinx communities to include people of Latin American, Caribbean, or Indigenous roots as well as those in the diaspora who live and work in the US or Canada, whose language of choice is usually English, but can also be Portuguese Spanish, or Spanglish. On the other hand, Latin American artists are those who live and work in their respective countries or they continue to identify with them, usually writing in Spanish, Portuguese, or in Indigenous languages. Due to the vast geographic area that includes almost all of the American continent, the historical tendency has been to create a gap or a fracture between Spanish, Portuguese, English, and the Indigenous languages, as they apply to national identity and belonging. What should remain evident, though, is that this is an open process permanently changing and filled with contradictory dynamics that interact in the construction–deconstruction–reconfiguration of Latin American and Latinx identity as it extends throughout the continent and is rooted in specific historical contexts. Putting Latin American and Latinx artists (as artists of Latinx America) in conversation is a powerful and empowering way to foment hemispheric dialogues, enhance cultural exchanges, as well as expand on our understanding of the historical and political past, present, and future that links the Latinx Americas.

With this anthology we intend to bring all these constructions together to showcase the connections, similarities, differences, and influences Latinx and Latin American artists have had on the theatre of the Americas for generations. Theatre, after all, can help smooth interactions among the diverse ethnic groups and cultures that constitute the hemisphere as we consider the influence that one group has had upon the other. To do so, we first provide an overview of the historical definitions of the terms, constantly in flux, associated with the cultures of both Latin America and the diaspora in the US and Canada. Defining Latinx and Latin American identities provides a foundation to understand the complexities of the theatre being produced across the Americas. For example, Nuyorican artists are in dialogue with islanders of Puerto Rico and vice versa, the 1960s Chicano movement propelled artists to create new theatrical forms, Dominican artists from the island and from the US are in continuous movement, and Afro-Latinx artists provide a major influence to both Latinx and Latin American playwrights and directors, among other exchanges. Understanding the rich history behind such a vast geographical territory implies an awareness of the identity markers that have circulated to categorize the theatre produced in the Americas.

DEFINING THE LATINX AMERICAS

The first hurdle when constructing a hemispheric approach to Latinx and Latin American theatre is tracing the cartographic borders of the region. Geographically, Latin America refers to a set of nations belonging to the regions of North America, the Caribbean, Central America, and South America. Historically, this has meant that culturally and linguistically, the nations of these areas predominantly speak Spanish or Portuguese—two of the many languages descended from Latin. This historical construction has also meant an erasure of the Indigenous populations, something that many in the current academic fields are trying to remedy.

The first use of the term "Latin America" can be traced back to the 1850s and the writings of Michel Chevalier (1806–1879), the French economist, who used the term to differentiate the "Latin" peoples from the "Anglo-Saxon" peoples of the Americas, using language to create a geographic distinction.[2] This definition has proven to be a complicated and false dichotomy. After all, what is the logic that allows the inclusion in the same identity group of different countries where, together, more than four hundred autochthonous languages and three different European languages (Spanish, Portuguese, and French) are spoken; yet at the same time excludes others, such as the French-speaking province of Québec in Canada or Guyana, Surinam, and Belize? There are also other nations that are geographically and culturally related to Latin America, but that are political territories of other nations—such as Puerto Rico, which remains a territory of the United States. Then there are the issues of historical migrations, for example, the fact that almost 1 percent of the population of Latin America, over four million people, is of Asian descent.³ In addition, if by Chevalier's definition, all American nations that speak a language of "Latin" origin should be defined as "Latin American," how can the United States, where Spanish is and was one of the dominant languages, not technically be considered part of Latin America? This is especially significant if we consider that in 1847, Mexico encompassed territories as far north as Oregon and as far east as Texas. Further complicating these definitions is the fact that Indigenous peoples have inhabited the Americas for thousands of years before the European conquest, at no point identifying themselves as a single geographical entity or as descendants of a "Latin" culture.

To name a collective under one term is to give it existence by attributing characteristics and delimiting its specificity according to the prevailing ideological-cultural parameters of the time and the power relations of the historical moment. After all, identity terminology is always political, depending on who is using it. In the course of the formation and transformation of continental identity, there are several names that were given or that were used to define Latin America from within. This has been the case since the eighteenth century, when the American *man* became aware of *his* cultural specificity and *his* need for self-determination. Various names were given through the century, but "American" was the one that had the most acceptance, both by the patriots in South America (Bolívar, Martí, etc.) as well as those in North America (Washington, Jefferson, etc.). The inclusion of the term in the US constitution connected the name "American" with the concept of freedom and the Manifest Destiny, which at the same time made it possible for the US to appropriate this denomination and force the rest of the continent to continue searching for a unifying name for their nascent and disunited republics.⁴

For these reasons, Latin America and its disparate nations aimed to find a cohesive terminology for their identity that encompassed all that united them. Two concurrent denominations confused and problematized identity formation and nationalist tendencies: "Hispanoamérica" and "Ibero-América." These identity markers served as a starting point in a process of categories that aimed to be inclusive of a growing set of characteristics but, instead, ended up erasing entire nations and peoples of Black and Indigenous descent. The process for this terminology went from the exclusively Spanish ancestry of "Hispanic American," to the more open term "Ibero-American," which includes Brazil with a mainly Portuguese culture, to finally reach the "Latin American" terminology that aims to bring together the countries and societies that compose the continental roots: Spanish, Portuguese, and French along with Indigenous and African civilizations. Today, there is a notable increase in Indigenous inclusivity and political participation that has given new light to the use of the name Abya Yala, first approved by the World Council of Indigenous Peoples in 1977. Abya Yala refers to the entire American continent in the Kuna language, which means land of plenitude and maturity. The adoption of this term by the Indigenous communities reflects the ongoing reconception of the inter-American lens needed to understand the relationships of oppression forged since the conquest.

Thus, considering that Latin America has a rich and diverse history of Indigenous cultures, European colonization, African slavery, and global migration, it is a daunting task to describe its people under a single ethnic category or identifier. This is perhaps why the communities of Latin American descent in the US and Canada are so often separated from their counterparts south of the border. People in the US and Canada who have origins in a Latin American country occasionally self-identify or are referred to as Latin American, but many prefer the terms Latina/o, Latinx, Hispanic, Chicanx, among others. It is common knowledge that the term Hispanic was first introduced in 1970 by the US Census Bureau, following the protests of groups such as the National Council of La Raza. They wanted an alternative category to classifying Mexican, Cuban, and Puerto Rican immigrants as "white," which was already a problematic concept because it does not refer to racial identification, rather an ethnic category. The term Hispanic is highly problematic because of the diverse cultures and ethnic identities that make up Latin America, in addition to its limitations as it refers to people with origins in Spanish-speaking countries. The term Latina/o had been informally used in academic circles since the 1970s and emerged as an official category in the 2000 US Census Bureau as an addition to the linguistic reference of Hispanic, signaling instead people living in the US who have ethnic or cultural origins in Latin America.

THE TERM LATINX

Further complicating this terminology is the fact that Latina/o indicates gender identity, so individuals who identify outside of the gender binary, or those seeking a more inclusive term, searched for a new option. David Bowles explains that:

> [R]adical feminists in the 90s (and perhaps as early as the 70s) would sometimes on posters and in graffiti literally "x" out the "o"

at the end of words that were meant to include men, women, and non-binary folk all together.[5]

Thus, by the mid-2000s the term Latinx began to be used "in activist circles primarily in the U.S. as an expansion of earlier gender-inclusive variations such as Latino/a (with the slash) and Latin@."[6] Our choice for utilizing the term "Latinx" instead of Latino, Latina, or Latin@ is a conscious one. By embracing the "x," we welcome the inclusivity of LGBTQ+ people, and those who believe that language should represent *all* of us. Moreover, Ed Morales suggests that "the term *Latinx* is the most recent iteration of a naming debate grounded in the politics of race and ethnicity."[7] For us, the term "Latinx" is also a way to call attention to the invisibility and openness to different Latinx stories, backgrounds, races, ethnicities, and identities. As Adriana Zavala states:

> [T]he X in LatinX is about addressing structured absence. But it also marks presence. It says I am here and I will be counted. The X also insists on queering structures of knowledge in order to make this presence visible.[8]

However, and as Deborah R. Vargas, Nancy Raquel Mirabal, and Lawrence La Fountain-Stokes also suggest when they chose Latina/o over Latinx in their *Keywords for Latina/o Studies*, our use of Latinx does not dismiss other terms used such as Latino/a, Chican@, or Latin@. Other scholars and artists have also began using the term Latiné or Latine to call attention to Spanish phonology.[9] We are aware that language and terms evolve, and we understand that a variety of terms exist because *we* need them. Thus, we use this space to welcome different iterations and modifications to the term.

The inclusivity ingrained in the term calls attention to the variety in racial, national, and gender this anthology emphasizes. In other words, while we are aware that Latinx as a term is more inclusive, we are also cognizant of the important racial and identity constructs that do not quite fit within this term. As Suzanne Bost and Frances Aparicio clearly state when defining the field of Latina/o studies in the 2000s, identity is subjective, and it is central to keep in mind that "most US Latinos/as define themselves first as belonging to a particular national, subnational, or binational group, like Boricua or Cuban-American, and only to a larger Latinidad for the purposes of pan-ethnic solidarity or inclusion."[10] This "pan-ethnicity," or collective umbrella that we bring forth, presents the idiosyncrasies and the localized nature of each artist while still promoting a Latinx American perspective. This is why each artist in the collection has been chosen to be part of this diverse group, where identities, nationalities, race, gender, language, and accents enrich the theatre production of the Latinx Americas.

RACIAL PROXIMITIES IN LATINIDAD

To widen the scope of this terminology one must also emphasize the specificity of racial diversity that is usually not as central in Latinx academic discussions. For instance, the term "Afro-Latinx" is central to some of the artists in this volume.[11] Indeed, Afro-Latinx has emerged as an identity marker that aims to question and problematize the proximity to whiteness that is often associated with Latinidad. Scholars Miriam Jiménez Román and Juan Flores explain how this term applies to "people of African descent in Mexico, Central and South America, and the Spanish-speaking Caribbean, and by extension those of African descent in the United States whose origins are in Latin America and the Caribbean."[12] Afro-Latinxs have been a central part of the Latinx American experience since they were forcefully brought to the Americas via the trans-Atlantic slave trade. The influence of an African heritage can be felt across the continent, and not just in the Caribbean or Brazil, to where it is often relegated. Afro-Latinxs are a large part of the mixed-race Latinx American constituency that extends from South to North, with their own ethnic and racial experiences of Latinidad. As Daphne Sicre has explained, understanding the mixed identity that encompasses Latinidad has proven to be complicated for an academic system in which "institutionalized racism privileges whiteness and denigrates the complex, mixed heritage of Indigenous, European, and/or African peoples."[13] In this volume, we include the experiences of Afro-Latinx artists who are embracing their multidimensional identities, thus complicating and enlarging definitions of racial and ethnic belonging across the Americas.

In bringing Latin American and Latinx playwrights and directors together as key figures of theatrical production, both in and outside of the US, we are aware of the varied racial, ethnic, and identity politics that are in place. Understanding the centrality of difference, and specifically a non-homogenous approach to defining Latinx America, opens the discussion of who we are, where we come from, how we identify, and how we would like to be seen. José Esteban Muñoz reaffirms the use of the term "brown" in his posthumous study on *The Sense of Brown*, as a necessary category that encompasses:

INTRODUCTION

[P]ersonal and familial participations in South-to-North migration patterns ... people who are brown by way of accents and linguistic orientations that convey certain difference ... in which one's spatial coordinates are contested, and the ways in which one's right to residency is challenged by those who make false claims to nativity.[14]

This anthology explores the variety and wealth of ethnic and racial backgrounds that both Latinx and Latin American artists bring.

VISIBILIZING ARTISTIC PRODUCTION

It is also appropriate to think about the fluid exchange of cultures, languages, and traditions that people of Latinx America have shared and how their cultural production has expanded and continues to attract generations of artists and audiences. Nevertheless, their artistic contributions contine to be ignored by mainstream theatre producers and academic institutions. For example, even though Latinx artists are major contributors to theatrical production in and of the US, they are usually missing from mainstream theatre anthologies, or if we are lucky, only one or two Latinx artists make the cut "representing" the field, usually making no distinctions between Latinx and Latin America. In a similar fashion, but from a visual art perspective, Arlene Dávila decries the invisibility portrayed to Latin American and Latinx artists, where "the racial politics of the art world become normalized ... through the racialization of selected categories [Latinx, African American, Caribbean, etc.] while 'the mainstream' continues to signal 'white' as the norm."[15] This book aims to make visible artists whose influences and productions have been key in the construction of a Latinx American theatre that goes beyond the perceived notions of race that corners them within a limited category.

Theatre studies in the US have taken a similar stand, categorizing Latinx or Latin American playwrights, directors, and artists as "ethnic others." For Dávila, "racist and Eurocentric ideas of universality in the arts still impact these identifications, fostering a continuous tiptoeing around identifying or embracing any identity that is nonwhite."[16] While in the visual arts, Latinx artists have been "an appendage to 'Latin American Art'," in theatre studies in the US and Canada, both Latinx and Latin American playwrights have been utterly marginalized. These theatre artists have grappled with a lack of understanding and representation when it comes to ethnic diversity. In an interview with

Cuban American visual and performance artist Coco Fusco, border performance artist Guillermo Gómez-Peña describes the flux, the in-betweenness of identities and the Latinx American experience, both at the US–Mexico border and beyond. He affirms that:

> [T]he state of identity is multileveled in the Southwest and in the border region. There is no such thing as a permanent, static, homogeneous sense of identity for Chicanos or for Mexican immigrants ... I am Mexican, but I am also Chicano, and I am also Latin American.[17]

It is within these networks, these contact zones (in Mary Louise Pratt's terms), that this book brings together an exchange of voices, cultural and linguistic backgrounds, ethnicity, race, and nationalities. Each entry in this collection emphasizes the theatrical productions and the artistic distinctions that each artist brings to the stage. We celebrate and welcome their differences as we seek to highlight the various cultural forms that compose the Latinx American experience. This is why we propose to study them in synch to foreground their work as productive channels for cultural advancement. Both sets of artists bring out multidisciplinary connections in transnational and trans-American ways, questioning and problematizing borders, geographies, languages, and histories that enrich how we understand the theatre of the American continent.

MAPPING LATINX AMERICAN THEATRE

Due to the vast magnitude of Latinx and Latin American artists, we had to make some difficult choices of who and why some artists were included while others were not. We have chosen to focus this anthology from the mid-twentieth century to today. The reason behind this choice is because the 1960s was a watershed moment for Latin American theatre as the phenomenon of collective creation took hold across the continent, making it a unique Latin American experience. Miguel Rubio, director of the Peruvian company Yuyachkani (founded in 1971), indicates that this period:

> [I]s a paradigm, a dream shared by many, a great illusion and, also the result of the conviction that we were part of a great theatrical revolution that was following in the footsteps of a great social revolution and of which we had no doubt about its possibility or its imminence.[18]

Ultimately, we are talking about a theatrical movement that arises from the continental influence of the Cuban revolution (1953–1959), that is, whose questioning of bourgeois morality merged with regional social situations among which major students and labor movements were key. Collective creation refers to a creative process in which members of a group share the various and numerous activities that lead to the performance, which implies that at the end of the process there is no single "author," but rather, the show is the product of the work of the whole group. The collective theatre experience is a tradition deeply linked to Latin American political transformations, echoing an anti-hierarchical structure that Brazilian Augusto Boal championed with his Theatre of the Oppressed in the 1970s. Moreover, as this anthology shows, its impact has been so pervasive that it continues to influence theatre creation today. Due to the magnitude of this history, we were forced to leave out some of the major founders of this movement, such as the Colombian Teatro Experimental de Cali (TEC) and their founder, Enrique Buenaventura, Libre Teatro Libre from Argentina, or Teatro Escambray from Cuba. These are companies that worked in their respective countries to foment an understanding of theatre as a means of communicating and processing the conflicting relationship between the ideals of the social revolution of the 1960s and the imminent explosion of political repression in the 1970s and 1980s. Nevertheless, they are highly regarded companies about whom much has been written and whose influence is obvious throughout the entries in this collection.

In Latinx theatre, the Chicano movement of the 1960s, which gave rise to Brown Power, is a key moment that shifts our understanding of cultural production from not just Mexican Americans living and working in the US, but also as a collective capable of representing their own histories and experiences. This, in turn, prompted sociopolitical changes that had a major impact in different Latinx communities. And, as Muñoz states, this Brown Power movement:

> [A]ttempted to articulate a refusal of dominant logics and systems of thought, an insistence on thinking and doing otherwise [and] was intimately linked to modes of knowledge production and institutional practices that would ultimately congeal as ethnic, Latino, or Chicana/o studies.[19]

The Chicano movement, which began as educational activism in Los Angeles as well as the farmworker strikes led by Cesar Chavez and Dolores Huerta in the Central Valley, had an "ideological base [that] was cultural nationalism, modulated at times by Marxist social critiques of capitalist class systems or new appreciations for Indigenous ancestry and history."[20] Luis Valdez and the Teatro Campesino (founded in 1965) have been a prime example of both Chicano activism and theatre that pushed the boundaries between theory, practice, and social justice by providing immigrant farmers a voice and a cultural space. Parallel to this movement, women and LGBTQ+ artists denounced the male-centeredness of most Chicano organizations. Such is the case of Latinx feminism in the United States that developed alongside the work and struggle of Black, Indigenous, and Asian American feminisms in the 1970s and 1980s. In the theatre, the centrality of playwright Cherríe Moraga's work, and her writings with Gloria Anzaldúa, made a strong impact on how plays and female characters were staged. Moraga's writings as well as those of other feminists of the time (Barbara Smith, Audre Lorde, and Hattie Gossett) helped forge a generation that "foregrounded the conceptual, affective, and institutional resources within academia that continue to shape scholarly production in Latinx feminists today."[21]

Our goal in this anthology is to provide a mapping of the most influential and productive artists in our field, including those artists who have been influential by being teachers, mentors, producers, or even activists. This means that we did not just focus on artists with long careers and well-known published plays, but we also looked at each artist's influence in the theatre as a whole. Some have worked extensively on providing a foundation for other theatre artists. Cuban American playwright and director María Irene Fornés, a well published author, for instance, is a prime example for her invaluable mentorship and influence on many Latinx playwrights that participated in her teachings and leadership at the International Arts Relations (INTAR) in the 1980s and 1990s. The same can be said about the influential work by Argentine Griselda Gambaro, whose plays have been translated and published worldwide, bringing issues of gender, sexism, human rights, and autocratic governments to the stage. There are also examples of lesser-known artists and theatre groups, such as Salvadorean playwright and community activist Quique Avilés, who has committed much of his work to social justice and immigration reform through the formation of different Latinx theatre collectives in Washington DC that explore topics of undocumented migrants, gentrification, gender, race, and class. Or, for instance, Chilean Mapuche group KIMVN Teatro, who have brought Indigenous issues to center stage as both artists and activists. Others, such as Lola Arias and Lin-Manuel Miranda have reached international, even mainstream fame, and have carved an important place for Latin American and Latinx experiences and perspectives within the mainstream audience in the US and abroad.

As the title of this series specifies, our task was to find Latinx and Latin American playwrights and directors that are considered key in the field. However, we would also like to emphasize the importance of theatre spaces and institutions that have been forged since the 1960s to today in Latinx America. Therefore, many of the entries make connections to spaces of theatrical encounters, to collective groups of theatre, and to institutions and theatres that have helped morph and build what today is Latinx American theatre.

There is a great number of theatre companies of historical significance that have helped shape the Latinx theatre scene in the US. One such influential institution is Puerto Rican Travelling Theatre (PRTT) founded in 1967 and directed by Miriam Colón (1936–2017) as a traveling theatre group based in New York City. One of Colón's main contributions was not seeing language as a barrier, and thus, instituting a bilingual approach to creating theatre. As the Puerto Rican diaspora grew, especially in New York City during the 1960s and 1970s, so did the need for a cultural and intellectual center that spoke to the political and community needs of a growing population. Greats such as Marc Anthony credit Colón with opening doors for Latinx artists by welcoming a bilingual theatre movement.[22] Another such institution that helped form many artists was Teatro Pregones founded in 1979 and led by Rosalba Rolón (1951–) in the Bronx. After many years of collaborations between the two groups, in 2016 PRTT and Pregones naturally merged into one group known as Pregones/PRTT. Another key cultural center is The Nuyorican Poets Café founded in 1973 by the late Miguel Algarín (1941–2020), as a place of encounter for playwrights, poets, and musicians of color whose work was not accepted in other mainstream spaces. The Nuyorican Poets Café provided many Latinx artists, such as Miguel Piñero, Pedro Pietri, Tato Laviera, and Piri Thomas, among others, with the setting to succeed in poetry, performance, and theatre, and to bring about issues central to the Latinx experience. And finally, the Repertorio Español, founded in 1968 by Gilberto Zaldívar and René Buch in New York City, sought to introduce Latin American, Spanish, and Latinx theatre to US audiences. From these foundational institutions, other contemporary collectives continue to foster a space for Latinx culture in theatre. Some worth mentioning here are Gala Hispanic Theater founded by Argentine Hugo Medrano in 1976 in Washington, DC; Culture Clash founded in 1984 by Richard Montoya, Ric Salinas, and Herbert Sigüenza based in San Francisco; Latino Theater Company founded by José Luis Valenzuela in 1985 and including members such as Evelina Fernández and Lupe Ontiveros based in Los Angeles; and Teatro Luna founded in 2000 by Coya Paz and Tanya Saracho based in Chicago. While these groups do not have specific entries, they are all ingrained and very much a part of this anthology through the artists who have either worked with them or have been mentored by them. There are other Latinx playwrights whose works have been extensively produced and have had an impact in the field, but we were unable to include them at this time. Some of these are Karen Zacarias, Carlos Morton, Edwin Sánchez, Monica Palacios, Tanya Saracho, Virginia Grise, Oliver Mayer, Guillermo Reyes, José Rivera, Matthew Lopez, and Marga Gómez, among many others.[23]

These gaps are further complicated when we consider Latin American theatre and its vast production from twenty nations and various languages. Many countries with enormous theatrical production and history are not as well represented, if we consider Argentina, Mexico, Chile, Uruguay, Colombia, and Peru as important theatrical producers, many of them with a long history of creating theatre spaces, schools, movements, and traditions. Collective creation, as previously mentioned, dominated the theatrical scene from the 1960s through the 1980s. These groups served as a foundation for contemporary theatre, giving rise to an extraordinary number of artists still very pertinent today. While we do not include individual entries for many of them, other anthologies and encyclopedias exist that provide a very complete history of their works.[24]

However, it is worth mentioning some of these names to contextualize the magnitude of Latin American theatrical production. For example, in Mexico the works of Luisa Josefina Hernández, Rodolfo Usigli, Emilio Carballido, and Rosario Castellanos belong to a generation of playwrights that modernized the stage allowing for a later group of internationally acclaimed artists to emerge, such as Sabina Berman, Estela Leñero, and Víctor Hugo Rascón Banda. In Argentina it is almost impossible to encompass the magnitude of the theatrical tradition, culture, and production. However, it is worth mentioning some extraordinary and highly influential playwrights since the 1960s to today. For example, Carlos Gorostiza, Eduardo Pavlovsky, Griselda Gambaro, Susana Torres Molina, Roberto Cossa, and Osvaldo Dragún made up an important generation of independent theatre-makers that opened doors to many other playwrights and theatre groups to come. Noted theatre teachers and playwrights, Daniel Veronese, Mauricio Kartun, and Ricardo Bartís, helped shape the more contemporary theatre practitioners in Argentina, including Rafael Spregelburd. In addition, a new generation of artists who explore the limits between film and theatre to great international acclaim includes Romina Paula, Mariano Pensotti, and Santiago Loza, among others. The list goes on, as the number of foundational figures for Latin American theatre ranges from the Brazilians Nelson Rodrígues, Osvaldo de Andrade, Grupo Macunaíma, Plínio Marcos, and Denise Stoklos, to the Chileans Ariel Dorfman, Egon Wolff, Isidora Aguirre, Jorge Díaz, Ramón Griffero, Teatro La Troppa, Teatro de la Memoria, and Alejandro Jodorowsky, to the Cuban group Teatro Buendía, José Triana, and Virgilio Piñera. But our goal is to include as many nations and backgrounds as possible, therefore we tried to find a balance between some of the most prominent figures in Latinx America while also providing space for other voices who have not been as prominently featured. We made a conscious effort to include those theatre artists that come from lesser-known theatrical traditions, even though they are major contributors to the field.

An important meeting place for Latin American artists has been through participation in international theatre festivals, which are important spaces for artistic exchanges. Festivals abound around the continent and foment international dialogue as they convene playwrights, actors, directors, and critics, along with artists from various countries. There have been several pioneering festivals. For the purposes of our anthology, one vital example was the V Festival of Chicano Theater and the I Latin American Encounter, which took place in 1974 in Mexico City. This encounter served as a bridge between Latinx and Latin American practitioners that allowed them to interact and see each other's work for the first time. The accessibility to artistic encounters and exhanges continues today as theatre festivals still thrive and evolve. As Vivian Martínez Tabares asserts:

> The large festivals have generated or given preference to a certain aesthetic that tends toward international standardization, directed to all types of audience and easily digested. The proliferation of festivals and the growth of networks and circuits interconnecting them, or their opening to fairs and markets, also favors an expedited mode of circulating spectacles legitimated by this route.[25]

Some of the most renowned examples include Festival Internacional de Teatro Manizales, Festival Iberoamericano de Teatro de Bogotá, and Festival Alternativo de Teatro in Colombia; the International Festival Cervantino in Guanajuato, Mexico; the International Hispanic Theatre Festival of Miami; the Festival Internacional de Buenos Aires;

Mayo Teatral in Havana, Cuba; Festival Transamériques in Montreal; the Muestra Internacional de Teatro de Mondevideo; and the largest festival today, Teatro a Mil, in Santiago, Chile.[26]

With the advent of technology and changes to social media, other new digital platforms have welcomed a new space of encounter and initiatives to promote the works of Latinx American artists, allowing audiences to learn and take part in the continued evolution of theatre. For instance, Latinx Theatre Commons, a flagship program of HowlRound,[27] first came together in 2012 led by playwright Karen Zacarias, and eventually produced a national convening for Latinx theatre artists to share their work and foster a connection between them. This has led to other productive initiatives, such as the Fornés Institute,[28] which aims to promote and preserve María Irene Fornés's legacy and impact in the theatre. Another important platform is Caridad Svich's NoPassport, a theatre alliance that welcomes cross-cultural advocacy and more importantly provides a space for publication of Latinx artists, as it is clear from many of the books published in this collection. Other digital platforms also provide connections between Latin America and the Caribbean. For example, the Cuban Theater Digital Archive,[29] established by Lilian Manzor at the University of Miami, provides access to theatrical materials that are mostly unavailable outside the island and fosters scholarly dialogue through digital resources, including teaching and learning materials. Finally, one of the first networks for theatrical research and archive is the Centro Latinoamericano de Creación e Investigación Teatral.[30] Founded in 1975, and with branches in different countries in Latin America, Spain, and Portugal, this Center aims to promote theatre artists and plays from these regions, and has become one of the most important archives, accessible for free and online, while also offering workshops, classes, and online courses. The CELCIT has its own flagship publication and offers a digital and physical library for theatre.

While it is clear that fifty spots are not enough to capture the history of the Latinx American theatre movement, we are hoping this is the first step in a holistic understanding of Latinx American theatre, both in and outside the US. It is our hope that this is a first contribution to further anthologies such as this one, and that we may continue creating spaces for all of these voices. To this end, we hope you enjoy this collection, and we invite you to learn and be inspired by the Latinx American theatre artists included here. And hopefully this will lead you to other voices that are still creating theatre today and transforming our understanding of Latinx American theatre.

Notes

1 A few anthologies that have combined Latin American and Latinx works include *Negotiating Performance: Gender, Sexuality, and Theatricality in Latin/o America* (Durham, NC: Duke University Press, 1994), edited by Diana Taylor and Juan Villegas; *Stages of Conflict* (Ann Arbor: Michigan University Press, 2008) and *Out of the Fringe: Contemporary Latina/Latino Theatre and Performance* (New York: Theatre Communications Group, 1999), edited by María Teresa Marrero and Caridad Svich; *Theatre and Cartographies of Power: Repositioning the Latina/o Americas* (Carbondale: Southern Illinois University Press, 2018), edited by Jimmy A. Noriega and Analola Santana.
2 Thomas H. Holloway, *A Companion to Latin American History* (Hoboken, NJ: Wiley-Blackwell, 2011), 4.
3 "Asians in Latin America," *Encyclopedia.com*, www.encyclopedia.com/humanities/encyclopedias-almanacs-transcripts-and-maps/asians-latin-america
4 For more information about the process of identity creation in the Americas see: Antonio Cornejo-Polar, "Mestizaje e hibridez: los riesgos de las metáforas. Apuntes," *Revista Iberoamericana*, 67.200 (2002): 867–870; Roberto Fernández-Retamar, *Pensamiento de nuestra América. Autorreflexiones y propuestas* (Buenos Aires: CLACSO, 2006); Ernesto Laclau, *The Making of Political Identities* (New York: Verso, 1994).
5 Irina Gonzalez, "What does "Latinx" Mean, Exactly?" *Oprah Daily*, August 11, 2020, www.oprahdaily.com/life/a28056593/latinx-meaning/
6 Ibid.
7 Ed Morales, *Latinx: The New Force in American Politics and Culture* (New York: Verso, 2018), 3.
8 Adriana Zavala cited in Arlene Dávila, *Latinx Art: Artists, Markets, and Politics* (Durham, NC: Duke University Press, 2020), 6.
9 A good example is when playwright Matthew López accepted the Tony award for best play, *Inheritance* (2021), where, according to *Los Angeles Times*, he became the first best play winner to use the term. Jessica Gelt, "'Latiné' vs. 'Latinx': How a Newly Crowned Tony-winning Playwright Cast his Vote," *Los Angeles Times*, September 27, 2021, www.latimes.com/entertainment-arts/story/2021-09-27/matthew-lopez-tony-awards-latine-latinx
10 Suzanne Bost and Frances R. Aparicio, "Introduction," in *The Routledge Companion to Latino/a Literature*, eds. Suzanne Bost and Frances R. Aparicio (London: Routledge, 2013), 2.
11 One current example is the debate over the lack of Afro-Latinx representation in the film *In the Heights*, directed by Jon M. Chu, written and produced by Lin-Manual Miranda and Quiara Alegría Hudes. Miranda recognized this erasure and apologized for not including Afro-Latinx actors in lead roles.
12 Miriam Jimenez Roman and Juan Flores, "Introduction," in *The Afro-Latin@ Reader: History and Culture in the United States*, eds. Miriam Jimenez Roman and Juan Flores (Durham, NC: Duke University Press, 2010), 1.

13 Daphne Sicre, "Afro-Latinx Themes in Theatre Today," in *The Routledge Companion to African American Theatre and Performance*, eds. Kathy A. Perkins et al. (London: Routledge, 2018), 272.
14 José Esteban Muñoz, *The Sense of Brown*, eds. Joshua Chambers-Letson and Tavia Nyongo'o (Durham, NC: Duke University Press, 2020), 3.
15 Dávila, *Latinx Art*, 3.
16 Ibid., 4.
17 Coco Fusco, *English is Broken Here: Notes on Cultural Fusion in the Americas* (New York: New Press, 1995), 153.
18 Miguel Rubio Zapata, *Raíces y semillas. Maestros y caminos del teatro en América Latina* (Perú: Grupo Cultural Yuyachkani, 2011), 10–11. All translations are our own.
19 Muñoz, *The Sense of Brown*, 3–4.
20 Sheila Marie Contreras, "Chicana, Chicano, Chican@, Chicanx," in *Keywords for Latina/o Studies*, eds. Deborah R. Vargas, Nancy Raquel Mirabal, and Lawrence La Fountain-Strokes (New York: New York University Press, 2017), 32.
21 Andrea J. Pitts and José Medina, "Introduction," in *Theories of the Flesh*, eds. Andrea J. Pitts, Mariana Ortega, and José Medina (Oxford University Press, 2020), 1.
22 Rosalba Rolón, "Miriam Colón: Opening Doors," *American Theatre*, March 9, 2017, www.americantheatre.org/2017/03/09/miriam-colon-opening-doors/
23 An important resource on Latinx theatre artists is Trevor Boffone, *Fifty Playwrights Project*, https://50playwrights.org, which has compiled a very comprehensive list.
24 See, for instance, Beatriz J. Rizk, Luis A. Ramos, and Nelsy Echávez-Solano, *Posmodernismo y Teatro en América Latina: Antología crírica* (Lawrence, KS: LATR Books, 2013); Eladio Cortés and Mirta Barrea-Marlys, *Encyclopedia of Latin American Theater* (Westport, CT: Greenwood Publishing Group, 2003); Don Rubin and Carlos Solórzano, *World Encyclopedia of Contemporary Theatre: The Americas* (London: Routledge, 2000).
25 Quoted in Jean Graham-Jones, "International Festivals in Latin America: Festival Santiago a Mil and Festival Internacional de Buenos Aires," in *Cambridge Companion to International Theatre Festivals*, ed. Ric Knowles (Cambridge: Cambridge University Press, 2020), 227.
26 Vivian Martínez Tabarez, "Festivales de teatro," *Encliclopedia Latinoamericana*, http://latinoamericana.wiki.br/es/entradas/t/teatro-festivales-de
27 https://howlround.com/ltc
28 https://fornesinstitute.com
29 http://cubantheater.org
30 CELCIT-Latin American Center for Theatrical Creation and Research, www.celcit.org.ar/historia/acerca-del-celcit/

Works cited

"Asians in Latin America," *Encyclopedia.com*, www.encyclopedia.com/humanities/encyclopedias-almanacs-transcripts-and-maps/asians-latin-america

Bost, Suzanne and Frances R. Aparicio. "Introduction." In *The Routledge Companion to Latino/a Literature*, edited by Suzanne Bost and Frances R. Aparicio, 1–10. London: Routledge, 2013.

Contreras, Sheila Marie. "Chicana, Chicano, Chican@, Chicanx." In *Keywords for Latina/o Studies*, edited by Deborah R. Vargas, Nancy Raquel Mirabal, and Lawrence La Fountain-Strokes, 25–28. New York: New York University Press, 2017.

Cornejo-Polar, Antonio. "Mestizaje e hibridez: los riesgos de las metáforas. Apuntes." *Revista Iberoamericana*, 67.200 (2002): 867–870.

Dávila, Arlene. *Latinx Art: Artists, Markets, and Politics*. Durham, NC: Duke University Press, 2020.

Fernández-Retamar, Roberto. *Pensamiento de nuestra América. Autorreflexiones y propuestas*. Buenos Aires: CLACSO, 2006.

Fusco, Coco. *English is Broken Here: Notes on Cultural Fusion in the Americas*. New York: New Press, 1995.

Gelt, Jessica. "'Latiné' vs. 'Latinx': How a Newly Crowned Tony-winning Playwright Cast his Vote," *Los Angeles Times*, September 27, 2021, www.latimes.com/entertainment-arts/story/2021-09-27/matthew-lopez-tony-awards-latine-latinx

González, Irina. "What Does 'Latinx' Mean, Exactly?" *Oprah Daily*, August 11, 2020, www.oprahdaily.com/life/a28056593/latinx-meaning/

Graham-Jones, Jean. "International Festivals in Latin America: Festival Santiago a Mil and Festival Internacional de Buenos Aires." In *Cambridge Companion to International Theatre Festivals*, edited by Ric Knowles, 224–238. Cambridge: Cambridge University Press, 2020.

Holloway, Thomas H. *A Companion to Latin American History*. Hoboken, NJ: Wiley-Blackwell, 2011.

Jimenez Roman, Miriam and Juan Flores. "Introduction." In *The Afro-Latin@ Reader: History and Culture in the United States*, edited by Miriam Jimenez Roman and Juan Flores, 1–18. Durham, NC: Duke University Press, 2010.

Laclau, Ernesto. *The Making of Political Identities*. New York: Verso, 1994.

Martínez Tabarez, Vivian. "Festivales de teatro." *Encliclopedia Latinoamericana*, http://latinoamericana.wiki.br/es/entradas/t/teatro-festivales-de

Morales, Ed. *Latinx: The New Force in American Politics and Culture*. New York: Verso, 2018.

Muñoz, José Esteban. *The Sense of Brown*, edited and with an Introduction by Joshua Chambers-Letson and Tavia Nyongo'o. Durham, NC: Duke University Press, 2020.

Pitts, Andrea J. and José Medina. "Introduction." In *Theories of the Flesh*, edited by Andrea J. Pitts, Mariana Ortega, and José Medina, 1–8. Oxford: Oxford University Press, 2020.

Rolón, Rosalba. "Miriam Colón: Opening Doors." *American Theatre*, March 9, 2017, www.americantheatre.org/2017/03/09/miriam-colon-opening-doors/

Rubio Zapata, Miguel. *Raíces y semillas. Maestros y caminos del teatro en América Latina*. Lima, Perú: Grupo Cultural Yuyachkani, 2011.

Sicre, Daphne. "Afro-Latinx Themes in Theatre Today." In *The Routledge Companion to African American Theatre and Performance*, edited by Kathy A. Perkins, Sandra L. Richards, Renée Alexander Craft, and Thomas F. DeFrantz, 272–277. London: Routledge, 2018.

FIFTY KEY FIGURES IN LATINX AND LATIN AMERICAN THEATRE

CARMEN AGUIRRE (SANTIAGO, CHILE/VANCOUVER, CANADA, 1967–)

Born in Santiago, Chile in 1967, Carmen Aguirre and her family fled to Canada when she was only six years old, a result of the 1973 *coup d'état* led by General Augusto Pinochet against socialist President Salvador Allende. Her family resettled in Vancouver as refugees, but only five years later, her mother and stepfather took her and her younger sister back to South America, moving constantly between Perú, Bolivia, and Argentina, as part of the underground resistance against Pinochet's regime. Thus, Aguirre's teenage years were divided between an underground life in South America and, with her father, a life in the Vancouver refugee community. For four years she was part of the resistance, dedicated to flying planes and smuggling goods across the Chilean border. In 1989, after elections were held in Chile for the first time since the *coup* and the resistance dissolved, Aguirre returned to Vancouver to train as a theatre artist at Studio 58.

When Aguirre began her career, the Latinx theatre scene in Vancouver was small, to say the least. Yet in 1994 she founded the Latino Theatre Group (LTG) with non-actors from her local community, generating a space for representation and storytelling. They collectively developed plays around a pan-Latinx immigrant experience in Canada, most notably *¿Qué pasa with la raza, eh?* (1999) and created over twenty-five forum theatre pieces in the span of eight years.

Her work after LTG has been primarily autobiographical, a genre she has expanded as both playwright and performer. Most of her texts deal with her life experiences as well as the larger testimonies of her community, often told from the perspective of a young girl. *Chile con Carne* (1995), a one-woman show, captures the experience of Manuelita—a recurring character in Aguirre's plays—an eight-year-old Chilean refugee in Vancouver during the mid-1970s, doing her best to fit in. *The Trigger* (2005) is based on Aguirre's own experience as a rape survivor at the age of thirteen, a story of resilience and sisterhood, to be performed by five women, with the same performer playing the role of Carmen and the rapist. In *The Refugee Hotel* (2009), set in a downtown hotel in Vancouver in 1974, we see Manuelita as the leading voice, joined by many others who inhabited the world of displacement: her family, those who greeted them in Canada, and those who were exiled with them. *Anywhere but Here* (2020), a story of long travel and family dynamics set in 1979, shows us a Chilean family's road trip from Vancouver to Chile, relying on the tropes of magic realism while exploring the Latinx-Canadian experience at the US–Mexico border. Delving into different theatrical forms and highlighting diverse perspectives, Aguirre's plays recreate worlds of nostalgia, both in time and space, where loss and trauma co-exist with her dark humor and a child's innocence, sometimes from the perspective of the individual's inner struggles, other times, speaking through the collective.

In sophisticated ways, Aguirre's work as a performer explores the relationship between audience and autobiography by using the body as a living archive. She experiments with the aesthetic and narrative possibilities of transmuting personal history into a very physical encounter with her audience. In her solo play, *Blue-Box* (2012), the power of the body of the performer is foregrounded. As she speaks of her body as a site of pleasure and a site of trauma, she gets close to her spectators, makes eye contact, singles out audience members, and uses their bodies to stage her memories. Years later, Aguirre took this a step further, incorporating the audiences' bodies as much as her own in her dance-lesson/performance titled *Broken Tailbone* (2019). During this "dance lesson," the audience shares in her vulnerability, calling attention to the self-consciousness of performing personal history through the body moving to the beats and sways of salsa music. *Broken Tailbone* is a fascinating example of how Aguirre, a well-known public figure in Vancouver, has crafted her public persona around the real-life value of her autobiographical experience.

Through her work, Aguirre expands Canadian history by generating public acts of remembrance that incorporate the Chilean refugee experience, as well as other less visible migration stories that intersect with hers through different forms of allyship. Thus, Aguirre interweaves her personal journey, be it in her coming-of-age stories or her struggles as a Latinx actress, with a global history of oppression. Her award-winning memoirs, *Something Fierce: Memoirs of a Revolutionary Daughter* (winner of the Canada Reads Award, 2011), and *Mexican Hooker #1: And Other Roles Since the Revolution* (2016), have given her international visibility, amplifying even further the presence of Latinx culture in Canada's mainstream society. In addition to her published plays, an invaluable contribution to Latinx theatre artists everywhere, she adds over eighty film, television, and stage acting credits and is Core Artist at Vancouver's Electric Theatre Company.

Aguirre's style as a playwright and performer has evolved hand in hand with her theatre activism. Famously in 2003, Aguirre withdrew her play, *The Refugee Hotel*, from being produced at a high-profile theatre when the director failed to cast the play with non-white actors. In a 2020 keynote address at the Canadian Latinx Theatre Artist Coalition event "Coyuntura," Aguirre reflected:

> I've spent my entire adult life putting my storytelling skills at the service of stories that are rarely told on our stages. Performed by actors of color with people of color at the helm. Important in terms of representation, and equally important in terms of labor. Of actually giving people of color work.[1]

Co-founder of the Canadian Latinx Theatre Artist Coalition (2020), Aguirre continues to be vocal on the ways in which Latinx culture is represented and materially supported, engaging critically with different movements toward inclusion and the larger public discourse through the arts.

Martha Herrera-Lasso González

Note

1 *Coyuntura Keynote Address*, April 24, 2020, www.youtube.com/watch?v=VE9ShQ3f2tc&ab_channel=CanadianLatinxTheatreArtistCoalition

Major works

Anywhere but Here, 2020.
Broken Tailbone, 2019.
Blue Box, 2012.
The Refugee Hotel, 2009.
The Trigger, 2005.
¿Qué pasa with la raza, eh?, 1999.
Chile con Carne, 1995.
In a Land Called I Don't Remember, 1995.

Published works

Anywhere but Here. Toronto: Talonbooks, 2021.
Chile con Carne & Other Early Works. Toronto: Talonbooks, 2019.
Blue Box. Toronto: Talonbooks, 2012.
The Refugee Hotel. Toronto: Talonbooks, 2010.
The Trigger. Toronto: Talonbooks, 2008.

Further reading

Aguirre, Carmen. "What is the Purpose of Art in the Face of Human Suffering?" In *Canadian Association for Theatre Research/Association*

Canadienne de la Recherche Théâtrale Conference. Brock University, vol. 26. 2014.

Etcheverry, Gabrielle. "Carmen Aguirre, *The Refugee Hotel*." In *Fronteras Vivientes*, ed. Natalie Alvarez. Toronto: Playwrights Canada Press, 2013. 274–278.

Habell-Pallan, Michelle. "'Don't Call Us Hispanic:' Popular Latino Theater in Vancouver." In *Latina/o Popular Culture*, ed. Michelle Habell-Pallán and Mary Romero. New York: New York University Press, 2005. 174–189.

Herrera-Lasso González, Martha. "Of Bodies, Cunts and Revolutions: Carmen Aguirre's Blue Box." *Alt Theatre Journal*, 10.1 (2012): 21–24.

Rabillard, Sheila. "Carmen Aguirre's The Refugee Hotel and the Space Between Limited and Unlimited Hospitality." *Theatre Research in Canada/ Recherches théâtrales au Canada*, 36.2 (2015): 216–237.

Rivera-Servera, Ramón H. "Moving from Realism to Hip-Hop Real: Transnational Aesthetics in Canadian Latina/o Performance." In *Latina/o Canadian Theatre and Performance*, ed. Natalie Alvarez. Toronto: Playwrights Canada Press, 2013. 133–150.

Verdecchia, Guillermo. "Hasta La Victoria Siempre! The Persistent Memory of Revolutionary Politics in the Plays of Carmen Aguirre." In *Latina/o Canadian Theatre and Performance*, ed. Natalie Alvarez. Toronto: Playwrights Canada Press, 2013. 179–199.

LUIS ALFARO (LOS ANGELES, CALIFORNIA, 1963–)

Luis Alfaro is a multi-faceted queer Chicanx theatre artist whose impact has been both on and behind the stage. He's a playwright, performer, and director, whose works have been staged in major regional theatres across the United States, garnering critical acclaim. But he's also a dramaturge, producer, and teacher, who has, behind the scenes, influenced an entire generation of new playwrights, and whose commitment to community-building has helped establish a national Latinx theatre network.

Born and raised in Los Angeles, Alfaro emerged on the scene in the late 1980s as part of the multiculturalism movement brought on by new voices and new genres. Alfaro's first solo performance piece, *Downtown* (1990), combined spoken word, video, and movement to address growing up queer and brown in Los Angeles. The solo piece became one of the era's central examples of new queer performance. Alfaro's charismatic stage persona combined with his incantatory poetry, introduced audiences to the emerging new field of solo performances based on identity politics and cultural critique. *Downtown* put Alfaro on the map, so to speak. He performed the piece in alternative venues in Los Angeles, including community centers, schools, and galleries, and at benefits for Latinx and LGBTQ and HIV/AIDS causes before touring throughout the United States in the alternative performance venues that were existent throughout the 1980s and 1990s. During the late twentieth century, audiences were more open to issues of multiculturalism and, thus, were drawn to performances by artists addressing the intersections of race, sexuality, and class, among other identity markers. Alfaro's autobiographical writings as a queer Chicanx working-class individual were especially well received in this context. In fact, he was awarded the prestigious MacArthur Foundation Fellowship early in his career (1997) for his innovative and socially engaged creativity. Alfaro emerged from the Los Angeles poetry and performance communities, and most of his work addresses contemporary life in Los Angeles, especially the lives of those living in East Los Angeles, the historically working-class Mexican American neighborhood, or in the Pico Union district, another Latinx immigrant community near downtown Los Angeles.

Along with Monica Palacios and Alberto "Beto" Ariaza, Alfaro was one of the founding directors in 1993 of *Teatro Viva!* a queer and Latinx HIV/AIDS theatre group committed to HIV educational outreach efforts to underserved populations throughout Southern California. The trio performed bilingual skits in the tradition of Teatro Campesino that combined humor, music, and improvisation in nontraditional settings outside of the theatre to reach a demographic often neglected by traditional HIV/AIDS groups and standard HIV prevention strategies. Alfaro has been central to both community-based projects such as *Teatro Viva!* and mainstream theatre venues such as the Mark Taper Forum, the most prestigious regional theatre in Los Angeles. He worked as co-director of the Latino Theatre Initiative with Diane Rodriguez at the Mark Taper Forum from 1995 to 2003, and then as director of New Playwright Development from 2003 to 2005. At the Mark Taper he commissioned countless new plays by Latinx playwrights and performers, serving as literary dramaturge for many of these playwrights, and creating a community of Latinx playwrights, directors, actors, and designers who traditionally had been left out of the Mark Taper's networks.

In the 1990s, Alfaro produced works that departed from the autobiographical tenor of his solo performances. In plays such as *Breakfast, Lunch, and Dinner* (2003), *Bitter Homes and Gardens* (1993), and *Straight as a Line* (1998), Alfaro wrote about family and domestic issues that featured characters from a multiplicity of ethnic and cultural backgrounds, defying the expectations that his work be limited exclusively to Latinx themes. In *Straight as a Line*, the play's two characters are Asian-British, living in New York City and Las Vegas. While the play is about HIV/AIDS, it's an acerbic comedy. Formally, it's divided into seventeen short sketches featuring a mother/son relationship that ends in the son's death from AIDS.

Alfaro explores different dramatic forms and representational content to address contemporary political and cultural pressure points. In all of his work, he is committed to representation and the importance of speaking your voice. In *Black Butterfly, Jaguar Girl, Piñata Woman and other Superhero Girls, Like Me* (1998), for example, Alfaro created a series of monologues for Latinx actresses highlighting the specific lives of young girls growing up in East Los Angeles. These monologues—reminiscent of Ntozake Shange's 1976 classic *For Colored Girls Who Considered Suicide/When the Rainbow is Enuf*—are performed by a cast of five Latinas who express the challenges facing girls who look different than those in glossy magazines, and whose position in their families and neighborhoods leave little space to be seen and heard on their own terms. The piece, which was inspired by the writings of Alma Cervantes, Sandra Munoz, and Marisela Norte, celebrates young urban Latinas, and is now a staple of youth theatres. It offers multiple audition monologues that have been especially useful for prospective early career Latina actors. Alfaro's mid-career works showcase a playwright of tremendous versatility grounded in community-based political action and empowerment.

Alfaro's twenty-first-century works build on his earlier foundation in solo performance and playwriting. In *St. Jude* (2013), his beautiful tribute to the complicated relationship with his father, Alfaro revisits some of his earliest childhood memories in light of his father's recent devastating stroke. It is both a memory play and a play about becoming, or in Alfaro's words, a play about "going from 'what I am' to 'who I was'." While an homage to his father, this solo performance also unveils the dynamics of a Latinx family. Alfaro often performs his work as if it were a work-in-progress, his script placed inside a thick black binder that itself is readily visible on a podium placed center-stage. Alfaro's work, however, is fully rehearsed and deliberately directed. The visible script suggests a liturgical text, and the stripped-down performance becomes a ritualized spiritual journey into the past.

Beginning in 2003, Alfaro began adapting classical Greek tragedies for contemporary Latinx contexts. He's written three so far: *Eletricidad* (2003), based on Sophocles' *Elektra*; *Mojada* (2013), based on Euripides's *Medea*; and *Oedipus El Rey* (2008), based on Sophocles' *Oedipus the King*. These plays share a desire to present the quotidian life of Latinx immigrants in tragic dimensions. They deal with pressing issues such as immigration, exile and deportation, gang warfare, prison and crime, gentrification, urbanization, and unemployment. The main characters are all Latinx, primarily but not exclusively first generation or recently arrived. The casts are intergenerational, and the tensions, as in the Greek tragedies, are both between and among the communities.

Alfaro is also interested in questions of faith and destiny, and he presents multiple belief systems—from indigenous spirituality to urban nihilism—by which these characters act, live, and die. The plays follow the familiar patterns of communal ritual. Audiences already know what's going to happen. Alfaro revives and revises the plays so that we experience the intensity of the play's action and leave in a shared cathartic sense of awe. He does not set out to propose Latinx experience as somehow worthy of the category of "universal," yet the affiliation with Greek tragedy somehow grants that understanding. Nor is he out to ride the coattails of the Greeks into the Western canon. In Alfaro's Greek trilogy, the specificity of the Latinx experience is rendered as dramatic and tragic as storytelling allows.

Alfaro continues to revise the plays from the Greek trilogy for each new production. Sometimes he resets the play within the particular Latinx neighborhood of the city producing the play. *Mojada*, for example, when it was produced in Chicago, was set in Pilsen, Chicago's Latinx neighborhood, and when it was produced in New York, Alfaro set the action in Corona, Queens. Other topical issues specific to the neighborhoods, including streets and parks, for example, are also introduced. The plays are among the most successful ones by a contemporary Latinx playwright.

Alfaro's writings spotlight the complexity of life among Latinx communities, giving voice to people often usually excluded from mainstream representation, or who, when rendered visible, exist in demeaning stereotype. Alfaro's commitment to art and social practice, and belief in the idea that the artist has an exemplary role in the culture, places him within a long history of progressive artists/activists both within Chicanx and Latinx traditions.

David Román

Major works

Mojada (2013)
St. Jude (2013)
Oedipus El Rey (2008)
Eletricidad (2003)
Breakfast, Lunch, and Dinner (2003)

Black Butterfly (1998)
Straight as a Line (1998)
Bitter Homes and Gardens (1993)
Downtown (1990)

Published works

Electricidad, Mojada, and *Oedipus El Rey*. In *The Greek Plays of Luis Alfaro*, edited by Rosa Andújar. London: Methuen Drama, 2021.
Bitter Homes and Gardens. In *Latino Plays from South Coast Repertory: Hispanic Playwrights Project Anthology*, edited by Jose Cruz Gonzales and Juliette Carrillo. New York: Broadway Publishing, 2000.
Straight As a Line. In *Out of the Fringe: Contemporary Latino/Latina Plays and Performances*, edited by Caridad Svicch and Maria Teresa Marrero. New York: Theatre Communications Group, 1999.
Downtown. In *O Solo Homo: The New Queer Performance*. New York: Grove Press, 1998.

Further reading

Cheng, Meiling. *In Other Los Angeleses: Multicentric Performances*. Berkeley: University of California Press, 2002.
Habell-Pallán, Michelle. *Loca Motion: The Travels of Chicana and Latina Popular Culture*. New York: New York University Press, 2005.
Muñoz, José Esteban. "Queer Theater, Queer Theory" in Alisa Solomon and Framji Minwalla, eds., *The Queerest Art: Essays on Lesbian and Gay Theater*. New York: New York University Press, 2002.
Perez, Daniel Enrique. *Rethinking Chicana/o and Latina/o Popular Culture*. New York: Palgrave Macmillan, 2009.
Román, David. *Acts of Intervention: Performance, Gay Culture, & AIDS*. Bloomington: Indiana University Press, 1998.
Román, David. "Latino Performance and Identity." *Aztlan: A Journal of Chicano Studies*, 22:2 (Fall 1997): 151–167.

LOLA ARIAS (BUENOS AIRES, ARGENTINA, 1976–)

For over twenty years, the Argentine theatre director, writer, and performer Lola Arias has managed to reshape understandings of documentary theatre worldwide. Her tantalizing repertoire of theatrical plays, songs, poems, installations, live concerts, video games, and urban performances blurs the lines between reality and fiction, stage and screen, fantasy, and activism. She has worked with actors, non-actors, musicians, war veterans, deported children, dancers, refugees, activists, policemen, families of all sorts, babies, and even turtles. Her projects have traveled around the Americas, Europe, and Asia, making Arias one of the most important contributors to contemporary theatre coming from Latin America.

Born in 1976 in Buenos Aires, Argentina, Arias is part of a wave of directors and creators, mostly born during the dictatorship (1976–1983), who might be loosely associated with a "post-trauma" generation. This wave of directors has learned to respond to the traumatic past through an autonomous and provocative aesthetic platform. In Arias's stylish production, loss and mourning are not only attached to pain, but also to humor and hope. Through Arias's work, audiences learn to consider theatre as a space for transformation where life can be expanded. Her plays might touch upon the traces of Latin American dictatorships, the reverberations of the disappeared German Democratic Republic, the cleaning staff at budget hotels around the world, the disparate forms of embracing motherhood, or the imaginaries of stateless teenagers looking for refuge in a strange world. Despite their hardy themes, Arias's productions bear a playful style in which excerpts of poetry, dance, and live music usually intertwine. They ultimately shed light on how lives depend on others in ways that cannot be controlled.

In Arias's productions, objects are charged and infused with life. Old clothes, toys, family pictures, letters are brought back on stage to test their resonances in the present. They are not only individual spoils, but also cultural treasures. On the verge of being forgotten, they become surfaces on which to travel in time. History can then be written backwards, enabling spectators to grasp how memory reshapes the present. Thus, Arias's theatre emerges as a collective endeavour: even if an individual story seems to be at the foreground, the audience can follow an entire cast manipulating objects and cameras and ultimately blurring the boundaries between one and another in an affective experience of body-to-body transmission. Thus, Arias's productions deconstruct an idea of testimony attached to the individual self. In her "re-enactments," rather to be attached to the individual, testimony is deconstructed and expanded to speak on behalf of multiple communities.

Not only does Arias look for stories that can intrigue or disturb, but she also searches for people who can fully embark upon processes of transformation. Spectators are confronted with the illusion that there is no script, and that her shows are just real people speaking. Significantly, her productions have thrived to create new ensembles, or families-by-choice; even if these families are enacted by former enemies playing a punk rock number on stage as in *Campo minado/ Minefield* (2016).

Although Arias has captured international attention as an author mostly dealing with documents, her early work was closer to fiction. Released during a huge economic and social crisis, her first piece, *A Kingdom, a Country or a Wastland, in the Snow* (2001), turned all possible taboos upside down. Twisted Greek myths, cannibalism, parricide, and incest co-existed with a leak of water, which kept on unattended falling on stage throughout the show. *Striptease/Revolver Dream/Love is a Sniper* (2007) offered a fictional trilogy on love projected through time. In *Striptease*, a baby was on stage at all times, alongside her real mother. The baby's movements—her crawling, playing, feeding from a bottle or throwing a toy from her cradle—inevitably marked the pace of the performance. This audacious live choreography not only made spectators more self-conscious of their own presence in the darkness, it also involved a revelatory moment in which Arias understood that "the theatre I was starting to do was persistently looking for 'unpredictability'."[1]

Arias's encounter with Stefan Kaegi, one of the creators of Rimini Protokol to whom she was married, marked her exploration of a wide spectrum of live performances and urban space installations. At a time when police *razzias* had become commonplace in Brazilian favelas, they launched *Chácara Paraíso* (2007), the first piece that Arias wrote based on the lives of non-actors, which brought on stage armed personnel working for the Brazilian police force. One year later, Arias and Kaegi launched *Airport Kids* (2008), a social experiment with children from international schools and immigrant backgrounds. Arias also designed *Parallel Cities* (2010/2011) with Kaegi, a series of site-specific installations in Berlin, Buenos Aires, Zurich, Warsaw, Utrecht, Copenhagen, Cork, Singapore, and Calcutta. In *Maids*, one of the eight installations that belonged to *Parallel Cities*, participants were able to wander through different rooms in a budget hotel, following the traces of the people in charge of the cleaning. The installation highlighted the possibilities of a more empathic spectatorship.

A turning point in Arias's career was her trilogy based on children reconstructing their parents' lives. The series includes *My Life After* (2009), *The Year I was Born* (2012), and *Melancholy and Demonstrations* (2012). In the first, six actors born during Argentina's dictatorship dress up as their parents to reconstruct their past lives as guerrilla activists, exiled intellectuals, bank employees, priests, and military intelligence officers. As if it were a science-fiction film, a pile of clothes from the 1970s allowed the younger generation to travel back in time. In the Chilean sister-version, *The Year I was Born*, eight young actors had to align themselves, from right to left, considering their mothers' ideological position during Pinochet's dictatorship (1973–1990). Tension and conflict became visible on stage. For the series finale, *Melancholy and Demonstrations* (2012), Arias "took a long drink of her own reenactive medicine."[2] As director, writer, and performer, she embarked upon an exploration of her mother's depression, which had started with her birth at the end of the dictatorship. Despite becoming a "nightmare," the process also helped Arias to better understand her way of doing theatre.

For her series on warfare, Arias trespassed into a fundamentally closed and vertical masculine world and dedicated three pieces to explore the Malvinas/Falklands war (1982). The genesis of the project was *Veterans* (2014), a video installation made of five short films presented at the London Battersea Centre (BAC), in which former Argentine soldiers reconstructed their wartime memories. Then, Arias brought together veterans from both countries for the play, *Minefield* (2016), and then for the film, *Theatre of War* (2018). In this high-risk, highly exposed public encounter, ex-combatants put on their old uniforms, showed their war trophies and read their letters as they attempted to re-inhabit those bodies that went to war. Far from presenting them as war heroes, Arias exposed former enemies on a common ground of vulnerability. By contrast, the theatrical *mise-en-abîme* of the film *Theatre of War* turned the same performing veterans into the spectators of their own lives as they are enacted by younger stunt actors. The film, a genre of its own, deconstructs both traditional imaginaries of war and the very idea of documentary.

Arias's social experiments then became increasingly transnational. *Atlas of Communism* (2016) was the director's attempt to bring back to life the vanished German Democratic Republic through a repertoire of old songs enacted by a troupe of performers aged from eight to eighty years old. In *What They Want to Hear* (2018), she reconstructed Raaed Al Kour's case, a Syrian archaeologist who got caught up in the German bureaucracy, losing any legal status. In *Futureland* (2019), Arias created a video-game theatre production in which a group of vulnerable and stateless teenagers who arrived in Europe as "unaccompanied minors" envisioned their future.

As life migrated online during pandemic times obliging Arias to interrupt *Lingua Madre*'s rehearsals—an Italian-based experiment on motherhood—she curated the transnational Zoom participatory sessions *My Documents. Share Your Screen* (2020). While embracing the unpredictable, this transnational series displayed a dream list of artists sharing their most intimate obsessions on screen, from inside their homes.³

Cecilia Sosa

Notes

1 Richard Gough, "Raining in the Theatre, Lola Arias in conversation with Richard Gough," in *Lola Arias: Re-enacting Life*, ed. Jean Graham-Jones (Aberystwyth: Performance Research Books, 2019), 307.
2 Jean Graham-Jones, "Introduction," in *Lola Arias: Re-enacting Life*, ed. Jean Graham-Jones (Aberystwyth: Performance Research Books, 2019), 14.
3 The series ran from May 15 to June 20, 2020 and included live sessions from Wuhan, London, Mexico, and Berlin.

Major works

Futureland (2019)
Atlas of Communism (2016)
Minefield (2016)
Melancholy and Demonstrations (2012)
The Year I was Born (2012)
My Life After (2009)

In collaboration with Stefan Kaegi:

- *Parallel Cities* (2010/2011)
- *Airport Kids* (2008)
- *Chácara Paraíso* (2007)

A Kingdom, a Country or a Wasteland, in the Snow (2001)

Published works

Lola Arias: Re-enacting Life. Edited by Graham-Jones, Jean. Aberystwyth: Performance Research Books, 2019.
Minefield/Campo Minado. London: Oberon Books, 2017.
Mi vida después y otros textos. Buenos Aires: Random House, 2016.
Striptease/Sueño con revólver/El amor es un francotirador. Buenos Aires: Entropía, 2007.

Further reading

Blejmar, Jordana. "Autofictions of Postwar: Fostering Empathy in Lola Arias' Minefield/Campo minado." *Latin American Theatre Review* 50.2 (2017): 103–124.

Bulman, Gail. "Catharsis, Spectacle, and the Post-postmodern Theatre of Lola Arias." *Letras Femeninas* 37.1 (2011): 101–112.
Hernández, Paola. "Biografías escénicas: *Mi vida después* de Lola Arias." *Latin American Theatre Review* 45.1 (2011): 115–128.
Perez, Mariana Eva. "Their Lives After: Theatre as Testimony and the So-called 'Second Generation' in Post-dictatorship Argentina." *Journal of Romance Studies* 13.3 (2013): 6–16.
Sosa, Cecilia. "*Campo Minado/Minefield*: War, Affect and Vulnerability—a Spectacle of Intimate Power." *Theatre Research International* 42.2 (2017): 179–189.
Sosa, Cecilia. "Lola Arias: Expanding the Real," in *No More Drama* (Dublin: Project Press, 2011): 46–66.
Werth, Brenda. "The Body as Time Machine: Reenactment in Lola Arias's Documentary Performance," in *Reenactment Case Studies: Global Perspectives on Experiential History*, eds. Vanessa Agnew, Sabine Stach, and Juliane Tomann (New York: Routledge, forthcoming 2022).

QUIQUE AVILÉS (EL CARMEN, EL SALVADOR/ WASHINGTON, DC, 1965–)

Quique Avilés is a poet, actor, and community activist who addresses race, class, gender, gentrification, migration, and hybrid identity by telling the stories of immigrants. As a migrant, Avilés focuses on the experiences of the Salvadorean diaspora in the US. In the late 1970s Avilés founded *Teatro Nuestro*, a political kind of theatre that brought to the stage the US interventions in El Salvador and Nicaragua. In 1985 he founded the LatiNegro Theater Collective, which performed in schools, prisons, and community centers, and in 1999 the non-profit artistic organization Sol y Soul, which created socially conscious art with people from the community and gave rise to El Barrio Street Theatre in 2000. This was an activist group that dealt with topics such as tenants' rights, gentrification, workers' rights, and immigration through street performances. Not only a storyteller of the first- and second-generation immigrant experience, Avilés also has empowered the marginalized to tell their own stories through writing and performance workshops, being honored with an Award of Excellence from the Mayor's Office on Latino Affairs in 2011.

Some common traits throughout Aviles's theatre include the minimal use of props and wardrobe in his performances as well as the alternating use of English, Spanish, and Spanglish while reading his rhythmic and vernacular poetry. He presents characters who are real-life people or composites from his interviews. Scholars writing about his early performances *Latinhood* (1993), *Chaos Standing* (1997), and *Caminata* (2003) have noted that identity is represented as changing and dynamic, meaning that characters on the stage reject social constructs that exclude them because of nationality, gender, race, class, or language, and instead define themselves beyond those repressive parameters exploring a fluid understanding of immigrant identity. Linking Aviles's work to Chicano borderland drama, feminist and queer alternative art happenings, and guerrilla street theatre, Ana Patricia Rodríguez points out how his early work shows identity to be "*performative*, scripted, cited, reconverted and negotiated in daily exchanges within and between subjects."[1] This performative nature of identity remains a salient attribute in his subsequent performances.

Latinhood (1993) and *Chaos Standing* (1997) feature residents of Mount Pleasant, Columbia Heights and Adams Morgan, Washington, DC, neighborhoods where Salvadorans live among other Latinx, Black, and other immigrant communities, as well as an increasingly gentrified population. Early in *Latinhood* Avilés reads a poem with the same title that was published separately in the poetry collection *The Immigrant Museum* (2003) and introduces the performance's main theme by posing a series of questions about Latinx identity:

> what does it feel like inside?
> what color is this latinhood?
> how does it do what it does?

The answers are additional questions pointing out the diversity among the people labeled as Latinx, asking if it is "black ... brown ... indio ... white" or if it could also be:

> italian latin via buenos aires
> latin with a tinge of whiteness
> mestizo latin with korean roots?

The heterogeneity composing Latinx identity posited here in the poem is reinforced in the play with monologues by four characters who immigrated to Washington, DC. Coming from different Latin American countries, speaking different languages, and having different immigration statuses, these characters illustrate the variety of identities concealed by the label "Latino" used in the United States. Loco Culebra/Crazy Snake, one of the characters in *Latinhood* and a recurring one in Aviles's theatre, is performed by Avilés as a "snake narrator" who is a descendent of the feathered serpent god Quetzalcoatl-Kukulcan from Aztec and Mayan mythologies. Despite his own confession of insanity, which caused him to forget his name, age, and country of origin, Loco Culebra/Crazy Snake transmits his wisdom about the changing role of immigrants in American society throughout history. *Chaos Standing* (1997) also deals with race relations as the protagonist tells the stories of friends and family to illustrate to a reporter different dimensions of multicultural living. This play expands the focus on the Latinx population to also include immigrants and non-immigrants of different races living in Washington, DC. Although *Chaos Standing* offers hope in the example of children who have not yet acquired adult prejudices, it criticizes the racism that emerged when Salvadoreans began living in the same neighborhoods with Blacks, with whom they had rarely interacted before immigrating to the United States.

Caminata (2003) looks beyond Washington, DC, as the protagonist speaks with immigrants from seven countries living throughout the United States while trying to understand what it means to be an American. Eschewing a single, definitive answer, the performance encourages continual self-reflection and suggests hybrid identity, in which one feels a sense of belonging to both the country of origin and host country, as a possible way to constitute Americanness. Later performances respond to social transformation when immigrants have children. Speaking as himself in *The Children of Latinia* (2009), Avilés announces a shift in focus to the hybrid identity of second-generation immigrants, who, although born in the United States, "feel voiceless, segregated, unequal ... out of a sense of solidarity to their immigrant parents' oppression by proxy." In response to this sentiment, the performance proposes that they actively create their own identities while participating in civic engagement, offering the example of a teenage character of Guatemalan and Ethiopian heritage who designs Latinia for a school project. With its own flag, map and declaration of independence, Latinia is a mental homeland where he feels a sense of belonging and empowerment as an American, which he channels by participating in immigrants' rights marches. In *El Canuto del Rock* [The Rock and Roll Hour] (2008), which includes a performance by the DC-based Salvadorean punk band Machetres, a young adult, whose father is Black and mother Salvadorean, travels to El Salvador in search of her roots. There she meets a campesino who convinced a radio station to give him a rock show. The key message transmitted here is the importance of rejecting preconceived notions regarding identity. Just as a peasant defied social norms in becoming a DJ, so can members of Black and Latinx communities pursue their personal and professional dreams.

While Avilés includes autobiographical references in many performances, in *Tongue* (2014) he explains in detail what led him to become a writer. Although school had trained him for stage and television roles, he realized that there were limited parts for Latinx actors beyond stereotyping members of their community as criminals. Influenced by the Nuyorican Pedro Pietri's epic poem *Puerto Rican Obituary* (1973), which taught him that the writer's job is to manipulate language, "to invent it and reinvent it," Avilés decided to shape language to create new roles for the Latinx community, immigrants and their children on and off stage. His early performances tell the story of the Salvadorean diaspora in Washington, DC, during the 1980s as its members were labeled Latino and forged relationships with neighbors of different races and cultures. The scope of his work then expands to address immigrants from throughout the world living in different parts of the United States whose social activism is an intrinsic part of who they have become. Finally, his most recent performances present the perspectives of biracial second-generation immigrants as they negotiate identities while defending immigrants' rights. Rather than accept the identities cast for them, the characters in Avilés's performances actively seek to define themselves, encouraging audiences to also engage in this open-ended and transformative quest.

Elaine M. Miller

Note

1 Ana Patricia Rodríguez. "Second Hand Identities: The Autoethnographic Performances of Quique Avilés and Leticia Hernández-Linares," *Istmo: Revista virtual de estudios literarios y culturales centroamericanos* 8 (2004), http://istmo.denison.edu/n08/articulos/second.html

Major works

Tongue (2014)
The Children of Latinia (2009)
El Canuto del Rock [The Rock and Roll Hour] (2008)
The Immigrant Museum (2003)
Caminata: A Walk through Immigrant America (2002)
Chaos Standing (1997)
Latinhood (1993)

Further reading

Avilés, Quique. "A Third Citizenship." *Washington History* 31, no. 1/2 (2019): 29–34.
Linares-Hernández, Leticia. "Stories from Our Unincorporated Territories." In *The Wandering Song: Central American Writing in the United States*, edited

by Leticia Hernández-Linares, Rubén Martínez, and Héctor Tobar. 9–11. San Fernando, California: Tía Chucha Press, 2017.

Villalta, Nilda. "Despiadada(s) ciudad(es): El imaginario salvadoreño más allá de la guerra civil." PhD diss., University of Maryland, 2004.

JOSEFINA BÁEZ (LA ROMANA, DOMINICAN REPUBLIC, 1960–)

Josefina Báez is a self-proclaimed "Dominicanyork" performance artist, dancer, director, poet, writer, and educator whose work is known for its formally and linguistically playful quality that defies categorization within traditional genres of theatre and performance. Her own autobiography is her primary source for material—a cornerstone concept of the performance practice that she uses and teaches called "Performance Autology." Her genres are spoken word and solo performance, which were popularized as she matured as an artist in the 1970s and 1980s. Báez produces work that challenges established notions of nationality and belonging while creating space for imagining more complex and transnational modes of identity.

Báez's experience as a woman of African descent that immigrated from La Romana, Dominican Republic to the United States at a young age plays a foundational role in her work. Her lineage is linked to Afro-descendant sugar-cane workers of the Dominican *bateyes*—shanty-town settlements that have historically popped up in sugar industry regions such as La Romana, once the headquarters of one of the largest sugar-cane mills in the Americas. Báez immigrated to New York with her family in 1972—before the establishment of the famously Dominican-dominant Washington Heights—and spent her formative years in a community on the West Side that was populated mainly by other Black American and Puerto Rican working-class families. Over the years she has maintained a strong connection with La Romana, traveling back often to visit extended family.

This life-on-the-move finds its parallel in her formation as a performance artist committed to the study of embodied and popular forms of performance both in New York and abroad. She began her career in the late 1970s as a performer in New York's Teatro 4, a community-based theatre group operating in Spanish Harlem. Part of her early years as a performance artist were dedicated to the study of classical, modern, and jazz dance in the American Dance School and at the New York Dance Troupe as well as Indian dance under the tutelage of masters in both New York and New Delhi. Additionally, in the 1990s, she received formal training in Cuba from Flora Lauten, director of the Buendía Theatre Group, before shifting her focus to studying Meyerhold's "theatrical biomechanics." Throughout her career, she has worked professionally all over the world as both a dancer and actress in locations including Brazil, Cuba, Mexico, France, Finland, Russia, and Spain. Based on the techniques learned through these varied experiences among others, Báez co-founded the theatre group Latinarte in 1986; it operates today as Ay Ombe Theatre under Báez's direction.

Centered in an in-between space that she begins to refer to as "El Nié" in her performance text *Levente no. Yolayorkdominicanyork*, Báez's work seeks to capture the experience of home for those whose lives are characterized by displacement, migration, and exclusion. "El Nié," which is a common Dominican slang term for "it is neither one thing nor the other," often inspires comparisons to Mary Louise Pratt's "contact zone" or Gloria Anzaldúa's metaphor of the borderlands due to the way it evokes the embodiment of cultures both in contact and in tension with one another. This concept can also be understood in dialogue with that of other border artists such as Guillermo Gómez-Peña who similarly embrace a poetics of "inbetweenness" in their performance practice. For Báez, whose mostquoted line from any work might be "home is where theatre is" (*Dominicanish*), performance is this liminal space where "El Nié" as home can be interrogated and inhabited.

Like this conceptualization of "home," Báez's works are characterized by fragmentary and mutable scripts and the use of non-traditional venues making a history of her performance trajectory somewhat elusive. Her *Wandering Soul Series* (2001) involves an ongoing series of "apariciones" [apparitions or appearances] that take place with little preparation or warning and involve her walking masked, costumed, and ghostlike into a public space either in La Romana or New York. For example, for one such "aparición," she visited defunct local businesses in La Romana as a multivalent commentary on the displacement of Dominicans due to a globalizing economy and the sense of permanent displacement experienced by migrants who attempt to return "home." In a similar ongoing fashion, *Aside from You/A Part of You* (1995) is an intimate performance event that takes place in someone's home after sharing a meal. It is a collective exercise where, for example, Báez might take the time to synchronize breathing with participants. The exercise invites participants who are often Dominican migrants themselves to build community around shared concerns.

As the structures of these works suggests, Báez's work is known for pushing the bounds of what might be considered a Latinx American theatre and performance canon. Even her most recognized and studied work, *Dominicanish* (1999), pushes these boundaries on a linguistic level. Beyond simple bilingualism, a trait that is commercially acceptable to a certain extent within the general field of Latinx literature, *Dominicanish* is known for employing a multiplicity of languages, dialects, and registers. Not only does the non-linear and fragmented work include a mix of Dominican Spanish and New York English but it also includes popular sayings, teenage slang, song lyrics, acronyms, and quotes from ancient Indian fables. Scholars have further noted how this use of language speaks to a transnational conceptualization of "home" that is disconnected from and has the space to critique national identity. Unlikely to have the exact same background that Báez brings to her work, through this use of language, the audience is invited to aesthetically confront and consider the experience of fragmentation and displacement on the stage in front of them. The fact that the work continued to transform during the ten years that Báez performed it and exists in multiple published iterations further defies canonical restrictions.

What further sets Baéz's work apart is its grounding in her simultaneous and non-binary negotiation of US, Latinx, and Black American realities and histories. This is an experience that, expanding on W.E.B. Du Bois's "double-consciousness," Juan Flores and Miriam Jiménez Román call a state of "triple-consciousness."[1] Following, among others, Silvio Torres-Saillant's critique of both a historical Dominican disavowal of Africanness and the racialized exclusion of Dominicans from the Latinx cultural imaginary, many scholars emphasize how Báez's embrace of her own Blackness in her work contradicts the anti-Blackness of both the US and Latinx America. Scholars have understood *Dominicanish* as an affirmation of Black American aesthetics and knowledge, a contradiction of Dominican nationalist and anti-Haitian—coded as anti-Black—ideology, a critique of both the myth of mestizaje and US multiculturalism, and an exploration of the lived experience of Blackness beyond national boundaries. Other works such as *Bliss. Co-Creating. Lecturance* (2017) and her performance text *Levente no. Yolayorkdominicanyork* demonstrate similar characteristics. Furthermore, Lorgia García-Peña argues that Báez's incorporation of Indian Kuchipudi dance concretizes the historic presence of East Indians who were brought to the Caribbean as indentured servants after slavery was abolished. In *Bliss*, the accompanying presence of Balinese instruments alongside Afro-Caribbean ones also speaks to the expansive nature of Báez's aesthetic. This rhizomatic way that Báez continues to explore belonging—as branching out in web formation rather than simply splitting along a border line—aligns her with a common characteristic of Caribbean theory and cultural production and challenges the established (post)colonial hierarchies of the Americas.

Megan Bailon

Note

1 Flores, Juan and Miriam Jiménez Román. "Triple-Consciousness? Approaches to Afro-Latino Culture in the United States." *Latin American and Caribbean Ethnic Studies* 4, no. 3 (2009): 319–328.

Major works

Bliss. Co-Creating. Lecturance (with Carlos Snaider; 2017)
Aparecer, Al parecer, A perecer (Wandering Soul Series) (2001)
Dominicanish (1999)
Apartarte/casarte [Aside from You/A Part of You] (1995)
Lo Mío Es Mío [What's Mine Is Mine] (with Claudio Mir; 1994)

Published works

Como la una/Como uma. New York: I. Om. Be. Press, 2013.
Comrade, Bliss Ain't Playing. New York: Latinarte, 2013.
De Levente: 4 textos para teatro performance. New York: I. Om. Be. Press, 2013.
Levente no. Yolayorkdominicanyork. New York: Latinarte, 2012.
Dominicanish: A Performance Text. New York: Graphic Art, 2000.

Further reading

Báez, Josefina. "Inner Dance. Outer Joy. Autology. A Route." In *Theatre and Cartographies of Power: Repositioning the Latina/o Americas*, edited by Jimmy A. Noriega and Analola Santana, 264–267. Carbondale: Southern Illinois University Press, 2018.
Cornet, Florencia V. "Performing New Nationalism / Performing a Living Culture: Josefina Báez's Dominicanish." In *African American Arts: Activism, Aesthetics and Futurity*, edited by Sharrell D. Luckett, 51–68. Lewisburg: Bucknell University Press, 2019.
Durán Almarza, Emilia María. "'At home at the border': Performing the Transcultural Body in Josefina Báez's *Dominicanish*." In *Transnationalism and Resistance: Experience and Experiment in Women's Writing*, edited by Adele Parker and Stephenie Young, 45–68. Amsterdam: Rodopi, 2013.
García-Peña, Lorgia. "Performing Identity, Language, and Resistance: A Study of Josefina Báez's *Dominicanish*." *Wadabagei* 11, no. 3 (Fall 2008): 28–45.
Irizarray, Roberto. "Traveling Light: Performance, Autobiography, and Immigration in Josefina Báez's *Dominicanish*." *Gestos* 42 (2006): 81–96.

Ramírez, Elizabeth C., and Catherine Casiano. "The Dominican Experience in Josefina Báez's Dominicanish." In *La Voz Latina: Contemporary Plays and Performance Pieces by Latinas*, edited by Elizabeth C. Ramírez and Catherine Casiano, 171–175. Urbana: University of Illinois Press, 2011.

Stevens, Camilla. *Aquí and Allá: Transnational Dominican Theater and Performance*. Pittsburgh: University of Pittsburgh Press, 2019.

SABINA BERMAN (MEXICO CITY, MEXICO, 1955–)

Sabina Berman is Mexico's leading living playwright. Born in 1955 to Polish-Jewish immigrants who met in Mexico City, she is successful in many genres, but her plays stand out as her hallmark because of their incisive humor, profound treatment of social issues, and superior productions. Berman's talent as a writer, producer, director, and television personality is exemplified by the multiple awards she has garnered. From accolades at international film and theatre festivals and nominations to the Academy Awards, to national awards for playwriting (including for children), journalism (print, television, film), and screenplays, Berman's work has been recognized repeatedly for its accessible yet sophisticated irreverence, and she is a key player on Mexico's intellectual scene. It is unusual if not unprecedented for someone who started as a poet and then embraced theatre to have an audience with the most fascinating and influential people in their country. Yet, over the years, Berman, through television programs like *Shalalá*, has connected with large audiences and dialogued with everyone from mothers of disappeared people to the president of Mexico. Over decades, Berman's myriad published plays (including one, *La grieta* [The Crack], which was distributed to thousands of retirees via the Mexican social security system in 1999) and sold-out performances in Mexico City and beyond add to this ability to reach people; and when Berman reaches people, especially through theatre, she is likely to change their way of thinking.

This is not to say that Berman's plays are dogmatic—quite the opposite. Take for example her hit play *Between Pancho Villa and a Naked Woman* (1993) ("Pancho" was added to the title of the English translation by Shelley Tepperman), which critics hail for Berman's uncanny ability to denaturalize social constructions. The play is about Gina, a Mexican woman navigating the macho myth of Villa, which lives on in her supposedly progressive lover. Sharon Magnarelli explains that instead of "simply denouncing (or, inversely, perpetuating) traditional gender roles (male or female), Berman shows them to be [historically based] citational performances."[1] This interpretation of the play—and the way it precedes and complements powerhouse theoretical works like Judith Butler's *Gender Trouble*—encapsulates most critical and audience responses. Yet Berman tells of a conversation with a man who had seen the play several time and lamented the loss of Villa's macho power (in one scene, Villa rides onto the stage straddling a large canon, which goes limp and emits a diminutive cannonball). Berman's strength is that she accepts these varied interpretations, noting: "And, just like with reality, the viewer sees themselves reflected."[2] Some authors turn to dogmatic dialogue to craft a specific message; Berman's feminist humor is elegantly nuanced. Other authors write pages of stage directions to control productions; Berman resists this temptation, though she often produces and/or directs her own plays, adaptations, and films, often alongside producer Isabelle Tardan. She sees art as a means to understand both the human condition and the complex social issues (chauvinism, power, corruption, fraud, violence) she regularly confronts: "Art doesn't have to be useful, yet I write because nothing has been more useful to me than certain works of literature to find meaning in the world."[3]

It is tricky to place Berman's play productions and publications on a strict timeline. Her plays, which she began to write and stage in the late 1970s, are routinely retitled as she rewrites, repurposes, and incorporates new ideas from specific productions. There was a time when it was an international sport to track down her playscripts, though now her major works (not all versions of each palimpsest, and not all translations) are published. The plays Berman chose to include in *Puro Teatro* (2005), her collected works, signal their importance: *The Agony of Ecstasy*, *Los dientes* [The Teeth], *En el nombre de Dios* [In the Name of God], *La grieta* [The Crack], *Muerte súbita* [Sudden Death], *Between Pancho Villa and a Naked Woman*, *Molière* and *Feliz nuevo siglo, doktor Freud* [Happy New Century, Doktor Freud, titled Freud Skating on Thin Ice in the translation by Kirsten F. Nigro], plus the children's plays *La maravillosa historia de Chiquita Pingüica* [The Marvelous Story of Little *Pingüica*], *Caracol y colibrí* [Snail and Hummingbird], and *El árbol de humo* [The Tree of Smoke]. Berman also considers the more recent *El narco negocia con dios* [A Narco Negotiates with God] (2012), and *Testosterona* [Testosterone] (2014) to belong squarely among her major works. There is always a new Berman play in the works, and her remarkable record of success continues, for example, with the March 2019 premiere, in Mexico City's Teatro Helénico, of *Ejercicios fantásticos del YO* [Fantastic Exercises of the SELF], which starred Gael García Bernal. Her plays also include *Yankee* (premiered in 1980 as *Bill*), *Krisis* (1996), *Aguila o sol* [Eagle or Sun] (1985), and *Puzzle* (1981). Kirsten F. Nigro, Shelley Tepperman, and Adam Versényi have been the most prolific in translating Berman's plays to English, and, in turn, Berman has adapted English language performances for the Mexican stage. These include the Australian performance piece *Puppetry of the Penis* (2004) and *eXtras* (2003), a wildly successful adaptation of Marie Jones's play *Stones in His Pockets*.

The production *eXtras* included the famous actors Demián, Bruno and Odiseo Bichir and is an excellent example of Berman's ability to draw a crowd with outstanding productions, with very positive reviews that included "renowned intellectuals as Olga Harmony and Carlos Fuentes."[4] *Stones in His Pockets*, which is about extras in a Hollywood film being shot in Ireland, with the concomitant exploitation and stereotypes, fits well as a theme on the Mexican stage, and *eXtras* is a good reminder that people and places underscore Berman's tremendous success. The Bichir brothers are only one example of the A-list stage, film, and television actors who have appeared in Berman's productions, and she has also collaborated on movie projects with the likes of Alfonso Cuarón and Alejandro González Iñárritu.

Writers, directors, producers, and actors are the "who" in Berman's theatre. The "where" is also critical to understanding the importance of Berman's plays. She has been widely produced throughout the Americas and Europe. College campus and regional theatres often stage her plays—they travel incredibly well. Her most recent production, *Testosterona*, premiered in Argentina, Madrid, and Mexico City. For decades, Berman has been an almost constant presence in large and small Mexico City performance spaces. One of the main areas for high-quality theatre in Mexico City is a series of venues behind the National Auditorium, where many of Berman's plays have been produced. One of these theatres, the Julio Castillo, was the location for Berman's hit play *Molière*, which, like *eXtras* and other Berman productions, explores the interplay between comedy and tragedy. At the time of the staging (2000) the theatre was being renovated, we were told, which allowed the layout to be reversed: the stage was in the middle of the theatre, the audience sat "backstage" and viewed the set, beyond which was the original theatre seating and the fictional audience. Berman, it seems, has the power, along with her creative team, to transform theatres, and she has certainly transformed Mexican theatre. To be a spectator of a Berman play is to witness the perfect combination of commercial and independent theatre, local and universal content, and, in the end, the devastating balance of comedy and tragedy.

Stuart A. Day

Notes

1 Sharon Magnarelli, "Tea for Two: Performing History and Desire in Sabina Berman's *Entre Villa Y Una Mujer Desnuda*," *Latin American Theatre Review* 30.1 (1996): 55.
2 Jacqueline Eyring Bixler, "Performing Culture(s): Extras and Extra-Texts in Sabina Berman's eXtras," *Theatre Journal* 56.3 (2004): 437.
3 Sabina Berman, *Puro Teatro* (Mexico City: Fondo de Cultura Económica, 2005), 269.
4 Ibid., 438.

Major works

Testosterona [Testosterone] (2014)
El narco negocia con Dios [A Narco Negotiates with God] (2012)
Feliz nuevo siglo, doktor Freud [Freud Skating on Thin Ice] (2000)
Molière (1998)
Between Pancho Villa and a Naked Woman (1993)
Muerte súbita [Sudden Death] (1988)
El suplicio del placer [The Agony of Ecstasy] (1978, premiered under the title *El jardín de las delicias*)

Published works

El Narco Negocia Con Dios; Testosterona. Introduction by Stuart A. Day. México, D.F.: Ediciones El Milagro/LATR Books, 2013.
The Theatre of Sabina Berman: the Agony of Ecstasy and Other Plays. Translated by Adam Versényi. Carbondale: Southern Illinois University Press, 2003.
La Grieta. In *Diálogos dramatúrgicos México-Chile*. Edition and Introduction by Stuart A. Day. México: Tablado IberoAmericano, 2002.
Molière. Translated by Shelley Tepperman. Toronto: Playwrights Union of Canada, 2002.
Between Pancho Villa and a Naked Woman. Translated by Shelley Tepperman. *Theatre Forum* 14 (1999): 91–108.
Krisis. *Tramoya* 52 (1997): 51–100.
Teatro De Sabina Berman. Mexico City: Editores Mexicanos Unidos, 1985.

Further reading

Bixler, Jacqueline Eyring. *Sediciosas Seducciones: Sexo, Poder y Palabras En El Teatro De Sabina Berman*. México, D.F.: Escenología, A.C., 2004.
Day, Stuart A. "It's My National Stage Too: Sabina Berman and Jesusa Rodríguez as Public Intellectuals." In *Mexican Public Intellectuals*, edited by Debra A. Castillo and Stuart A. Day. 117–138. New York: Palgrave, 2014.
Unruh, Vicky. "'It's a Sin to Bring Down an Art Deco': Sabina Berman's Theater among the Ruins." *PMLA/Publications of the Modern Language Association of America* 122, no. 1 (2007): 135–150.

AUGUSTO BOAL (RIO DE JANEIRO, BRAZIL, 1931–2009)

Augusto Boal, Brazilian theatre maker, author, and political figure, is better known as the founder of Theatre of the Oppressed, the Rainbow of Desire, and Legislative Theatre, all interactive, community-centered art forms meant to liberate participants from the oppressive impositions of society and empowering them to become critically engaged actors of their own lives. Boal believed that in the hands of the common people, theatre could become a catalyst for social change. Raised in Rio de Janeiro, he earned a degree in Chemical Engineering in the early 1950s that led him to pursue graduate studies at Columbia University, in New York. While there, he rekindled his childhood passion for theatre, studying with Professor John Gassner, joining the Writer's Group, and attending sessions at the Actor's Studio as an auditor. Upon finishing his degree, Boal returned to Brazil to work with the company Teatro de Arena, in São Paulo.

In the early 1960s *coup d'états* and some of the most repressive dictatorships in Latin America were taking place. In response, the theatre became inherently political and invested in national identity and active citizenship. Teatro de Arena was focused on producing thought-provoking and politically engaged work by national playwrights. Boal and his collaborator at the time, Gianfranco Guarnieri, were sponsoring the Seminário de Dramaturgia, a playwriting school attracting young talent from all over the country and producing their work.

Inspired by Piscator and Brecht, Teatro de Arena called themselves an activist theatre company meant to "influence reality and not merely reflect it."[1] They developed their very own style, often setting their productions within the frame of a fable, myth, historical event, or historical figure of importance to Brazilian history and experimenting with the role of actors as narrators and collective storytellers. Songs and live music were popular elements in their productions, leading to important collaborations with master composers like Caetano Veloso and Chico Buarque. The company became a great success and all the while, Boal's cultural activism intensified. In 1971, following the success of plays such as *Arena Conta Zumbi* [Arena Tells of Zumbi] (1965), and *Arena Conta Tiradentes* [Arena Tells of Tiradentes] (1967–1968), the company was preparing the third sequel *Arena Conta Bolivar* [Arena Tells of Bolivar] when Boal was arrested, and the production was banned from opening. While imprisoned, Boal was tortured, and shortly after his release, he self-exiled to Argentina.

Although Boal's contributions to the theatre are vast, he is better known for his work *Theatre of the Oppressed* (1973), published while in

Argentina. Here, he exposes a new system for theatre making where the process is shared with the spectators, giving them agency to intervene the action. The theatre director turns into the master of ceremonies facilitating interaction between the actors and the spectators. This role is called the joker (*coringa*). It encourages and guides participants into dramatic action. The Theatre of the Oppressed is the result of years of practice touring rural communities with Teatro de Arena and the development of the company's work and thought process, heavily influenced by Brecht's *Didactic Theatre* and Paulo Freire's *Pedagogy of the Oppressed*.

The main premise of Theatre of the Oppressed is that theatre is a tool for liberation. Boal argues Aristotelian theatre is coercive because in it, the audience is a passive receptor of information with no power to affect change. This model has become mainstream because it asserts the power of the dominant culture over the global majority, maintaining the status quo. Boal's model flips the power structure of the theatre-making process by inviting the audience to make the creative decisions that the playwright and the director would traditionally make. This liberates spectators from the "imposed finished visions of the world"[2] the mainstream theatre traditionally forces upon them, while raising consciousness in spectators about the social conditions of their lives.

In Theatre of the Oppressed, spectators become spect-actors,[3] active observers/participants with agency to transform the dramatic situation. They tackle complex situations on the stage that they might one day face in real life and they get to rely on the help of the community in the room to collectively seek solutions to the problem. Ultimately, this "rehearsal of revolution"[4] propels participants into thinking and acting for themselves in their real lives, emancipating themselves from the oppressive impositions the dominant culture places on sex, gender, race, ethnicity, economic status, and the like.

To transform spectators into spect-actors, Theatre of the Oppressed proposes a four-phase process. Phase one and two center on developing body awareness and expressive capabilities in all participants. This is achieved in a workshop setting, through a series of physical games and group activities. Boal compiled most of these games and exercises in *Games for Actors and Non-Actors* (1992). The third phase of the process is exploring theatre as language. Here participants play with collective forms of theatre making to start intervening in the dramatic action. The final phase is theatre as discourse, where spect-actors appropriate theatre-making tools and language, producing their own spectacles.

For theatre as language and as discourse Boal developed a series of techniques that allow participants to explore the role of actors.

Newspaper Theatre, where participants question the way everyday events are portrayed and disseminated to the masses, and Image Theatre, where participants use tableau and physical expression to have discussions around situations of oppression, are most commonly used in workshop settings. Other techniques such as Invisible Theatre require trained actors to perform previously rehearsed scenes in public spaces, without the audience ever knowing they witnessed a planned performance.

Forum Theatre is perhaps Boal's most popular and worldwide-known technique. Here actors perform a previously rehearsed scene, centering on a protagonist facing a situation of oppression. Then, the scene is performed a second time, but this time the joker invites the audience to freeze the action when they see an injustice occur and to take the role of the protagonist on stage to attempt to solve the issue. While multiple spect-actors take turns attempting to change/transform the situation in favor of the oppressed, everyone else present in the room is invested in dialogue and problem-solving. In Forum Theatre, the whole room is physically and mentally invested in transforming the reality of the scene in favor of the oppressed character(s). This shifts the attention from the stage to the community building unfolding in the room.

After a few years in Argentina, Boal self-exiled to Europe, settling in Paris where he continued to experiment with his techniques, touring Europe and subsequently the world with workshops, masterclasses, and lectures on Theatre of the Oppressed and its techniques. While in Europe, it became evident that people's economic realities and experiences with oppression were quite different than in Brazil and South America, leading Boal to question the efficacy of his work in a Euro-centric context. In Latin America, his work had emphasized communal liberation and empowerment toward social change; but in Europe, it was moving toward an exploration of self-liberation. In this context, Boal developed the Rainbow of Desire, a series of techniques meant to explore participants' internalized oppression, something Boal called "the cop in the head."[5] The Rainbow of Desire focuses on participants' own life experiences, giving each person a chance to explore their desires and internalized oppressions while receiving encouragement and support from the ensemble. This approach is often associated with psychodrama and other therapeutic uses of theatre making.

In 1986 Boal returned to Brazil, settling in Rio de Janeiro and opening Brazil's first Center for the Theatre of the Oppressed (CTO-Rio). Soon after, he got involved in local government, running for city council in 1992 and winning. He used his theatre-making system to engage with his constituents, holding public meetings where people named community problems and used theatre to enact situations where possible policies were played out, unveiling the advantages and disadvantages of the law. Citizens then used this information to vote in support or opposition to the policies. Using this method called Legislative Theatre, Boal was able to pass thirteen out of forty proposed legislations.

Of course, Boal's work has not escaped criticism. Scholars and practitioners alike have criticized his methods and politics by pointing to the contradiction between its Marxist origins and the predominantly middle-class, euro-centric audience that benefits from it. Nonetheless, Theatre of the Oppressed continues to be a worldwide system of theatre making practiced all over the world and recognized as a catalyst of social change. Former students and collaborators of Boal, including his son, Julian Boal, continue to uphold his legacy, inspiring theatre companies, community organizations, NGOs, and even established institutions such as colleges and universities to study and apply his methods in formal and informal settings alike.

Gina Sandí-Díaz

Notes

1. Augusto Boal, *Theatre of the Oppressed* (New York: Theatre Communications Group, 1985), 168.
2. Ibid., 155.
3. Augusto Boal, *The Rainbow of Desire* (London: Routledge, 1995), 40.
4. Boal, *Theatre of the Oppressed*, 141.
5. Augusto Boal and Susan Epstein, "The Cop in the Head: Three Hypotheses," *TDR* 34.3 (1990): 35.

Major works

Torquemada, Teatro del Centro (1972)
Arena Conta Bolivar [Arena Tells of Bolivar], Teatro de Arena (1971) [Censored]
Arena Conta Tiradentes [Arena Tell of Tiradentes], Teatro de Arena (1967)
Arena Conta Zumbi [Arena Tells of Zumbi], Teatro de Arena (1965)
Chapetuba Futebol Clube, Teatro de Arena [Cahpetuba Futbol Club] (1959)

Published works

The Aesthetic of the Oppressed. London: Routledge, 2006.
Hamlet and the Baker's Son. London: Routledge, 2001.
Legislative Theatre. London: Routledge, 1998.

The Rainbow of Desire. London: Routledge, 1995.
Games for Actors and Non-Actors. London: Routledge, 1992.
Theatre of The Oppressed. Translated by Charles A. and Maria-Odilia Leal McBride. New York: Theatre Communications Group, 1985.
Categorías de Teatro Popular. Buenos Aires: Ediciones Cepe, 1972.

Further reading

Boal, Julian and Kelly Howe, eds. *The Routledge Companion to Theatre of the Oppressed.* New York: Routledge, 2019.
Cohen-Cruz, Jan and Mary Schutzman, eds. *A Boal Companion: Dialogues on Theatre and Cultural Politics.* New York: Routledge, 2006.
Emert, Toby and Ellie Friedland, eds. *Come Closer: Critical Perspectives on Theatre of the Oppressed.* New York: Peter Lang, 2011.
Paterson, Doug. "A Brief Biography of Augusto Boal," *Pedagogy and Theatre of the Oppressed Website*, accessed January 31, 2021, https://ptoweb.org/aboutpto/a-brief-biography-of-augusto-boal/

GUILLERMO CALDERÓN (SANTIAGO, CHILE, 1971–)

Guillermo Calderón is one of Chile's most nationally and internationally recognized playwrights and directors. His plays—which have been performed in over twenty-five countries—are deeply political, taking on complex local and global issues. In addressing these concerns, Calderón has developed a meta-theatrical, self-critical dramaturgy that positions his plays as part of an ongoing practice of ideological questioning. In this process, Calderón does not shy away from paradoxes or dead ends. His plays offer no answers, instead they forge the space for politically thoughtful communities in the theatre.

Born in 1971, Calderón grew up during Augusto Pinochet's military dictatorship and came of age during Chile's democratic transition. This generational positioning deeply inflects his work and politics. Calderón trained as an actor at the University of Chile and, like many of his contemporaries, writes and directs his own work, resulting in a highly distinctive dramaturgy. Calderón does not work with a set company, though he favors collective, research-based processes, often with many of the same collaborators. The resulting plays are actor-centric but possess a strong literary quality, visual aesthetic, and authorial voice.

However, Calderón did not begin playwriting until his mid-thirties, which he attributes to an uncertainty about how to position his work in relation to Chilean politics. It was only with some distance from Chile—Calderón studied abroad in California, New York, and Italy—that he was able to begin writing. Fittingly, his first play, *Neva* (2006), foregrounds theatre's relationship to politics. In a St. Petersburg rehearsal room on Bloody Sunday, three actors (including Anton Chekhov's widow, Olga Knipper) gather to rehearse *The Cherry Orchard*. The rest of the cast is absent, having become embroiled in the massacre outside. As they await the cast, the actors gossip, discuss acting, and recreate the scene of Chekhov's death, unsettling the boundaries between art and life. When their conversation turns to politics, Masha fervently attacks the theatre as a bourgeoise distraction from the real urgency of politics. *Neva* stages an ironic ambivalence, as Calderón uses theatre as a platform to challenge its own value.

Neva was a tremendous success, launching Calderón's national and international career. Its run at the Teatro Mori in Santiago led to its inclusion in the 2007 Santiago a Mil International Festival, an international tour, and a 2013 run at the Public Theater in New York. However, Calderón did not feel the play resonated as politically radical as he had hoped. According to Calderón, the titular river *Neva* alludes to Santiago's Mapocho river—both "moving cemeteries" where the bodies of dissidents had been historically discarded.[1] However, he found that the implications of this connection were lost—evident to him when two of Pinochet's former ministers seemed to enjoy the production. In that moment, Calderón vowed to further radicalize his theatre. Thus, *Neva* not only launched his playwriting career, but it also launched a project to probe the limits and possibilities of political theatre.

In subsequent plays, Calderón renders his political discourse and its connection to contemporary events more explicit, tackling questions of nationalism and the militarized Chilean state (*Diciembre* [December], 2008), the student protest movement (*Clase* [Class], 2008), the legacy of dictatorship trauma and memorialization (*Villa*, 2011), the failures of the left (*Discurso* [Speech], 2011), the role of violence in resistance movements (*Escuela* [School], 2013; *B*, 2017), police corruption (*Mateluna*, 2016), the dynamics between the Global North and Global South (*Beben* [Quake], 2012; *Kiss*, 2014), and immigration and racism (*Dragón* [Dragon], 2019). Calderón incorporates similar dramaturgical and intertextual elements across his plays, creating a "narrative density" that allows them to speak "beyond themselves."[2] Each play is part of an ongoing critical project: they build upon and complicate each other, posing a prismatic critique of contemporary Chilean and global politics.

His plays take place at moments of crisis, highlighting, perhaps, the centrality of Chile's democratic transition in Calderón's thought: a revolution brews in Russia, wars threaten Chile on multiple fronts, students protest in the streets. From these moments, Calderón interrogates the possibility of real political change. Each play is set in places set apart from the events—a rehearsal room, an empty classroom, a safe house—and the theatre becomes a space for contemplation and debate. Indeed, the plays are structured primarily as dialectical debates, with ideological positions forming the primary marker of character and driving the dramatic action. This allows Calderón to test out, advance, and critique various sides.

Throughout his works Calderón collapses the boundaries between the theatre and the real world. His design aesthetic is a heightened theatrical naturalism. The sets and costumes are minimal or obviously fake, cables hang visibly from the lighting grid, and the language is often excessively quirky, highlighting its theatricality. These choices advance a Brechtian alienation and emphasize the fact that theatre is a space shared by both actors and audiences. It is a theatrically *real*—rather than illusionistic or immersive—space for contemplation; but the crises that loom outside remind the audiences that the urgent stakes of politics lie *outside* the theatre's walls.

At times Calderón further collapses the boundaries between theatre and reality—to draw even more attention to these tensions. Calderón often stages *Villa*—a debate concerning the memorialization of a dictatorship-era torture center—at former sites of detention and torture (in Chile and abroad), using the powerful memories present at these sites to invite his audiences into affective communities. *Mateluna*, perhaps, represents Calderón's most extreme effort to collapse the boundaries between theatre and reality, as well as a direct challenge to *Neva*'s proposition of theatre's political irrelevance. The play is a response to the arrest of Calderón's friend and collaborator, Jorge Mateluna, a former militant in the anti-dictatorship resistance and pardoned political prisoner. Mateluna had advised Calderón and the cast in the making of *Escuela*. While the cast was on tour with that play, Mateluna was arrested for a bank robbery. However, the process by which he was identified was corrupted, and false evidence was offered in the trial that convicted him. The play constitutes the company's efforts to expose this police corruption and pressure the judicial system for his release. The first half of the play consists of a series of plays-within-a-play, detailing the cast's efforts to understand Mateluna's relationship to political violence. The second half of the play presents the exculpatory evidence in Mateluna's favor, using direct address, documentary materials, and staged recreations of the events. The play is thus an uneasy kind of documentary theatre, in which documentary evidence is revealed as unstable and manipulable and the theatricality of state power is laid bare. It is, ultimately, a convincing case. However, though the play has been successful in raising awareness of Mateluna's case—reaching over 4,000 spectators—Mateluna remains in prison (an appeal to reopen his case was denied in 2018). Although *Mateluna* is premised on the idea that art can engage meaningfully with politics, its limitations are apparent—both in the play's meta-theatrical engagements with theatre—as well as in the play's inability to achieve the goal of Mateluna's freedom.

Calderón often concludes his plays with an annihilating gesture. In *Diciembre*, two pregnant twin sisters open their false bellies and hundreds of beans pour out onto the floor. The beans—symbolic of the Chilean nation—suggest the unproductivity and failure of the nation-state. In *Mateluna*, the actors violently throw chairs and other props on the stage, expressing their rage at the injustice done to Mateluna. Rather than resolve his plays, Calderón brings them to their breaking point, suggesting, perhaps, that politics itself must break before a way forward can be found. For Calderón, this moment is not the locus of theatre's failure, but is instead its place of possibility, offering the opportunity to transcend the theatre's walls. He asserts:

> when plays reach a dead end they can be about pessimism, but at the same time it's theatre, it's art, so ... there's always a possibility of creativity, of gathering around the village to think collectively, feel emotions collectively, experience theatre collectively.[3]

Jennifer Joan Thompson

Notes

1 Guillermo Calderón, "Tres actores en escena, una estufa, algunas sillas. Diálogo entre Guillermo Calderón y Soledad Lagos a propósito de *Neva*," interview with Soledad Lagos, *Telondefondo* 6 (2007): 1.
2 Qtd. in Isabel Baboun Garib, "Guillermo Calderón: Tres motivos para una poética casi trágica," *Apuntes de Teatro* 131 (2009): 23.
3 Guillermo Calderón, "When a 'Kiss' Is Not Just a Kiss," interview by Elyse Dodgson, *American Theatre*, September 25, 2017, accessed February 13, 2019, www.americantheatre.org/2017/09/25/when-a-kiss-is-not-just-a-kiss/

Major works

Dragón [Dragon] (2019)
B (2017)

Mateluna (2016)
Escuela [School] (2013)
Beben [Quake] (2012)
Speech (2011)
Villa (2011)
Diciembre [December] (2008)
Clase [Class] (2008)
Neva (2006)

Published works

B. Translated by William Gregory. London: Oberon Books, 2017.
Kiss. *American Theatre* 34 no. 7 (2017): 53–69.
Neva. Translated by Andrea Thome. New York: Theatre Communications Group, 2016.
"*Villa.*" Translated by William Gregory, *Theater* 43 no. 2 (2013): 65–97.
Speech. Translated by William Gregory, *Theater* 43 no. 2 (2013): 99–119
Teatro I: Neva, Diciembre, Clase. Santiago: LOM Ediciones, 2012.
Teatro II: Villa, Discurso, Beben. Santiago: LOM Ediciones, 2012.

Further reading

Baboun Garib, Isabel. "Guillermo Calderón: Tres motivos para una poética casi trágica," *Apuntes de Teatro* 131 (2009): 20–28.
del Campo, Alicia. "Nuevos realismos para viejos discursos: las guerras prometidas y el fin del Chile neoliberal en *Diciembre* de Guillermo Calderón," *FIT 2008: El teatro iberoamericano en el siglo XXI* (2009): 121–131.
Hernández, Paola S. *Staging Lives in Latin American Theater: Bodies, Objects, Archives.* Evanston: Northwestern University Press, 2021.
Madarieta, Ethan. "'Marichiweu': Performances of Memory and Mapuche Presence in Guillermo Calderón's *Villa*," *Latin American Theatre Review* 25, no. 2 (2020): 81–103.
Opazo, Cristián and Carlos Benítez, "'A Little Respect': Mateluna, de Guillermo Calderón," *Revista Conjunto* 185 (2017): 8–15.
Pottlitzer, Joanne. "Forgetting Filled with Memory," *Theater* 43, no. 2 (2013): 57–63. Thompson, Jennifer. "Horizons of Impossibility: The Political Imperative and the Dramaturgy of Guillermo Calderón," *Theatre Journal* 72, no. 2 (2021): 169–187.

EL CIERVO ENCANTADO (HAVANA, CUBA, 1996–)

Cuban theatre and performance group El Ciervo Encantado produces works that deal with the origins of Cuban identity and the ongoing struggle for Cubans to survive during extended periods of economic crisis. Known for experimental theatre, performance, and street interventions, their works challenge spectators to draw upon their experiences of being Cuban, while dialoguing with and drawing from fundamental texts from national literature. Through their unique performance techniques, they redefine theatre and interpret history and the contemporary Cuban experience by exploring themes of independence, colonialism, slavery, censorship, exile, and economic lack.

Before forming El Ciervo, director Nelda Castillo (Cárdenas, 1953)—together with Flora Lauten (Havana, 1942)—founded Teatro Buendía in 1986. As an actor and director in this important group, she honed a theatrical language that centered on "the study of the possible relations between music, dance and interpretation, as well as the formulation of new forms of scenic writing and dramaturgy of the spectacle."[1] While working as an instructor at the nation's premiere art school, the Instituto Superior del Arte (ISA), Castillo formed El Ciervo Encantado in 1996 along with three of her students: Mariela Brito, Lorelis Amores, and Eduardo Martínez. Critical components of the group's creative process are exhaustive research and rigorous rehearsals that are a study of the actor's body. As Lillian Manzor and Jaime Gómez Triana have written, the physical and psychological approach of the group stems from Grotowski's "negative path," in which the actor reveals their true interiority by taking off everyday masks. Through this process, the group has developed alternate embodied routes through breathing and channeling movement from the energy center of the body. Further, Castillo notes that the group never "represents" characters, but rather each actor transforms to become that figure. Their pieces are inspired by Artaud's Theatre of Cruelty, as they seek to create a new theatrical language beyond words that involves gestures, sound, lighting, and movement to both shock and connect with spectators.

Their innovative theatre mines Cuban literary works for inspiration into their investigation of national identity. Many of these are banned works by exiled writers that circulate underground in academic and artistic circles. By working closely with these texts, the group has succeeded in creating works that resist the Cuban state's desire to articulate a singular way of being Cuban by including censored or marginalized queer, black, indigenous, and female voices. This diverse inclusion leads El Ciervo to create works that enjoy multiple interpretations through myriad textual origins that tend toward expressionism rather than a narrative plot. Their critical boldness has also created issues for the group in terms of censorship, such as during the 13th Havana Biennial in 2019 when their street performances were approved but consistently marginalized and edited by the state. These experiences are indicative of the endurance needed to remain artistic provocateurs in a state-controlled environment that tends to stifle experimentation.

El Ciervo's *oeuvre* can be divided into two periods. The first centers on memory (1996–2010), and the second on survival (2010–present). According to Castillo, the title of their first performance and the name of the group, *El ciervo encantado* [Enchanted Deer] (1996), is related to the hunt, but also to freedom. This performance explored historical writings about Cuban independence and centered on freedom of expression. Using texts from Cuban writer and patriot Esteban Borrero Echeverría, in addition to works by Carlos Manuel Céspedes, José Martí, and Virgilio Piñera, the play features three masked archetypal characters—indigenous, creole, and black—who are covered in wet body paint. Set to Cuban *son* music, the characters emerge from the afterlife to a transcultural Cuba represented through the mixing of paint on the actors' bodies that is melded through ritualized movements. Other theatrical works that uncover the relationship between body and collective memory include *De donde son los cantantes* [From Cuba with a Song] (1999), which used the late, exiled writer Severo Sarduy's eponymous novel as an inspiration for an exploration of queer nightlife culture before the revolution. *Pájaros de la playa* [Beach Birds] (2001) also utilized Sarduy's novel as a backdrop for a theatrical experience about pain, liberation, and dying of AIDS. *Visiones de la cubanosofía* [Visions of Cubanosophy] (2005) mines Alfonso Bernal del Riesgo's text on Cuban psychology for a deep exploration into the island nation's identity. Bernal del Risego's text is fleshed out with characters and texts from Cuban icons such as José Martí, whose presence on stage has been described as an all-powerful god who brings together the past and the future as a figure in the hearts and dreams of all Cubans. Rounding out this period on memory is *Variedades Galiano* [Galiano Variety Show] (2010), which takes its direction from Reina María Rodríguez's novel of the same name, and also incorporates elements of Piñera's novel *La carne de René* [Rene's Flesh] as well as poetry by Flor Loynaz, Lezama Lima, and Luis Eligio Pérez. As Norge Espinosa notes, it's not as though these texts are the inspiration for *Variedades*, but rather that the deterioration of the origin texts signals a sense of ruin that is a poetic solution of Cubanness.[2]

The group's thematic focus on survival since 2010 is an artistic response to ongoing severe economic crises and the government's inability to provide for its citizens. With the loss of actors and a reconfiguration of the group in 2010, most of El Ciervo's works became shorter in length and—in Brechtian style—often involved significant audience interaction. *Cubalandia* (2011) treats Cuba's dual currency economy and features Brito as a loquacious street-savvy figure who moves through the serpentine ways in which Cubans negotiate this duality. A nearly voiceless character in *Rapsodia para el mulo* [Rhapsody for the Mule] (2012) performs the pain of endurance as experienced by the Cuban people in the form of a mule. Based on Lezama Lima's poem, it viscerally communicates the limits of the physical and the humane. *Triunfadela* [Triumphantland] (2015) features a grotesque, clown-like figure that challenges the construction of an essential Cuban identity in the post-revolutionary period. After the re-establishment of US–Cuban relations, *¡Guan melón, tu melón!* [One Melon, Two/Your Melon] (2016) tackles newly stimulated tourism practices. Here, art school student Yindra Regüeifero performs autobiographical scenes about how the unofficial tourist economy allows her to make ends meet. Next, *Departures* (2017) and *Arrivals* (2018) utilize documentary approaches, and treat actor Brito's personal experiences with migration, separation, exile, and subsequent return to one's native country. Their most recent works are shorter and more performance based. *PIB* [GDP] (2019), *Zona de silencio* [Zone of Silence] (2020), and *La anunciación* [The Annunciation] (2020), treat the dehumanization of Cuban citizens as they grapple with economic pressures, voicelessness, and the possibility for rebirth.

This group's exploration, while focusing on Cuban independence, memory, and survival, also acknowledges a Cuba that is not yet here. This layering of historical, literary, visual, and musical influences, in conjunction with an embodied language of the group's creation, has cemented their reputation as one of the country's most innovative and critical groups, and one of the most difficult to categorize.

Bretton White

Notes

1 "Teatro Buendía," Hemispheric Institute, accessed February 1, 2021, https://hemisphericinstitute.org/en/hidvl-collections/itemlist/category/125-buendia.html
2 Norge Espinosa, "Variedades Galiano Dossier." *La jiribilla*, no. 570: Año X, April 7–13, 2010.

Major works

Zona de silencio (2020)
Arrivals (2018)
Departures (2017)
Guan melón, tu melón (2016)

Rapsodia para el mulo (2012)
Cubalandia (2011)
Variedades Galiano (2010)
Visiones de la cubanosofía (2005)
Pájaros de la playa (2001)
El ciervo encantado (1996)

Published works

Castillo, Nelda. *El Ciervo Encantado: Textos de la Memoria*. Havana: Letras Cubanas, 2012. [Includes *El ciervo encantado*, *Un elefante ocupa mucho espacio*, *De donde son los cantantes*, *Pájaros de la playa*, *Visiones de la cubanosofía*, *Variedades Galiano*]

Further reading

Gárciga, Thais. "Departures: desgarre de memorias que no coagulan." *La jiribilla*, no. 824: Año XVI, April 22–28, 2017. www.lajiribilla.cu/articulo/departures-desgarre-de-memorias-que-no-coagulan

Gómez Triana, Jaime. "El Ciervo Encantado: Nuevas formas del teatro cubano," *INTI*, 71/72 (Primavera-Otoño 2010): 287–385.

Mansur, Nara. "Visiones de la Cubanosofía Dossier." *La jiribilla*, no. 570: Año X, April 7–13, 2010. www.lajiribilla.co.cu/2012/n570_04/570_06.html

Manzor, Lillian, and Jaime Gómez Triana. *El Ciervo Encantado: An Altar in the Mangroves*. New York: Hemi Press, 2015. https://ciervoencantado.hemi.press/

White, Bretton. *Staging Discomfort: Performance and Queerness in Contemporary Cuba*. Gainesville: University of Florida Press, 2020.

MIGDALIA CRUZ (NEW YORK CITY, NEW YORK, 1958–)

Migdalia Cruz is an award-winning and internationally produced multi-platform playwright, lyricist, translator, and librettist of more than sixty works. She was born in the Bronx to a family of Puerto Rican immigrants who only spoke Spanish at home. Although she has an MFA degree in playwriting from Columbia University, she learned to write plays with María Irene Fornés, her mentor, at International Arts Relations' (INTAR) Hispanic Playwrights-in-Residence Laboratory (HPRL). However, by the time Cruz joined HPRL, she had already held positions in various theatres (assistant house manager, properties with Mabou Mines, assistant director, dramaturge). This experience gave Cruz a knowledge of theatre from the inside which contributes to her plays' unique treatment of the spectacular. The first Latina to win a Commendation of The Susan Smith Blackburn Prize for Women Playwrights (1991) and winner of the 2013 Helen Merrill Distinguished Playwright Award, her plays break boundaries that cross genres, media, languages, and nations.

Cruz's plays are characterized by resilient women who are survivors of the physical and psychological trauma inflicted by patriarchal society and religion. Her characters are in a constant search for freedom and home. Since her early plays, the female body has been an ongoing site of contestation. As a matter of fact, the female body literally and metaphorically carries the inscriptions of violence as well as the marks of displacement and poverty. This is the case in one of her earlier plays, *Miriam's Flower* (1990), where the main character's process of healing is through the carving of flowers on her body as stigmata. In Cruz's early experimental musical fantasy *Welcome Back to Salamanca* (1988), the fleshiness of María's female body is first presented as meat to be consumed by males, but María ends up being the one eating them.

Her characters also break the parameters of traditional female beauty, like Miranda, in *Cigarettes and Moby Dick* (1996), who sees herself as homely because of low self-esteem. Or in *Fur* (1995), a complicated love story where most primal instincts are performed, where one female character is covered in thick, black hair and exhibited as a freak. Beauty, for Cruz, is "the transformation of women from sexual object to spiritual being."[1] They are victims who love and dream of a different life and a different future. Although they end up killing, it is only through that violent act that they reach physical and spiritual autonomy. In the end, her characters are all rebels seeking individual freedom in extreme circumstances. Paradoxically, Cruz's use of violence opens up a space in which her audience can see that the characters' situations are constructed and, as such, can change. If her characters are able to heal in the midst of systemic violence, there is hope for communal healing.

Theatre allows Cruz to explore taboo subjects, especially those related to eroticism. She dares to enter the "forbidden" territories of incest, masturbation, nudity, homoerotic and heterosexual acts, exploring the limits of what is acceptable onstage and on the page through impactful visual and linguistic images. Theatre is also the site through which Cruz tells the stories of forgotten historical figures such as Lolita Lebrón, a member of the Puerto Rican Nationalist Party; Roberto Cofresí, a Puerto Rican pirate; and Robert Johnson, a Blues master from Mississippi's Delta region.

It is through Cruz's unique theatrical language that her readers find beauty in what is ugly. She writes short scenes, like her mentor Fornés, often times incorporating a narrative voice. Her plays are non-linear, with open and fragmented structures. Each character speaks their own lyrical idiolect of English which signals their social position and age group. Code switching poetically shows off their multidialectical abilities. Her use of ellipsis suggesting pauses is as important as spoken language. Though most of her characters have Spanish-sounding names and many of the stories come from the playwright's experiences, the force of her writing shows that the Nuyorican/Latina female experiences are an American experience, a human experience.

Cruz's attention to language goes beyond its connection to sociocultural identity. She is interested in language's connection to power and its performative possibilities. *Satyricoño* (2016), for example, is a dystopic musical that incorporates actors along with bunraku puppets playing the masses, Nino Rota's music from Fellini's films, jazz, punk-rock, hip-hop, reggaeton, and jingles. Inspired by Petronius's and Fellini's *Satyricon*, Cruz riffs on various linguistic registers. This multiple use of linguistic and musical registers suggests that characters also find "home" in the performance of languages and the hybridization of musical traditions.

Just as her plays cross linguistic registers, they also incorporate a varied musical repertoire. But music is never used to create ambiance, as is often the case on the US stages. The musical crossings in Cruz's plays mix high culture and popular forms and perform the blurring of generic boundaries characteristic of her playwriting. *Cigarettes and Moby Dick*, for example, uses Edith Piaf and Celia Cruz, as well as The Trammps' "Disco Inferno." The "burn, baby burn" refrain of the song, a metaphor for the musical heat on the dance floor, literalizes on stage the passionate lovemaking between the two characters. But the refrain also reminds us of the phrase chanted at the Los Angeles Watts Riots by those protesting police brutality. The best example of Cruz's playwriting in relation to music is *Da Bronx Rocks* (2007), a site-specific work performed from a barge moored on New York's East River as part of Mabou Mines' *Song for New York: What Women Do While Men Sit Knitting*. She worked with Lisa Gutkin who composed tunes from Nigerian "call and response" to Puerto Rico's disappearing *baquiné* to Bosnian riffs.

Reviews of her plays often underscore the dual set of feelings they elicit: funny and sad, familiar and foreign, erotic and repulsive, mysterious and mundane. She lets the audience see the effects of her characters' individual attempts to wrestle with responsibility. Her poetic realism creates imaginative works that break with theatrical structures as they question the very fabric of our contemporary societies. Although her plays are considered "risky" by the theatrical establishment because they challenge the audience's cultural comfort zone, her theatre always makes us feel more human. In her own words, "it gives us a chance to feel something and to see that we are not alone ... [It] haunts our sensibilities and resonates in our memories."[2]

Lillian Manzor

Notes

1. Migdalia Cruz, "Fur," in *Out of the Fringe: Latina/Latino Theatre and Performance*, eds. Caridad Svich and María Teresa Marrero (New York: Theatre Communications Group, 2000), 72.
2. Migdalia Cruz, *336 CPW Newsletter* (Spring 1997).

Major works

Lives of the New Kind of Saints (2020)
Satyricoño (2018)
The Book of Miaou: Don't Drink Everything Your Mother Pours You (2017)
El Grito del Bronx (2008)
Salt (1997)
Fur (1995)
Miriam's Flowers (1990)

Published works

El Grito del Bronx and Other Plays. Southgate, CA: No Passport Press, 2010. [Includes *Yellow Eyes*; *Salt*; *From the Country to the Country of the Bronx: Da Bronx Rocks: A SONG*.]
Frida. In *Puro Teatro: An Anthology of Latina Theatre, Performance, and Testimonios*, edited by Nancy Saporta Sternbach and Alberto Sandoval Sánchez. Tucson: University of Arizona Press, 2000.
Lucy Loves Me. In *Latinas On Stage: Criticism and Practice*, edited by Alicia Arrizón and Lillian Manzor. Berkeley: Third Woman Press, 2000.
The Have-Little. In *Contemporary Plays by Women of Color*, edited by Roberta Uno and Kathy Perkins. New York: Routledge, 1996.
Miriam's Flowers. In *Shattering the Myth: Plays by Hispanic Women*, edited by Linda Feyder. Houston: Arte Público, 1992.

Further reading

Escoda Agustí, Clara. "I Carve Myself into My Hands." *Hispanic Review* 75.3 (Summer 2007): 289–311.
García, Armando. "Freedom as Praxis: Migdalia Cruz's Fur and the Emancipation of Caliban's Woman." *Modern Drama* 59.3 (2016): 343–362.
Lopez, Tiffany Ana. "Violent Inscriptions: Writing the Body and Making Community in Four Plays by Migdalia Cruz." *Theatre Journal* 52 (2000): 51–66.

Perales, Rosalina. "El Bronx también existe: Teatro breve de Migdalia Cruz," *Ollantay Theater Magazine* 18.35–36 (2010): 118–127.

Sandoval-Sanchez, Alberto. "Nuyorican Fairy Tales: Allegories of Existence and Bare Survival in Migdalia Cruz's and Eddie Sánchez's Theater." *Hispanic Issues Online* 20 (Spring 2018): 252–284.

Santana, Analola. "Teatro Latino en los Estados Unidos: La estética teatral de Migdalia Cruz." *Cuadernos de Literatura* 37 (January–June 2015): 361–379.

NILO CRUZ (MATANZAS, CUBA/MIAMI, FLORIDA, 1961–)

Almost inevitably the first thing anyone says about Nilo Cruz was that he is the very first Latinx playwright to have won the Pulitzer Prize for drama, for his play *Anna in the Tropics* (2002, as of this writing there are two more Latinx winners of Pulitzer Prizes: Quiara Alegría Hudes in 2012 and Lin-Manuel Miranda in 2016). The second thing people marvel at is that *Anna* won the prize before it had a New York City debut, almost the *sine qua non* for consideration, and that none of the prize committee members saw its world premiere Coral Gables production. This means that, unusually enough, the play was awarded the prize based solely on the text. And Cruz has remained famous for the writerly qualities of his work. Ben Brantley, in his *New York Times* review of the New York production, famously said it was "better on the page than on the stage,"[1] a backhanded tribute to the lyricism of the play.

Indeed, all of Cruz's plays are notable for their highly poetic quality; in his interview with Jody McAuliffe, at various points he describes his work as: "lyrical," "magical," "theatrical," "formal." In the same interview he comments on his preference for "heightened language," and for drama that deals with emotions (without being sentimental).[2] His work, he feels, speaks most strongly to a Latinx sensibility that values the metaphorical, the involvement of the whole body and self rather than (as he says is typical of Anglo-American drama) theatre from the neck up. Furthermore, he refuses to limit his imagination to what Caridad Svich and Maria Teresa Marrero in their 2000 collection *Out of the Fringe* identified as significant challenge in production of Latinx drama: mainstream audiences expect the plays to be either satisfyingly exotic or acceptably ethnic. Cruz tends not to explicitly address ethnicity, nor the thematics of immigration, nor the mainstream version of Latinx magic realism. He is, accordingly, less interested in succeeding with the standard Broadway audience, which is largely elite, white, and elderly, than reaching out to Latinx and regional theatre audiences who he finds more deeply appreciate his work.

Nilo Cruz was born shortly after the Cuban Revolution, in 1961, in Matanzas, Cuba, and he came to the US with his parents when he was ten years old. Young Cruz thought of himself as a poet but was drawn to theatre by a charismatic teacher at Miami Dade Community College. He was working as a cargo loader at the airport when he had the opportunity to take a workshop with the great Cuban American playwright María Irene Fornés; after seeing his direction of a scene from her play *Mud,* she invited him to International Arts Relations (INTAR) in New York City. She recommended him to continue studying, and during his graduate work at Brown University, he had the mentorship of Pulitzer Prize winning playwright Paula Vogel. Beginning in 1995 he embarked on a long collaboration with the McCarter Theatre in Princeton, and with its artistic director Emily Mann. They produced a number of his subsequent plays, including *A Park in Our House* (1995), *Two Sisters and a Piano* (1998), and *Anna in the Tropics* and *Bathing in Moonlight* (2016).

While most of his plays are written in English, he has worked on versions of both *Anna* and *Exquisita agonía* [Exquisite Agony] (2018) in Spanish (*Exquisita agonía* was produced at Repertorio español in New York City in 2018 and GALA Hispanic Theatre in Washington, DC in 2020). While Emily Mann says she sees the influence of Chekhov, García Lorca, and Tennessee Williams in his style, scholar José Esteban Muñoz argues that all his work is written under the sign of "cubanía," a way of seeing and structure of feeling that is deeply and specifically Cuban. Cruz himself points to the importance of a childhood profoundly influenced by three women: his grandmother, his mother, and an older sister.

Some of the political threads that connect Cuba to his plays can be found in *Two Sisters and a Piano*. Before its revision into a full-length play for live production onstage, it was originally written as a shorter radio play. It is set in Cuba in 1992 and focuses on two artistic sisters who are under house arrest. The play eschews the easy critique of Cuban revolutionary politics, to hone in on the inner lives and desires of these political prisoners: the writer, Maria Celia, is prohibited from writing; the musician, Sofia, has access, but only for a while, to an out-of-tune piano. In his analysis of this play, José Esteban Muñoz rightly points out that it frustrates a Western sense of plot, speaking instead "to the emotional life world of *cubanía,*"[3] in which the characters represent different aspects of the nation during the difficult times of the Special Period, but without falling into political cliché or strident ideological positioning.

Like *Two Sisters, Hortensia and the Museum of Dreams* (2001) is set in Cuba, this time during Pope John II's historic visit in January 1998.

Two stories intertwine in this play. The first tells of a brother and sister who are facing reunion after Operation Pedro Pan separated them from each other in the US and from their family left behind in Cuba decades ago. The second story, which gives the title to the play, involves an Afro-Cuban elder who maintains a reliquary. The two siblings have been stalled in their full development to adulthood by the abrupt childhood exile, and the play forces the audience to take note of their stuttering re-engagement with their home country through the use of a Tibetan bell, which rings intermittently throughout the play to indicate suspension of reality, contrasting with the Afro-Cuban musical theme associated with Hortensia.

Anna in the Tropics brings Cuba across the straights to Ybor City, Florida. Set in a cigar-rolling factory in 1929, on the edge of the Great Depression as well as the transformation of the tobacco industry to machine-made cigarettes, the play focuses on the way all the characters in this small world are affected by the new lector (reader) they hire for the factory, a man named Juan Julian, who chooses Tolstoy's *Anna Karenina* as his text, rather than the newspapers and political tracts that were more common reading fare in actual cigar factories of the time. The play, then, nostalgically traces a shift in labor from artisan to cog in a factory wheel, but the emphasis, as is typical of Cruz, is not the social, but rather the affective transformation in his characters.

Other plays depart from the specificity of "cubanía," such as *Lorca in a Green Dress*, which offers a surreal homage to the Spanish playwright and poet, in a play even less traditional in structure. Through fragments of dialogue and music, the play re-enacts scenes from Lorca's life. It is set in Purgatory, imagined as a Dali-esque landscape of dreams, that sometimes seems like a cabaret show. A series of spirits embody moments and affects: Lorca in bicycle pants, Lorca in a green dress, Lorca with blood, etc. Despite its biographical inspiration, this play takes Cruz far from realist territory, deepening the emphasis on nonlinear drama, full of the magical, mysterious, musical elements he loves. This unconventional, non-plot-driven, symbol-heavy play is a harbinger of the kinds of work Cruz will continue to develop in the following decade, right up to his most current play as of this writing, *Exquisita Agonía*, a dream-like story of an opera singer's efforts to recuperate her lost love by searching out the person who received her deceased husband's heart in a transplant operation.

There are only a handful of scholarly studies that look closely at the work of this great Cuban American playwright, perhaps because his elusive work defies easy categorization within either Latinx or mainstream American theater. He is a dramatic poet of love, loss, mystery, a writer of ideas, and a generator of surreal images. As Hilton Als wrote in a glowing review, where other playwrights give us mind-numbing talk, "Cruz conducts arias with his pen."[4]

Debra A. Castillo

Notes

1. Ben Brantley, "The Poetry of Yearning, the Artistry of Seduction," *New York Times*, November 17, 2003, https://go-gale-com.proxy.library.cornell.edu/ps/i.do?p=AONE&u=nysl_sc_cornl&id=GALE%7CA227198686&v=2.1&it=r&sid=ebsco
2. Jody McAuliffe, "Nilo Cruz" (interview), *South Atlantic Quarterly* 99.2/3 (2000): 461–470.
3. José Esteban Muñoz, "The Onus of Seeing Cuba: Nilo Cruz's *Cubania*," *South Atlantic Quarterly* 99.2/3 (2000): 456.
4. Hilton Als, "Ghosts and Hosts," *New Yorker*, January 23, 2006, 94.

Major works

Exquisita Agonía [Exquisite Agony] (2018)
Bathing in Moonlight (2016)
Sotto Voce (2014)
The Color of Desire (2010)
Lorca in a Green Dress (2003)
Anna in the Tropics (2002)
Hortensia and the Museum of Dreams (2001)
A Bicycle Country (1999)
Two Sisters and a Piano (1998)
Night Train to Boliña (1995)

Published works

Sotto Voce. New York: Theatre Communications Group, 2016.
The Color of Desire/Hurricane: Two Plays. New York: Theatre Communications Group, 2011.
Beauty of the Father. New York: Dramatist's Play Service, 2007.
Anna in the Tropics. New York: Theatre Communications Group, 2003.

Further reading

Del Busto Ramirez, Kimberly. "The Lost Apple Plays: Performing Operation Peter Pan." *Studies in Twentieth and Twenty-First Century Literature* 32.2 (2008): Article 6.
Delgadillo, Theresa. "Another Cubanía, Another Latinidad." *Latino Studies* 16.3 (2018): 341–360.

Mann, Emily. "Nilo Cruz" (interview), *Bomb*. December 1, 2003, 70–75.
Rossini, Jon. "The Pleasure of Reading: Cruz, Tolstoy and the Pulitzer." *Gestos* 20.40 (2005): 63–77.

CUATROTABLAS (LIMA, PERÚ, 1971–) AND MARIO DELGADO (1947–2016)

The year of 2021 marks the fiftieth anniversary of Grupo de Teatro Cuatrotablas, a theatre group that laid the foundation for an innovative theatrical language in Peru. Based in the city of Lima, and questioning Eurocentric frameworks for artistic creation, Cuatrotablas embraced ancestral cultures both as a source of aesthetic and political worldmaking, and as a site of knowledge production. Likewise, the group's quest for their own artistic language developed a collaborative theatrical form based on a shared community. Known as *teatro de grupo*, or group theatre, it conceptualizes and puts into practice creative processes in which each member of the group participates in an artistic dialogue oriented by social struggles, bringing together art and life.

Since its inception in 1971, Cuatrotablas aimed to create a new theatrical language that would emerge from and engage with diverse idiosyncratic histories in Latin America. The Cuban Revolution (1959), different socialist projects throughout the region, repressive military dictatorships in the 1970s and 1980s, and social movements of resistance, shaped a new generation of theatre artists that weaved stage languages with a strong and long-lasting political activism. Along with groups like Teatro Experimental de Cali (1955) and La Candelaria (1966) in Colombia, Libre Teatro Libre in Argentina (1969), Augusto Boal's Theatre of the Oppressed (1960s) in Brazil, and its fellow compatriots Yuyachkani (1971) in Peru, Cuatrotablas was part of a new wave of theatre practices. They reimagined theatre's relationship with the written text, exploring forms of bodily, musical, and lyric theatrical playwriting. One of the driving forces behind these experimentations was Mario Delgado (1947–2016), founding member and director of the group. He understood and designed his group's practices as embodied research. The very notion of *teatro de grupo* echoes his commitment to a persistent life project: he gave everything to and for Cuatrotablas, and by the end of his life, his passing in poverty would be a reminder of what still must be done to acknowledge and reward the social importance of artistic labor.

In dialogue with the *teatro de grupo* tradition, two influential figures on Cuatrotablas' work were Jerzy Grotowski (1933–1999), especially with his book *Towards a Poor Theatre* (1968), and Eugenio

Barba (1936–) and his concept/practice of "Third Theater," explored with the Odin Teatret. These European directors were in close dialogue with Latin American theatre collectives, exploring new artistic practices that intertwine life and theatre, and theatre and sociopolitical practices. Cuatrotablas parallels its artistic influence in experimental theatrical practices, both nationally and internationally, with these renowned directors. Together they created artistic networks across the world, gathering for groundbreaking transnational projects.

The founding members of Cuatrotablas came together through their first piece, *Tu país está feliz* [Your Country Is Happy] (1971), a political-musical collective creation. Among them were Mario Delgado, Soledad Mujica, Aurora Mendieta, Ana Gorriti, Hilda Collantes, Nora Curonisy, Manuel Cervantes, Walker Cooper, Enrique Avilés, Marco Iriarte, Alberto Chávez, Tito Falvy, Stojan Vladic, and Douglas Tarnawieski, performing roles both on and off stage. From this first ensemble, Cuatrotablas reinvented itself through different moments in recent Peruvian history, shaping ten artistic *generaciones* or "cohorts" of subsequent ensembles that included the group's youngest members, who would continue training and working together while other members left the ensemble to pursue independent projects.

Cuatrotablas's method focuses on the actor's training of body and voice, first warming-up the body to reconnect the actor with their spine and balance; secondly, inviting a learning process of self-reflection and questioning of the artistic creation; later, following a process of *construcción* or building of movements meant to find precision, physically and mentally; and finally, improvising on stage to freely explore creative possibilities for non-lineal narratives. For the group, improvisation is the latest stage of individual and collective creation, because it is only possible to improvise on the basis of what is well-known and well-researched. Cuatrotablas focuses on the creative process of physical and intellectual daily training, to analyze and rewire the ways in which the performers' bodies have lost and can regain self-physical-consciousness.

The *Oye* saga (1971–2004) is the best example of Cuatrotablas's search of a theatre of their own and an expression of their method. Built as a collective creation, born on the stage through the actors' theatre training, the piece was based on poems and songs on the contradictions of a national identity in a country culturally, socially, and politically fractured. The foundational *Oye* (1972) weaves a ludic narrative comprised by a series of vignettes where the actor-characters invite the audience to reflect upon their own context and their role in society. This is why the appellative "*oye*" ("hey!" or "listen!") is an invitation to the audience to join the actors in a concerted effort to understand their national history and to act in order to transform it. Further reinventions addressed societal issues in different moments of recent history: *Oye nuevamente* (1983) was inspired in the multiplication of informal small businesses in the chaotic capital city of Lima; while *Oye nuevamente hoy* (1997) was inspired by the actors' migration stories, reflecting upon their personal and collective past.

Oye, like most of Cuatrotablas's pieces, was conceived for a circular stage, close to the audience, and meant to be performed in any space: public squares, schools, universities, and small towns in different Peruvian regions and internationally. The characters dress in everyday clothes and the stage is void of settings or furniture: based on their laboratory's physical training, the actors' bodies build the scenery; for example, they gesture actions like rowing on a boat, and this action would conjure on stage the ships that landed in the New World; or they would climb on each other, creating a human mountain to plant the national flag. They barely use props, adding just some cubes and objects that will accompany the narrative of their bodies.

Within Cuatrotablas's legacy, the Arguedian cycle deserves a separate mention. Working with texts by Peruvian writer and ethnographer José María Arguedas (1911–1969), the group explores the fissures and connections between orality, theatricality, and the written word. *Arguedas o el suicidio de un país* [Arguedas or The Suicide of a Country] (2007), *Los ríos profundos* [Deep Rivers] (2008), *Los Ernestos* (2010), and *Arguedas, entre cantos y cuentos* [Arguedas, Between Songs and Stories] (2010) navigate tension and reconciliation, in a constant process of connecting the actors' life experiences with their country's history. Through songs and dance in both Spanish and Quechua, these pieces revisit Andean traditions on stage as a way to reconnect with new senses of belonging. Arguedas's writing is a point of departure for an eclectic theatricality made possible through a collage of music, words and songs, rituality, and the personal research of each performer, who brings to the stage their experiences of migration, bilingualism, and cultural diversity.

In May 1978, Cuatrotablas organized the first "Encuentro Ayacucho," in the city of Huamanga, in the Central Peruvian Andes. This was a point of encounter for different experimental theatre groups, coming from Latin America, Europe, and Asia. From avant-garde stage explorations, to the reincorporation of ritualistic theatricalities, to the dialogues opened by the Odin Teatret and Butoh traditions, "Encuentro Ayacucho" was a trans-disciplinary and trans-cultural experience that reshaped the theory and practice of theatre and performance across cultures. Most importantly, Cuatrotablas engaged with the community of Ayacucho, transforming an artistic encounter into a collective learning effort. The Ayacucho *Encuentros* have gathered every ten years, the most recent of which occurred in 2018 in the wake of Mario Delgado's passing. From a desire to find a theatrical language that would intertwine thinking and doing, and from a persistent effort to transverse individual and sociopolitical realities, Cuatrotablas stands as a central referent of Latin American theatre. Its tenth cohort of artists has found ways of staying current and continues bringing their pieces to small towns in the deepest regions of Peru, to keep learning and growing with their audiences. Cuatrotablas's collective resilience for fifty years is a testament to how theatre can be transformative, and above all, a site for political imagination.

Leticia Robles-Moreno

Major works

La ciudad sin ti [The City Without You] (2017)
El banquete de Mariátegui [Mariategui's Banquet] (2011)
Los ríos profundos [Deep Rivers] (2010)
Arguedas, el suicidio de un país [Arguedas, The Suicide of a Country] (2006)
La nave de la memoria [The Ship of Memory] (2001)
Oye nuevamente hoy [Listen Again Today] (1996)
El pueblo que no podría dormir [The Town that Couldn't Sleep] (1992)
Oye nuevamente [Listen Again] (1983)
La agonía y la fiesta [The Agony and the Festival] (1982)
Oye [Listen] (1972)
Tu país está feliz [Your Country Is Happy] (1971)

Further reading

Espinoza Domínguez, Carlos. *Mario Delgado: La sabiduría del eterno discípulo*. Lima: San Marcos, 2009.
Ramos-García, Luis, and Mario Delgado. *La nave de la memoria: Cuatrotablas, treinta años de teatro peruano*. Lima, Minneapolis: Asociación para la Investigación Actoral, 2004.
Rizk, Beatriz J. *Imaginando un continente: Utopía, democracia y neoliberalismo en el teatro latinoamericano. Tomo II: Colombia, Venezuela, Perú, Chile, Argentina, Bolivia*. Lawrence: LATR Books, 2010.
Salazar, Hugo. "Cuatrotablas, Yuyachkani y la identidad nacional." *Latin American Theatre Review* (Spring 1987): 81–83.
Seda, Laurietz, ed. *Teatro contra el olvido*. Lima: Universidad Científica del Sur, 2012.
Vargas Salgado, Carlos. "José María Arguedas: Memoria y teatralidad en los Andes." *Revista de Crítica Literaria Latinoamericana* 39.77 (2013): 303–324.

MARÍA IRENE FORNÉS[1] (HAVANA, CUBA/NEW YORK CITY, 1930–2018)

María Irene Fornés, considered by many to be the mother of Latinx playwriting, was an influential and award-winning playwright, director, and teacher. Born in Havana, Cuba, Fornés, the youngest of six children, immigrated to the United States in 1945 with her sister Margarita, and mother Carmen, a former schoolteacher. Earlier that year, her father Carlos, a low-level bureaucrat in Cuba's civil service, died of a heart attack at the age of fifty-three. Fornés and her sister were raised by their mother in New York City, where she resided for the rest of her life. Fornés wrote and directed more than fifty plays that were produced throughout the United States and internationally including in Cuba, Peru, England, France, Germany, Spain, Denmark, Sweden, Russia, and India. *Tango Palace* (1963) was her first produced play and *Letters from Cuba* (2000) was her final play. She won an unprecedented nine Obie Awards and her play, *What of the Night?* (1990) was a finalist for the Pulitzer Prize in Drama. Fornés eschewed identity politics yet her work has been described as feminist, Latinx, lesbian, and avant-gardist. She was also an influential educator, teaching playwriting across the US, and especially through her founding of the Hispanic Playwrights in Residence Lab (HPRL, 1981–1992), at International Arts Relations (INTAR), a New York City theatre committed to producing works by Latinx writers, where she trained many celebrated Latinx playwrights of the late twentieth century. During her final years, Fornés suffered from Alzheimer's disease, and was cared for by family, friends, former students, and colleagues, while she resided at the Amsterdam House in New York City, where she died in 2018. Her later years are poignantly captured in the award-winning documentary film, *The Rest I Make Up* (2018), directed by Michelle Memran.

Largely an autodidact, Fornés never completed high school after her arrival to New York City, yet she pursued an artistic path. In the early 1950s, she studied with Abstract Expressionist painter, Hans Hofmann (1889–1966), whose push-pull theory examining dynamic visual energies informed her future theatre work. In 1953, while painting in Paris, Fornés attended the original production of Samuel Beckett's *Waiting for Godot*, directed by Roger Blin. At the time she

---

1 Note, this entry includes diacriticals on Fornés' name unless they were not included in the original publication. During her lifetime, Fornés chose not to include accents on her published work. Since her death, Fornés scholars use diacriticals to more precisely highlight Fornés's Cuban-American identity as well as emphasize the proper pronunciation of her name.

did not speak French but was hugely inspired by the performance. She began writing in 1961 while in a relationship with writer Susan Sontag (1933–2004). To help Sontag with momentary writer's block, she began writing a short story by opening a cookbook at random and using the first word of each sentence on the page as inspiration. When Fornés began writing plays, this use of found materials influenced her theatrical process. In the early 1960s, Fornés became a member of the Actors Studio Playwrights' Unit, where she learned acting techniques from Lee Strasberg (1901–1982) and Gene Frankel (1919–2005) and applied their pursuit of replicating authentic human emotion and behavior to her playwriting.

Fornés's groundbreaking and award-winning plays are celebrated for their powerful female characters, linguistic exactitude, culturally diverse narratives, and theatrical experimentation. Her works often explore female characters searching for expression, empowerment, and education. She believed that a playwright ought to write what intrigues her, which may or may not be related to her cultural background. Consequently, she created plays, through spare, poetic, and visceral dialogue, that examined diverse cultural worlds including eight Anglo women preparing an educational fundraiser in 1935 New England (*Fefu and Her Friends*, 1977), a European family in Budapest confronting nuclear war (*The Danube*, 1982), a Cuban American family struggling to survive in the 1940s Bronx (*Sarita*, 1984), a military household in Latin America dealing with torture and oppression (*The Conduct of Life*, 1985), and British actors seeking to stage Ibsen's *Hedda Gabler* in 1890s London (*The Summer in Gossensass*, 1998). Fornés experimented with theatrical forms to create site-specific works, plays that emphasized character exploration, and plays inspired by objects found at thrift shops and flea markets such as 1930s chiffon dresses (*Fefu and Her Friends*), a 1901 domestic servant's diary (*Evelyn Brown, A Diary*, 1980), Hungarian language lesson records (*The Danube*) and an ironing board, axe, and pitchfork (*Mud*, 1983).

As a key figure in the Off-Off Broadway movement, which generated numerous collectives, she championed experimental theatre creation through the co-founding of the New York Theatre Strategy (NYTS, 1973–1979), a collective that presented over twenty experimental works including her seminal play, *Fefu and Her Friends*. In 1978, several Off-Off Broadway playwrights, including Sam Shepard, Murray Mednick, and herself, founded the Padua Hills Festival and Workshop (Padua, 1978–1995), in Southern California, which became an annual haven for the production and teaching of experimental playwriting. Fornés directed, wrote and taught at Padua, where she created early versions of plays such as *The Danube*, *The Conduct of Life*, *Mud*, and *Oscar and Bertha* (1989). She would often develop a play at Padua and later stage the work in New York City or in a US regional theatre. Fornés also explored the intersections between music and theatre. Her Obie award-winning 1965 musical, *Promenade*, for which she wrote the book and lyrics with music by Al Carmines, whimsically follows two escaped convicts as they careen through urban class conflict. It was produced Off-Broadway for 259 performances, the longest run in her production history. She collaborated with numerous composers such as Leon Odenz, who wrote songs for her play *Sarita* utilizing different musical styles, including guaguancó, guaracha, tango, bolero, swing, boogie, and gospel. Additionally, in 1997, *Manual for a Desperate Crossing (Balseros/Rafters)*, an opera by Robert Ashley for which she wrote the libretto, considers the plight of Cuban émigrés who made the treacherous journey from Cuba to Florida aboard makeshift rafts.

In 1973, she directed a production of her play, *Molly's Dream*, and from then on directed the original productions of all of her own plays. For Fornés, directing helped her achieve her playwriting vision. She combined a keen eye for detailed physical work with visual poetry and an environmental use of space. In *Fefu and Her Friends*, performed in a loft, Fornés utilized various spaces to serve as the living room, lawn, kitchen, study, and bedroom of Fefu's country home. During the play's second part, she divided the audience into four groups that each migrated to the distinct spaces to witness the characters' intimate conversations. In 1984, at Padua, she developed an early version of *The Conduct of Life*, staging the play outdoors on a terrace overlooking a large field and a two-lane road. Additionally, Fornés directed her own adaptations of classic works by Calderón de la Barca, Chekhov, and Ibsen.

As an influential playwriting teacher, she trained over forty playwrights at HPRL, whose works have largely shaped the field of Latinx theatre. Her innovative playwriting method encompasses an experiential practice based in physicality, orality, and community, to help writers generate dynamic, new play material. The elements of the "Fornés playwriting method" include centering movement, guided visualization, basic drawing, found materials (aural, written, and visual), and communal writing.

She wrote and directed her final play, *Letters from Cuba* (2000), based on letters from her brother Rafael, which was produced Off-Broadway during her residency at the Signature Theatre. While Fornés wrote primarily in English, several of her plays were also translated into Spanish and produced in the US and Latin America. Her work continues to be championed by artists and scholars who formed the Fornés Institute[1] that aims to preserve and amplify Fornés's legacy through workshops, convenings, and advocacy.

Anne García-Romero

Note

1 www.fornesinstitute.com

Major works

Letters from Cuba (2000)
The Summer in Gossensass (1998)
What of the Night?: comprised of four short plays: *Nadine*; *Springtime*; *Lust*; and *Hunger* (1989)
The Conduct of Life (1985)
Sarita (1984)
Mud (1983)
The Danube (1982)
Fefu and Her Friends (1977)
Molly's Dream (1973)
Tango Palace (1963)

Published works

Fefu and Her Friends. New York: PAJ Publications, 2017.
What of the Night? Selected Plays. New York: PAJ Publications, 2008.
Letters from Cuba and Other Plays. New York: PAJ Publications, 2007.
Promenade and Other Plays. New York: PAJ Publications, 2002.

Further reading

Alker, Gwendolyn. "Fornesian Animality: Maria Irene Fornes's Challenge to a Politics of Identity." *Journal of Dramatic Theory and Criticism*, 35.1 (2020): 9–28.
Cummings, Scott T. *Maria Irene Fornes*. London: Routledge, 2013.
Delgado, Maria and Caridad Svich, eds. *Conducting a Life: Reflections on the Theater of Maria Irene Fornes*. New York: Smith and Kraus, 1999.
Fornés, María Irene, and Robb Creese. "I Write These Messages That Come." *The Drama Review: TDR*, 2.4 (1977): 25–40.
García-Romero, Anne. *The Fornes Frame: Contemporary Latina Playwrights and the Legacy of Maria Irene Fornes*. Tucson: The University of Arizona Press, 2016.
Kent, Assunta Bartolomucci. *Maria Irene Fornes and Her Critics*. Westport: Greenwood Press, 1996.

Marranca, Bonnie. "The Real Life of Maria Irene Fornes." *Performing Arts Journal*, 8.1 (1984): 29–34.

Moroff, Diane. *Fornes: Theater in the Present Tense*. Ann Arbor: University of Michigan Press, 1996.

Renganathan, Mala. *Understanding Maria Irene Fornes' Theatre*. Champaign: Common Ground, 2010.

Robinson, Marc, ed. *The Theatre of Maria Irene Fornes*. Baltimore: Johns Hopkins University Press, 1999.

Svich, Caridad. "The Legacy of Maria Irene Fornes: A Collection of Impressions and Exercises." *PAJ: A Journal of Performance and Art*, 31.3 (2009): 1–32.

GRISELDA GAMBARO (BUENOS AIRES, ARGENTINA, 1928–)

Griselda Gambaro is an iconic figure in the arts, highly regarded worldwide for her plays, novels, short stories, and essays. Her theatre has played a central role in pioneering avant-garde aesthetics and exemplifying the engagement between theatre, human rights, and activism. She is a self-proclaimed feminist in action, and her work lays bare the shifting power dynamics that have shaped discourses on gender and violence in Argentina from the 1960s to the present. Her critique of prescribed gender and sexuality roles, treatment of gender violence, scrutiny of motherhood, and portrayals of resistance to patriarchal structures, prominent in much of her work, resonate powerfully in the context of recent feminist mobilizations and mass protest against gender violence in Latin America.

Gambaro's earliest plays of the 1960s, including *The Walls* (1963), *El desatino* [The Blunder] (1965), *Siamese Twins* (1965), and *The Camp* (1967), are non-realist works comprising what critics consider her avant-garde period. *El desatino* and *Siamese Twins* premiered at the Center for Audiovisual Experimentation, housed at the Torcuato di Tella Institute in Buenos Aires, the epicenter of avant-garde aesthetics in the visual arts, music, theatre, and dance in Argentina during the 1960s. These plays fueled a debate among artists and scholars based in and outside of Argentina about how to interpret the nonsensical and violent realities they depicted. Critics identify Gambaro's use of diegetic sound, physical language, enclosed spaces, and a general sense of disorientation as signs of her familiarity with Artaud's theatre of the absurd. David William Foster calls Gambaro's *The Camp* "probably the purest example of theatre of cruelty in Latin American drama."[1] In this two-act play, diegetic space is key to creating the nightmarish atmosphere. Audiences hear children laughing, moaning, and crying from offstage; there are dogs barking ferociously, gun shots, and the odor of burning flesh. Yet in spite of what some critics have identified as clear affinities with Artaud's theatre of the absurd, Gambaro insists that European definitions of the avant-garde are not suitable for describing her theatre, which, according to the playwright, aligns more closely with the tradition of *grotesco criollo* and reflects the specific absurdity of the world in which Argentines were living at the time.

In the late 1970s after her novel *Ganarse la muerte* [To Earn One's Death] (1976) was banned by the military dictatorship, Gambaro and her family spent three years in exile in Barcelona. Though her artistic production was interrupted during this decade, prior to exile, Gambaro wrote *Information for Foreigners* (1973), one of her plays that has generated most scholarly interest. Described as a chronicle in twenty scenes, the play is interactive and takes its cue from the environmental theatre of the 1960s in its exploration of the collapse between the audience and actors' space. Spectators are divided into groups and led by guides through the labyrinthine rooms of a residential house depicting disturbing scenes: in one scene actors re-enact the Milgram Experiment; in another a young woman is being tortured. The guides offer explanations "for foreigners," taken directly from the newspapers during the early 1970s, which document the disappearances of real individuals. Gambaro weaves in verbatim accounts of the disappearances from the press and situates the action in the specific context of Argentina, marking a departure from the unspecified settings found in her drama of the previous decade. In *Information for Foreigners* Gambaro focuses newfound scrutiny on the role of spectatorship, forcing hypothetical audience members to acknowledge the ethical implications of watching violence.

Gambaro's shift to more politically engaged theatre continues with her participation in Argentina's Teatro Abierto [Open Theatre], one of the most important theatrical and sociopolitical movements organized in opposition to the military dictatorship. Running from 1981 to 1985, Teatro Abierto brought playwrights, directors, actors, and other theatre practitioners together in defiance of the state-orchestrated repression and censorship that had substantially immobilized the artistic community. Gambaro was one of three women out of twenty-one playwrights invited to participate in the inaugural run in 1981.[2] She presented *Saying Yes* (1974), a one-act play depicting a senseless and grisly murder in a barbershop, in an exploration of the relationship between terror and the everyday. Though premiered in the framework of Teatro Abierto, *Saying Yes* reflects dominant themes in Gambaro's dramaturgy from the 1960s and 1970s, notably her preoccupation with the relationship between victim and victimizer.

Gambaro's attention to the binary relationship between victim and victimizer goes hand in hand with her interest in how power relations determine human behavior. Her plays of the 1980s reveal an innovation that disrupts this binary significantly. Characters begin to question and rebel against their oppressors and many of these characters are women. Her plays of the 1980s also reveal a definitive pivot toward a more realist aesthetic. Dolores, the main character in *Bad Blood* (1982), exemplifies this new role for women in Gambaro's work, rebelling against her tyrannical father. And though she ultimately succumbs to the oppressive patriarchy she fights against, the silence that remains after her death is one that screams in protest: "I am quiet but my silence screams!"[3] Set against the backdrop of the repressive nineteenth-century regime of Juan Manuel Rosas, *Bad Blood* initiates a series of plays in which Gambaro employs allegory and adaptation of classical texts in order to discuss the dictatorship. Premiering at the very end of the dictatorship, it is also the first of Gambaro's plays to attract a more mainstream audience.

Gambaro's plays of the 1980s and early 1990s explore themes that were prominent in cultural expression during the post-dictatorship such as memory, justice, and mourning. Gambaro's most famous work, *Furious Antigone* (1986), directed by longtime collaborator Laura Yusem, is a poignant example of Gambaro's engagement with memory politics of the post-dictatorship period. The play premiered at the Goethe Institute in Buenos Aires. *Furious Antigone* was envisioned as an homage to the Mothers of Plaza de Mayo, the organization of women who during the dictatorship protested publicly to demand justice and the return of their disappeared children. Often considered Gambaro's most significant innovation in this play is the decision to use Antigone's death as a point of departure. Gambaro's Antigone returns from death and thus embodies the mantra of the Mothers of the Plaza de Mayo, demanding the return of their disappeared children alive (Aparición con vida). Gambaro's *Furious Antigone* is one of the first and most moving performances to attempt to represent the rituals of mourning of the disappeared in the post-dictatorship period and it has resonated across contexts where mass violence and systematic disappearance have occurred.

Gambaro's plays of the 1990s begin to show more subtle and diverse examples of women's roles and a break with the Antigone motif, which runs through much of her work. Premiered in 1990 and directed by

Yusem, *Penas sin importancia* [Sorrows of No Importance], for example, depicts Rita, pregnant, living in economic hardship with an unfaithful husband in an apartment in contemporary Buenos Aires. In this rich intertextual work, drawing on Chekhov's *Uncle Vanya* and Roberto Arlt's *Trescientos millones* [Three Hundred Million], Rita defies convention and openly acknowledges the ambivalence she feels about being pregnant. No longer the mourning mothers presented in previous plays like *Furious Antigone* or *Loose Ends* (1991), Gambaro now offers a more complicated portrait of maternity, a trend that is visible in subsequent works in the late 1990s and early twenty-first century.

Gambaro's *De Profesión Maternal* [Of the Maternal Profession] (1999), *La persistencia* [Persistence] (2004), and *Querido Ibsen: soy Nora* [Dear Ibsen: It's Me, Nora] (2013) are three such plays that exemplify this shift toward exploring more nuanced portrayals of motherhood and family. In *De Profesión Maternal*, Leticia is reunited with her mother (Matilde) after a forty-five-year separation, only to realize that her mother is in a relationship with another woman. This is an important innovation, given the prevailing heteronormativity that structures most realist portrayals of family in twentieth-century Argentine theatre. In *La persistencia*, Gambaro radically transforms the Antigone motif and creates complete disengagement between maternity and mourning through her creation of Zaida, a mother who is overcome by hatred and desires to avenge, instead of to mourn, her son's death. In this play, the mother character is an excellent example of one of Gambaro's anti-heroines, embodying narcissism, cruelty, and vanity. Yet whether they are heroines or anti-heroines, women in Gambaro's plays are active subjects, "defying symbolic systems of representation dominated by masculine ideology."[4] And in one of Gambaro's most recent plays, *Querido Ibsen: soy Nora*, Gambaro again turns to the early modernists, this time drawing on Ibsen's *A Doll's House*. In this play, Gambaro introduces Ibsen as a character and in the dialogue that ensues onstage, Nora debates with Ibsen and expresses her dissatisfaction with various aspects of her representation. Like many of Gambaro's women characters since the 1980s, Nora rebels against oppression, but the main focus here is not on husbands or fathers, but rather on her author and the possibility of Nora intervening in the creation of her own identity.

At the time of this writing, Gambaro is in her early nineties and she continues to be active in the Argentine theatre scene. Her plays are staged regularly in Argentina and around the world. A lifelong feminist, Gambaro's nearly six decades of work have played a major role in shaping Argentine theatre and innovating new gender perspectives that have taken hold in recent years in Argentina and across Latin America. The feminist critique in her treatment of power relations; the exploration of oppressive gender roles; the explicit rebellion of women characters against their oppressors and the alignment of this rebellion with the activism of the Mothers and Grandmothers of Plaza de Mayo in her work of the 1980s and early 1990s; the critical questioning of motherhood; the explorations of the abject in depictions of antiheroines; and representations of non-heteronormative families all contribute to a nuanced and kaleidoscopic body of work that has made a revolutionary contribution to Latin American theatre.

Brenda Werth

Notes

1 David William Foster, "The Texture of Dramatic Action in the Plays of Griselda Gambaro," *Hispanic Journal* (1980): 62.
2 The other two women playwrights were Aida Bortnik and Diana Raznovich, who premiered *Papá Querido* [Dear Father] and *Desconcierto* [Disconcerted] respectively.
3 Griselda Gambaro, *Bad Blood* (translated by Marguerite Feitlowitz. Woodstock: Dramatic Publishing Company, 1994), 98.
4 Susana Tarantuviez, *La escena de poder: El teatro de Griselda Gambaro* (Buenos Aires: Corregidor, 2007), 18.

Major works

Querido Ibsen: soy Nora [Dear Ibsen: It's Me, Nora] (2013)
La persistencia [Persistence] (2004)
La señora Macbeth [Lady Macbeth] (2002)
De Profesión maternal [Of the Maternal Profession] (1997)
Antígona furiosa (1986) [Furious Antigone, 1992]
La malasangre (1981) [Bad Blood, 1994]
Decir sí (1974) [Saying Yes, 1996]
Información para extranjeros (1973) [Information for Foreigners, 1992]
El campo (1967) [The Camp, 1971]
Los siameses (1965) [Siamese Twins, 2011]
Las paredes (1963) [The Walls, 1992]

Published works

Siamese Twins. Translated by Gwen MacKeith. London: Oberon, 2011.
Loose Ends. Translated by Catherine Boyle. *Travesia*, 1.1 (2009): 118–144.
Saying Yes. Translated by Sebastian Doggart. In *Latin American Plays*. London: Nick Hern Books, 1996.
Bad Blood. Translated by Marguerite Feitlowitz. Woodstock: Dramatic Publishing Company, 1994.

Information for Foreigners, *The Walls*, and *Furious Antigone*. Translated by Marguerite Feitlowitz. In *Information for Foreigners: Three Plays by Griselda Gambaro*, Edited, Translated, and with an Introduction by Marguerite Feitlowitz; with an Afterword by Diana Taylor. Evanston: Northwestern University Press, 1992.

The Camp. Translated by William I. Oliver. In *Voices of Change in the Spanish American Theater: An Anthology*. Austin: University of Texas Press, 1971.

Further reading

Bulman, Gail A. "El grito infinito: Ecos coloniales en *La malasangre* de Griselda Gambaro." *Symposium: A Quarterly Journal in Modern Literatures*, 48.4 (1994): 271–276.

Graham-Jones, Jean. *Exorcising History: Argentine Theater under Dictatorship*. Lewisburg, PA: Bucknell University Press, 2000.

Magnarelli, Sharon. "Staging Shadows/Seeing Ghosts: Ambiguity, Theatre, Gender, and History in Griselda Gambaro's La señora Macbeth." *Theatre Journal*, 60.3 (2008): 365–382.

Pellettieri, Osvaldo. "La recepción del teatro de Griselda Gambaro (1965–1968)." In *El teatro y sus claves. Estudios sobre teatro iberoamericano y argentino*. Edited by Osvaldo Pellettieri. 117–126. Buenos Aires: Galerna, 1996.

Puga, Ana Elena. *Memory, Allegory, and Testimony in South American Theater: Upstaging Dictatorship*. New York: Routledge, 2008.

Taylor, Diana. *Theatre of Crisis: Drama and Politics in Latin America*. Lexington: University Press of Kentucky, 1992.

Trastoy, Beatriz. "Madres, marginados y otras víctimas: El teatro de Griselda Gambaro en el ocaso del siglo." *Teatro: Revista de Estudios Culturales/A Journal of Cultural Studies*, 16 (2002): 37–46.

Werth, Brenda. *Theatre, Performance, and Memory Politics in Argentina*. New York: Palgrave, 2010.

GUILLERMO GÓMEZ-PEÑA (MEXICO CITY, MEXICO/SAN FRANCISCO, CA, 1955–)

Born and raised in Mexico City, Guillermo Gómez-Peña is the best-known Latinx performance artist, having been awarded the McArthur Genius Grant (1991—the first Chicano artist to have received it), the American Book Award (1997), and the Guggenheim Fellowship (2019), among others. Spanning from the late 1970s to the twenty-first century, his art practice has relied on the concept of hybridity and border culture.

After studying Literature and Linguistics in Mexico's National Autonomous University (UNAM), Gómez-Peña moved to Los Angeles in 1978. A graduate of the California Institute of the Arts, his bilingual, multifarious training in literature, the visual arts, and critical theory continues to inform his artwork to the present. Through live interaction with the audience, applying humor, multilingual poetry, and an aesthetic of the grotesque, he creates an intentionally distorted mix of references to Latin American culture, high-tech, and countercultural punk-rock imagery. Unambiguously political, his work aims at blowing up dominant ideas on fixed ethnic and sexual identities, and delves into the gaps and clashes between mainstream American values and minority cultures seen as the Other, particularly immigrants.

His contributions to contemporary Latinx and Latin American theatre relate to his use of performance, not as a separate medium or discipline, but as an aggregated space that allows for unrestricted, transdisciplinary actions where paradox, ambiguity, and contradiction are not just tolerated, but encouraged. He sees performance and the centrality of the body as a utopian space of sorts that allows for the emergence of suppressed cultural and sexual identities and alternative social realities.

Gómez-Peña's first documented performances as a student in Los Angeles were endurance-based solo pieces characterized by austere visual aesthetics that dealt with the invisibility of Mexicans in California. For example, in *The Loneliness of the Immigrant* (1979), he laid down on a public elevator floor wrapped head-to-toe in fabric and tied down with a rope for 24 hours while people kept using it regularly. A text posted on the elevator door alluded to the "unbearable" loneliness of immigrants.

Also, in 1979, he co-founded the Cal Arts interdisciplinary performance collective Poyesis Genetica. In fact, a fundamental tenet of his practice to the present has been collaborating with other artists across disciplines and national borders in order to explore social justice issues via audience participation. In 1984 he was a founding member of Border Art Workshop/Taller de Arte Fronterizo, a pioneer arts project straddling the San Diego/Tijuana border comprised of artists, scholars, activists, and journalists. Their various projects often took place on site. For example, in *Border Wedding* (1988), Gómez-Peña and Emily Hicks theatrically and actually got married in front of about one hundred people while he stood on the Tijuana side of the fence and she on the San Diego side. This collective has been credited with inaugurating border culture both as an artistic and political category, as well as a theoretical academic notion that later permeated various scholarly fields, particularly Latinx theatre and performance studies.

In Gómez-Peña's work the "border" notion clearly interweaves with the critique of neocolonialism. One of his most resonant works in this regard is *Two Undiscovered Amerindians Visit the West*, later known by its video title, *The Couple in the Cage* (1992–1993), in collaboration with Coco Fusco. In this traveling performance piece, they toured five countries including Spain and the US where they exhibited themselves in public sites like parks and museums as a caged indigenous couple from a supposedly undiscovered Caribbean island. As it was 1992, their intent was to call into question the idea of discovery through satire while documenting the viewers' reactions. Significantly, the performers soon realized many in the audience believed they were actual "savages," which showed, according to Fusco "the dilemma of cross-cultural misunderstanding we continue to live with today."[1] This work is considered a milestone in art history in that it explicitly manifests the crossroads between theatre and anthropology by engaging "the history of how the West has constructed otherness by putting a cage around 'difference'."[2] As such, it is characteristic of the 'reverse anthropology' practice that underlies Gómez-Peña's work.

In 1993 in Los Angeles, California, the artist co-founded the ever-evolving performance troupe La Pocha Nostra with Roberto Sifuentes and Nola Mariano (now based in San Francisco). Still under his directorship in 2021, its name is a wordplay with *Pocho* (a derogative term for Americans of Mexican descent whose Spanish is "contaminated" by English) and *Nostra* (from *La Cosa Nostra*, the iconic Italian mafia organization).

La Pocha's work is characterized by the practice of body intervention in the form of quasi-torture devices (ropes, prosthetics, and needles), along with another practice common in twentieth-century body art: the leaving of the performer's body at the mercy of the audience's wishes, calling attention to the participatory theatrical tools that from the beginning have engaged audiences with his artwork. Gómez-Peña's collaborations with La Pocha aim to deconstruct hegemonic imaginaries—and power dynamics—behind the notion of the "true" America and its treatment of minorities and immigrants. In fact, Gómez-Peña has termed La Pocha's work as a "theatricalization of postcolonial theory."[3]

A significant feature of Gómez-Peña's influence on both Latinx and Latin American theatre artists is that of the openness of his workshops and methodology to explore theatrical innovations, where experimenting with various artistic languages allows for a non-hierarchical nature to creative and collective work.

Possibly his most theatrical work is *El Mexterminator: From Aztec to High-Tech* (with Roberto Sifuentes and Sara Shelton, 1985–2004). First, in the pre-performance step, artists gathered information about their own "cultural avatars" based on both their fears and erotic desire of minorities and foreigners. Then, they purposefully mingled the assorted ethnographic information, in order to create hybrid personas, which they called "living dioramas."[4] During the actual performance, at El Museo del Barrio in New York, the artists personified these monstruous creatures made out of bits and pieces of cultural stereotypes to interact with the audience and engage them in a dialogue with their fear and desire of the Other. As such, it was a theatrical performance based on reverse anthropology as a key foundation for participatory political art.

Throughout his artistic career, Gómez-Peña has embodied various hybrid personas based on iconic images of Mexicans and Latinxs such as Mariachis, wrestlers, boxers, and shamans, clad in sci-fi post-apocalyptic punk paraphernalia, and often wearing skirts or high heels. His work toys with the crisis of the contemporary Western world from a mixed subaltern perspective which understands the US better than mainstream Americans do, in order to explore—and resist—the persistence of racist, homophobic, and colonial cultural dynamics. In fact, he often purposefully exaggerates the "untranslatability" of minority cultures in his performances by peppering his English with street Mexican Spanish expressions, foreign language words, as well as uttering whole tirades in made-up languages.

Both artist and cultural critic, Gómez-Peña has also been a prolific author of poetry, performance, and transdisciplinary cultural theory volumes and articles. His contributions to theatre relate to his multifaceted open-ended approach to the stage, where barriers between creator and spectator, politics and theatre, "high-tech" and so-called Third World culture, are blurred. Theatricality in his works consists of an interdisciplinary, non-hierarchical, and collaborative mise-en-scène where fixed identities and cultural norms collide.

Paola Marín

Notes

1 Coco Fusco, "The Couple in the Cage," accessed February 22, 2021, www.cocofusco.com/the-couple-in-the-cage
2 Ruth Behar and Bruce Mannheim, "In Dialogue: The Couple in the Cage: A Guatinaui Odissey," *Visual Anthropology Review* 11.1 (1995): 119.
3 Guillermo Gómez-Peña, *Ethno-Techno: Writings on Performance, Activism, and Pedagogy* (London: Routledge, 2005), 245.
4 A diorama is a scene staged with three-dimensional live-size models, usually used in natural history museum exhibits.

Major works

The Most (un)Documented Mexican (2017–2020)

La Nostalgia Remix Series (2005–2016)
The Mexorcist (2005–2007)
The Mapa/Corpo Series (2004–2008)
The Mexterminator Project (1997–1999)
The Cruci-Fiction Project (1994)
The Couple in the Cage: Two Undiscovered Amerindians Visit the West (1992–1993)
Border Brujo (1988–1989)
Borderscape 2000 (1997–1999)
The Border Wedding (1988)
The Loneliness of the Immigrant (1978)

Published works

Posnacional 2 Glosolalia: Border Poetics Against the Wall (USA / México, 2020) (in collaboration with La Pocha Nostra). Self-published, 2020. http://book.flipbuilder.com/saulgarcialopez/

Documentado/Undocumented Ars Chamánica Performática (in collaboration with Felicia Rice). San Francisco: City Lights Publisher, 2017.

Conversations Across Borders: A Performance Artist Converses with Theorists, Curators, Activists (edited by Laura Levin). Chicago: Seagull Press, University of Chicago Press, 2011.

Exercises for Rebel Artists: Radical Performance Pedagogy (in collaboration with Roberto Sifuentes). London: Routledge, 2011.

Dangerous Border-Crossers: The Artist Talks Back. London: Routledge, 2000.

The New World Border. Prophecies, Poems & Loqueras for the End of the World. San Francisco: City Lights, 1996.

Warrior for Gringostroika: Essays, Performance Texts, and Poetry. Minneapolis: Graywolf Press, 1993.

Further reading

Foster, Thomas. "Cyber-Aztecs and Cholo-Punks: Guillermo Gómez-Peña's Five-Worlds Theory." *PMLA: Publications of the Modern Language Association of America* 117 (2002): 43–67.

Fox, Claire F. "Site Specificity, and the U.S.-Mexico Border: Guillermo Gomez-Pena's *Border Brujo* (1988–1990)." In *The Ethnic Eye: Latino Media Arts*, edited by Chon A. Noriega and Ana M. López, 228–243. Minneapolis: University of Minnesota, 1996.

Gómez-Peña, Guillermo. "Border Hysteria and the War Against Difference." *TDR: The Drama Review* 52.1 (2008): 196–203.

Luna, Violeta. "Body in Action: Cartographies for Socially Engaged Performance." *Karpa* 3.2 (2010): n.p. http://www.calstatela.edu/misc/karpa/Karpa3.2/Site%20Folder/violeta.html

Seda, Laurietz. "Trans/Acting Bodies: Guillermo Gómez-Peña's Search for a Singular Plural Community." In *Trans/acting: Latin American and Latino Performing Arts*, edited by Jacqueline Bixler and Laurietz Seda, 227–237. Lewisburg: Bucknell University Press, 2009.

Sheren, Ila. "Border Art." In the *Blackwell Companion to Modern and Contemporary Latin American and Latino Art*, edited by Robin Greeley and Alejandro Anreus, 385–397. Hoboken: Wiley-Blackwell, 2020.

QUIARA ALEGRÍA HUDES (PHILADELPHIA, PA, 1977–)

Quiara Alegría Hudes, who reminds audiences that her name translates as beloved happiness, is the first, and only, Latina Pulitzer Prize winner for Drama for her play *Water by the Spoonful* (2011). An icon in the Latinx theatre movement, Hudes is "west Philadelphia-born-and-raised" and self-transplanted to the Washington Heights section of New York City. A favorite of both audience and critics, Hudes continues to break down barriers between theatrical, literary, musical, and social activist categorizations—being equally prolific in her creation of domestic dramas, musical theatre, operatic libretti, and Latinx theatrical performance. As a playwright equally adept at drama, comedy, and musicals, Hudes stresses that "storytelling is a cleansing ceremony, cleansing by truth-speaking, where one must find the divinity within and honor the human spirit's vast complications."[1]

Hudes originally trained as a musician and composer, as is made clear through her knowledge of musical performance history in many of her plays and specifically in her musical productions. She received a BA in Musical Composition from Yale University, which prepared her to write in collaboration with renowned musicians, such as Michel Camilo, Erin McKeown, Nelson Gonzalez, the Cleveland Orchestra, and Latinx icon Lin-Manuel Miranda, with whom she received the 2008 Tony Award for Best Musical, as well as Pulitzer Prize finalist status, for the libretto of *In the Heights* (2005), and its subsequent Warner Brothers film adaptation screenplay (2021). Hudes is quick to note that her musical abilities are inherited, due to her matrilineal mentors, including her Aunt Linda who taught her music and was a composer for the Big Apple Circus for almost two decades. Hudes's mother, Virginia Sánchez, a "*santera* and shaman who taught her about the spiritual legacy of a Taína-Lukumí-Boricua,"[2] plays a major role in Hudes's upbringing as a mixed Puerto Rican-Jewish woman. Sánchez's bond with her daughter led to Hudes's drama-therapeutic beliefs that the interchange between music, writing, and spirituality can be taught to the larger community through theatre.

Further, Hudes collaborated with her sister Gabriela Sánchez to create the *Latinx Casting Manifesto*, which reflects Hudes's ever-increasing desire to diversify the theatrical palette of performance and representation. *Latinx Casting Manifesto* was originally created as a "tumblr" exercise in 2018 which sought to investigate the casting of Latina/x roles and the complaints against practices which often led to stereotypical and non-existent representation in popular entertainment. This project soon became a duo performance with both Sánchez and Hudes offering a "large-scale group meditation, part frank conversation on wellness and womanhood, part theater manifesto towards radical joy."[3] As is the case with Hudes's dramatic work, this foray into performance began with her strong political leanings and interest in social activism. The project was created as a bilingual, multimedia lecture, and talkback. In part, this performance piece served as a departure from the domestic drama, emblematic in her *oeuvre*, and led to Hudes's interest in Latinx biographical documentation and her eventual 2021 memoir, *My Broken Language*.

Her strong familial bond also led to the creation of the *Emancipated Stories Project* (2018) with her cousin and "muse" Elliot Ruiz, which serves as a platform for incarcerated persons to share their stories and in direct protest and opposition of the carceral state of the country's for-profit prison system. The goal of the project is to give voice and visibility to those trapped behind the bars of the American penal system, for the most part black, brown, and underrepresented in corridors of power, and to bridge the chasm between those inside and out. Ruiz himself serves as the inspiration for Hudes's celebrated trilogy, "The Elliot Plays," which are individually entitled *Elliot: A Soldier's Fugue* (2006; Pulitzer Prize finalist, 2007), *Water by the Spoonful* (2011; Pulitzer Prize winner, 2012), and *The Happiest Song Plays Last* (2013). These plays dramatize the lives of Hudes's own family in a semi-autobiographical framework, including her cousin Elliot's PTSD, and the importance of family and community in relation to social issues ranging from addiction, gentrification, to feminist Latinidades.

Her formal training as a playwright began with an MFA at Brown University under the tutelage of fellow Pulitzer and Tony Award winner, Paula Vogel. Her apprenticeship with, and encouragement from, Vogel was welcomed, particularly following the success of fellow Brown graduate, Vogel mentee, and Pulitzer Prize winner, Nilo Cruz. The education received at Brown quickly resulted in residences with New Dramatists and Page 73 Playwrights, where Hudes's talent led to early productions at mainstream theatres including The Culture Project, and the O'Neill Theatre Center, as well as opportunities at Latinx theatre companies including the Miracle Theatre in Portland.

Early successes with *Yemaya's Belly* (2003) and *Elliot: A Soldier's Fugue* featured Hudes's ability to create universal connections between the complexities of growing up Latinx and more rigid structures including the US military, gentrifying corporations, academic institutions of higher learning, the rigidity of the penitentiary system and the unwinnable war on drugs. With a careful adherence to the advancement of feminist causes and the deconstruction of patterned histories of *machismo* within struggling Latinx families, Hudes's writing centers the Latinx nuclear family and its pressure to survive, both financially and spiritually, within the promised American Dream. She is able to do so without utilizing tired and stereotypical depictions of the "dysfunctionality" of Latinidad. Hudes's familial characters suffer not due to, but despite, the fact that they are Latinx. Her post-millennial compositions do not replicate an earlier generation of Nuyorican dramaturgy (after all, she is from Philadelphia), which often featured impoverished and illicit criminal activity to detail the destruction of Latinx families. Rather, Hudes creates characters who live both within, and removed from, an America which categorizes brown and black Latinxs as the sociological problem, as seen in the earlier work of pioneers including Miguel Piñero, José Rivera, Migdalia Cruz, or Reinaldo Povod. Thus, Hudes creates a new form of *Ame-rícan* dramaturgy, composed of highly educated, patriotic, and proud Puerto Rican families caught in a web of miscommunication, and oftentimes, internalized complicity.

Compounding this categorization of Latinx problematic and criminal theatrical themes, Hudes's expert ability to create musical plays in celebration of her unique Latinidad, including *In the Heights*, *26 Miles* (2009), *Barrio Grrrl! The Musical* (2009), and *Miss You Like Hell* (2016) allows for both a cultural and popular music celebration of mixed genres of traditional composition. These recent plays weave music within all her work, musical or dramatic, and allows non-Latinx audiences the same aural-sensory experience and reception of twenty-first-century "musicalized" barrios including Washington Heights and West Philadelphia. Further, issues related to immigration, Latina representation on the arts, and the trauma of living as a Puerto Rican in the United States are investigated through the use of musical performance. Hudes is of the strong opinion that theatre artists must immerse themselves in all facets of performance and creation. This has led to an outpouring of commercially successful play productions throughout the country: the Public Theater, Miracle Theatre, Goodman Theatre, a residency at the Signature Theater in New York and dozens of regional residencies since 2006. Though stressing the need to self-produce work, Hudes has never seemed to lack major funding or grant opportunities following her graduation from Brown.

Daphne's Dive's successful 2016 run at the Signature Theatre welcomed Hudes along a long line of iconic twentieth- and twenty-first-century American playwrights: María Irene Fornés, Sam Shepard, Edward Albee, and Romulus Linney. The play features a return to the domestic drama, with which Hudes seems to engage with most fluidly. This west Philadelphia "bar play" (reminiscent of the work of O'Neill's *Iceman Cometh*, Lynn Nottage's *Sweat*, or John Patrick Shanley's *Savage in Limbo*), allows Hudes the comfort of creating characters defined by the *New York Times* as "a multicultural bunch, although the majority are Latino"[4] while exploring issues of race, ethnicity, economics, politics, and privilege. She has served as the Shapiro Distinguished Professor of Writing and Theater at Wesleyan University since 2014. Her work has carved her a prominent place in Latinx theatre, which, in her own words, matters because this is "our history; it's not written down, it's not recorded, it could disappear ... there's still more to say."[5]

Jason Ramírez

Notes

1. Trevor Boffone, "Quiara Alegría Hudes," *50 Playwrights Project*, https://50playwrights.org (2016).
2. www.quiara.com
3. www.quiara.com/latinx-casting-manifesto
4. Charles Isherwood, "*Daphne's Dive*," *New York Times* (2016).
5. Beth Stevens, "Quiara Alegria Hudes...," *Broadway Buzz* (2016).

Major works

Miss You Like Hell with Erin McKeown (2016)
Daphne's Dive (2016)
The Good Peaches (2016)
The Happiest Song Plays Last (2013)
Water by the Spoonful (2011)
Barrio Grrrl! The Musical (2009)
In the Heights with Lin-Manuel Miranda (2005)
Elliot: A Soldier's Fugue (2006)
Yemaya's Belly (2003)

Published works

My Broken Language: A Memoir, One World Publishers, 2021.
Miss You Like Hell, Theatre Communications Group, 2018
Daphne's Dive, Theatre Communications Group, 2017.
The Good Peaches, Theatre Communications Group, 2017.

The Happiest Song Plays Last, Theatre Communications Group, 2014.
In the Heights, Applause Libretto Library, 2013.
Water by the Spoonful, Theatre Communications Group, 2012.
26 Miles, Dramatist's Play Service, 2011.
Elliot: A Soldier's Fugue, Dramatist's Play Service, 2008.
Yemaya's Belly, Dramatists Play Service, 2008.

Further reading

Cázares, Gabriela. "Resisting Gentrification in Quiara Alegría Hudes and Lin-Manuel Miranda's *In the Heights* and Ernesto Quiñones *Bodega Dreams*." *American Studies* 56.2 (2017): 89–107.

Dufournaud, Daniel. "'When things are bad': Entrepreneurial Failure and Levinasian Ethics in Quiara Alegría Hudes's Water by the Spoonful." *College Literature* 47.3 (2020): 441–467.

Friedman, Sharon. "The Gendered Terrain in Contemporary Theatre of War by Women." *Theatre Journal* 62.4 (2010): 593–610.

Noriega, Jimmy. "'Don't Teach These Plays!': Latina/o Theatre and the Termination of the Tucson Unified School District's Mexican-American Studies Program." *Theatre Topic* 27.1 (2017): 37–48.

Ybarra, Patricia A. "How to Read a Latinx Play in the Twenty-First Century: Learning from Quiara Hudes." *Theatre Topics* 27.1 (2017): 49–59.

MANUELA INFANTE (SANTIAGO, CHILE, 1980–)

Since the early twenty-first century, Manuela Infante has stood at the forefront of contemporary Chilean theatre. Her critical, philosophical, and risky theatrical projects place her as a prolific theatremaker that challenges the meaning and methods of making theatre. Starting with her first stage appearance as a director and dramaturg in 2001, Infante's aesthetic proposals and poetics have guided her to approach the relationship between representation and reality. Her controversial debut, *Prat* (2002), not only initiates this exploration but also shows how cultural productions can reveal oppressive systems of power that constantly restrict communities.

Infante graduated from the School of Theatre at the University of Chile as a trained actor. Yet, her artistic interests led her to write and direct theatre. In 2001, she formed the group Teatro de Chile, which gained national and international recognition until they disbanded in 2016. As a multifaceted artist, she is also a musician, teacher, scriptwriter, and earned a Master's in Cultural Analysis from the University of Amsterdam. Her curiosity for philosophy and music has informed her theatrical practice, producing visually and sonically innovative works. In 2014, she was the first woman director of the National

Festival for Dramaturgy in Chile. Among her many residencies and distinctions, her latest is the 2019 Stückemarkt Commission prize for *Estado vegetal* [Vegetative State] (2017). She is also regularly featured at the Santiago a Mil International Festival.

Infante's first play, *Prat*, catapulted her as a major figure on the national stage and marked a turning point in Chilean theatre. Before its premiere, the media leaked *Prat*'s controversial script, making headlines in major national news outlets. The script challenges nationally established discourses by portraying war hero and navy officer Arturo Prat Chacón as an insecure and vulnerable adolescent awaiting battle during the War of the Pacific (1879–1883). By turning the officer into an antihero, the play not only sheds light on the constructedness of reality but also reveals the fabrication of national myths and heroes. In response, former military members and conservative politicians attempted to censor the play, calling it defamation of Prat, and took the case to the Supreme Court. This event made Teatro de Chile an artistic referent by producing a generational introspection—what is theatre's role in reflecting on who and what is allowed to be represented. Furthermore, those who opposed the premiere came from sectors that supported Augusto Pinochet's bloody dictatorship (1973–1989), and thus the controversy revealed that the regime's forces of coercion prevailed long after it ended. This revelation prompted Infante's generation to rupture from the censorship dynamics that confined artists' content and dissemination of their art.

The thematic interests of *Prat* and other postmodern inquiries informed Infante's early *oeuvre* in Teatro de Chile, including the stage as a site to define theatricality, the potentials of transmediality, how reality is played out and (de)constructed, and the relationship between history and myth. These examinations define works such as *Juana* [Joan] (2004) and *Cristo* [Christ] (2008), where she deconstructs the historical figures of Joan of Arc and Jesus Christ. Infante casts them as an accumulation of representations, thus exposing the processes that constitute reality as an invention. To catalyze these queries, she advanced a methodology established by Teatro de Chile. This method consists of prolonged collective investigation and improvisations, where a text emerged after an initial exploration onstage. This method led the group to show their research process as part of the end product, displayed "onstage as a mode of rehearsal, fragment, and remnant."[1]

Her postmodern inquiries and interest in questioning representation continue to nourish her current work. While her earlier theatre challenged historical discourses and revealed the construction of reality, her recent projects still explore these topics, but now focus on dismantling the social constructs of the human vs. nonhuman distinction and, thus, that of the object vs. subject. She identifies her latest practice as *nonhuman theatre*,[2] asserting that "theatre has never been human."[3] This statement dissociates her from traditional humanistic conceptions of theatre and affirms her artistic investment in refusing humans' centrality to the theatrical event. By delving into an innovative practice with nonhuman entities, her latest plays highlight marginalized human characters, such as people with disabilities, children, the elderly, and peasants. Infante's plays vindicate them as producers of alternative ways of being and capable of coexisting and communicating with objects and plants. The title of *Realismo* [Realism] (2016) recalls her earlier theatrical explorations, but the play goes a step further. It mocks realism in theatre by instead focusing on the objects that accompany different generations of a Chilean family. In doing so, the play portrays objects not as props, but as entities capable of having agency in the evolution of the family.

Estado vegetal further explores mimesis and the nonhuman. As a work that continues her exploration of representation, the play is not only about plants; it is a play that unfolds as a plant. It is a one-woman show that imitates the movement, communication, and other elements of vegetative existence in its content and form. By translating the principles of plant neurobiology to the stage, the actress's presence and Infante's dramaturgy make the audience consider the shared characteristics between plants and human beings. In Infante's words, her newest plays aim "to deconstruct the hierarchical pyramid that enforces the idea that inanimate objects or plants are below animals and people."[4] In emphasizing the nonhuman, these plays force spectators to simply contemplate obscurities and ambiguities generated by performances that suspend the meaning-making process. Today, Infante's bold scenic proposals situate her as a leading voice of contemporary Chilean theatre.

Carlos A. Ortiz

Notes

1 Andrea Jeftanovic, "Manuela Infante: La antidramaturga," in *Antología: un siglo de dramaturgia chilena: Tomo IV: Período 1990–2009*, eds. María de la Luz Hurtado and Mauricio Barría (Santiago, Chile: Comisión Bicentenario, 2010), 234. Author's translation.
2 Manuela Infante, "El teatro nunca ha sido humano," in *Santiago a Mil 2019: Clases magistrales*, www.teatroamil.tv/videos/clase-completa-manuela-infante
3 Ibid.
4 Ibid.

Major works

Estado vegetal [Vegetative State] (2017)
Realismo [Realism] (2016)
Xuarez (2015)
Zoo (2013)
Cristo [Christ] (2008)
Rey Planta [The Plant King] (2006)
Narciso [Narcissus] (2005)
Juana [Joan] (2004)
Prat (2002)

Published works

Zoo. Trans. by Alexandra Ripp. *Theater* 47, no. 2 (2017): 67–99.
Rey planta. In *Antología: un siglo de dramaturgia chilena: Tomo IV: Período 1990–2009*, edited by María de la Luz Hurtado and Mauricio Barría. 237–257. Santiago de Chile: Comisión Bicentenario, 2010.
Prat seguida de Juana. Santiago de Chile: Ciertopez, 2004.

Further reading

Francica, Cynthia. "Un universo de cosas: Materialidades y afectividades no humanas en *Realismo* (2016) de Manuela Infante." In *Lenguajes y materialidades: Trayectorias cruzadas*, edited by Pedro Moscoso-Flores and Antonia Viu. 327–353. Santiago: RIL editores, 2020.
Hernández Parraguez, Carolina. "Transmedialidad y crisis de la representación en *Cristo* de Manuela Infante y Compañía Teatro de Chile." *Revista Laboratorio* 18 (2019): 1–25.
Labbé, Carlos y Mónica Ríos. "Entre el texto, la puesta en escena y la performance del registro en la escritura de Manuela Infante y el Teatro de Chile." *INTI* no. 69/70 (2009): 207–219.
Opazo, Cristián. "Al abordaje de una huérfana: Lectura sumaria de *Prat* (2002), de Manuela Infante." In *Pedagogías letales: Ensayo sobre dramaturgias chilenas del nuevo milenio*. 147–174. Santiago de Chile: Editorial Cuarto Propio, 2011.
Ripp, Alexandra. "Power Play." *Theater* 42, no. 3 (2012): 93–101.

SARA JOFFRÉ (LIMA, PERÚ, 1935–2014)

Clotilde Sara Joffré González was an extraordinary theatre practitioner that felt passion for everything related to theatre. She is known as a groundbreaking woman playwright, director, critic, editor, researcher, and promoter of Peruvian theatre. Joffré began her relationship with the stage when she was a young girl, but it wasn't until 1957 that she debuted as an actress at the Club de Teatro de Lima (Lima's Theatre

Club). However, in 1961 she exchanged her role as an actress for one as a playwright when she wrote *En el jardín de Mónica* [At Monica's Garden] and *Cuento alrededor de un círculo de espuma* [Story Around a Foam Circle]. Both plays were poetic and metaphorical musings regarding childhood and human relations.

With the help of a travel award from the International Theatre Institute (ITI) and the British Council in 1964, Joffré became acquainted with Bertolt Brecht's theories and theatre, which she would disseminate in Peru through workshops, reading sessions, conferences, and other events. The circulation of Brecht's theories and plays sparked the interest of then nascent groups such as Yuyachkani and Cuatrotablas. After realizing how much influence Brecht's ideas permeated the Peruvian stage, in the year 2001 Joffré published the book *Bertolt Brecht en el Perú* [Bertolt Brecht in Peru].

Following her return from Europe, Joffré started to write plays that would criticize and expose Peru's social, political, economic, gender-related issues, and environmental maladies. Racism and discrimination toward the indigenous and Andean communities are exquisitely treated in her 1968 play *Se administra justicia* [Justice is Administered]. This piece presents an indigenous woman who seeks in vain justice for her fourteen-year-old daughter who was sexually assaulted by the nephew of a police officer. The title is ambiguous and ironic at the same time because it questions the way in which justice is manipulated in favor of men with lighter skin and power. In this play, we also come to understand how the police and the judicial systems are complicit and legitimize racism and discrimination towards women, particularly of Andean and indigenous heritage.

Continuing with her interests on Peruvian social issues, Joffré wrote *Una obligación* [An Obligation] (1974) about two men that confiscate a family's assets while a ten-year-old is alone in his home and his mother is outside working long hours. A parallel can be established between the robbers of the home and the political groups in power that loot the riches of the nation. A different play that tackles other forms of discrimination in the nation is *La madre* [The Mother] (1994), a monologue that shows an old actress, run down, who, due to her age, is only offered to play the role of a transvestite. Thus, this play criticizes the aesthetic canons required by employers and companies and how these are used to perpetuate gender and age discrimination.

Joffré not only wrote about Peruvian issues. In some plays, she incorporated universal personalities such as the Spanish conqueror Lope de Aguirre in *La hija de Lope* [Lope's Daughter] (1989); the French sculptor Camille Claudel, in *Camille* (1999); the German philosopher Walter Benjamin and the French philosopher and sociologist Jean Baudrillard in *Camino de una vía* [One Way Road] (2000). Fifty years after Joffré wrote *Se administra justicia*, her play *Bagua: Ni grande ni chica simplemente insondable nada más* [Bagua: Neither Big nor Small Just Unfathomable Nothing More] was posthumously published in 2017 and premiered in 2019 under the direction of Diego La Hoz. This is Joffré's most Brechtian play. One can see that at the end of her career the playwright goes back to Brecht, but now adding the environmental concerns that are affecting twenty-first-century Peru. She proposes the use of songs, dances, voice-over, paintings, helicopter, and gun noises, among many other things to make the audience think about the importance of the environment, discrimination against indigenous people and the significance of life. This intense play takes into consideration the massacre occurred on June 5, 2009, in Bagua, Peru where thirty-three Amazonian natives who were protesting the use of their lands by foreign mining companies were killed and more than 200 were injured by the police. *Bagua* demonstrates how racism and racial inequality are deeply institutionalized, embedded, and legitimized in Peru by the state and its representatives.

In addition to being a playwright, Joffré was an advocate for other emerging artists who needed to showcase their work. Her most important legacies were the creation of the Muestra de Teatro Peruano (Peruvian Theatre Festival, 1974–present) and the edition of the journal *Muestra: La Revista de los Autores de Teatro Peruano* [Muestra: The Peruvian Playwrights Theatre Journal] (2000–2014). Another important contribution was the founding of Homero, Teatro de Grillo's [Homer, Cricket Theatre] with members Homero Rivera, Roberto Ríos, Aurora Colina, and Alejandro Elliot. From 1963 to 1978 the group presented innovative theatre for children every Sunday. Their main purpose was to educate and entertain but most of all to present quality theatre for children. This pioneering group also published a ten-book volume entitled *Vamos al teatro con los grillos* [Let's go to the Theatre with the Crickets] (1965) that included most of the plays staged by their group. Joffré not only wrote, translated, and adapted plays for children but she also directed many of them, thus making her one of the first female theatre directors in Peru.

Even though at the beginning Teatro de Grillos staged theatre for children, little by little they started staging theatre for adults. Using Brechtian techniques such as slide projections, songs, and other devices, they were among the first to make the Peruvian audience think, understand, and make considerable and rational judgments about any political, social, economic, and racial issues presented in the plays.

The Muestra de Teatro Peruano, celebrated every other year since 1974, was born from the question: "Is there something we could call Peruvian Theatre?" Thus, the festival's main goal was to acknowledge and stage plays written and directed by Peruvian artists. Many contemporary theatre playwrights and groups, such as César de María and Roberto Sánchez Piérola, Yuyachkani, Cuatrotablas, Cuer2, Espacio Libre, Algovipasar, and Barricada Teatro, among many others, became known through this unique national festival. In the beginning, the festival only staged authors and directors residing in Lima. However, it soon started to include artists from all over Peru, and later different cities became its host, making it one of the most inclusive national festivals in Latin America.

As the managing editor and founder of *Muestra: La Revista de los Autores de Teatro Peruano*, her main goal was to only publish Peruvian authors. Every time Sara was out and about, she would take her copies of the journal and sell them personally to anyone interested in Peruvian theatre. Since Joffré was always willing to put the needs of others before her own, only one (*Camille* [1999]) of the forty-six plays published in the journal was a work written by her. In 2003 she put together a book entitled *Teatro hecho en el Perú* [Theatre Made in Peru] that includes all the articles she published in the newspaper *El comercio* from 1991 to 1998.

Sara Joffré should be recognized as one of Latin America's most important theatre practitioners. She was a trailblazer playwright and director, an avid researcher and critic, but overall, she was an unselfish artist that was always encouraging and advising young playwrights, directors and actors to showcase and publish their work, and loved seeing others shine on their own.

Laurietz Seda

Major works

Bagua ni grande ni chica simplemente insondable nada más [Bagua: Neither Big nor Small Just Unfathomable Nothing More] (2017)
El que hace salir el sol: Teatro en la escuela [Making the Sun Come Out: Theatre in the School] (2010)
Aparecen las mujeres [Women Appear] (2007)
Camino de una sola vía [One Way Road] (2000)
Camille (1999)
La madre [The Mother] (1994)
La hija de Lope [Lope's Daughter] (1989)
Una obligación [An Obligation] (1974)
Se administra justicia [Justice is Administered] (1968)
En el jardín de Mónica [At Monica's Garden] (1961)

Published works

Aparecen las mujeres. Alexandria, VA: Alexander Street Press, 2007.
Diáspora. Alexandria, VA: Alexander Street Press, 2007.
7 obras de teatro. Lima: Universidad Garcilaso de la Vega, 2006.
Obras para la escena. Lima: Fondo Editorial de la UNMSM, 2002.

Further reading

Geirola, Gustavo. "Entrevista a Sara Joffré." In *Arte y oficio del director en América Latina: México y Perú*, edited by Gustavo Geirola, 129–143. Argentina: Editorial Atuel, 2004.
Nigro, Kirsten. "Filling the Empty Space: Women and Latin American Theatre." *Studies in 20th Century Literature* 20.1 (1996): 251–270.
Seda, Laurietz. "Memoria y conciencia del Perú: El teatro de Sara Joffré." *Historia de las literaturas en el Perú.* Vol. 6, edited by Raquel Chang-Rodríguez and Marcel Velázquez Castro, 351–371. Lima: Pontificia Universidad Católica del Perú, Casa de la Literatura, Ministerio de Educación del Perú, 2018.
Vargas-Salgado, Carlos. "Sara Joffré: Soul of Peruvian Theater." *The Brechtian Yearbook* (2016): 1–3.

KIMVN TEATRO (2008–) AND PAULA GONZÁLEZ SEGUEL (SANTIAGO DE CHILE, 1983–)

Paula González is a Chilean theatre director, documentary filmmaker, playwright, actress, and musician. Her artistic interests range from Latin American folklore to classical music studies, including playing the violin for over twelve years. She studied acting at the School of Theatre at the Universidad Mayor in Santiago and directing from Alfredo Castro at Teatro la Memoria. She later earned a master's degree in Documentary Filmmaking from the University of Chile. In 2008, she and her sister, Evelyn González Seguel, founded KIMEN Teatro (*kimen* means "do you know me?" in Mapuzungun, the language of the Mapuche people). The group was later renamed KIMVN Teatro in 2016 (*kimvn* translates to "knowledge") and operates as a multidisciplinary collective that engages theatre, music, and audiovisual arts in its creative practice. KIMVN functions as a loose network of artists, under the leadership of González, who are invited to research and develop specific projects through a process of investigation and experimentation. The resulting works often feature a mixture of professional and non-professional performers and the productions have been presented in Argentina, Australia, Belgium, Brazil, China, Cuba, France, Mexico, and South Korea. To date, González has directed thirteen theatrical productions and has collaborated with more than 100 artists.

González self-identifies as a member of the Mapuche community, which includes indigenous groups from the southern regions of Chile and Argentina. She explains, "My great-grandmother was an ancestral authority of the Mapuche people. She was a *machi*, a woman who healed through plants, rituals, and ancestral medicine."[1] This connection to Mapuche culture and tradition fuels her creative work and process. Her art and identity are intertwined and aimed at bringing attention to Mapuche social, political, and historical issues. It was during her last year at the Universidad Mayor that she directed her first production with Mapuche women, who did not have acting training, from an urban indigenous community in Santiago. After collecting their stories for a year, she put them on stage in the first production by KIMEN Teatro with *Ñi Pu Tremen* [My Ancestors] (2009). Throughout the performance, the women recounted their memories of childhood and subsequent migration to the capital city. The production engaged many of the topics that would become prominent in the group's later works: a critique of state-sanctioned violence, racism, discrimination, marginalization, the effects of poverty, and gendered violence.

Inspired by the experience of its first production, KIMVN Teatro continues to utilize documentary research methods as part of its "continuous search of the ancestral knowledge of the Mapuche people through the rescue of orality, language, and culture."[2] The company also aims to bring awareness to the violations of human rights and other social and political issues that affect the Mapuche community. González's second production, *Territorio descuajado* [Dislodged Territory] (2011), draws upon multiple Mapuche perspectives to bring attention to the complicated and politicized issues of territoriality and space. The performance interrogates the effects of dispossession and marginalization on those families who emigrated from the south to live on the outskirts of Santiago. Based on testimonies and written by Marisol Vega Medina, the play offers a unique and often invisible perspective on the urban Mapuche experience.

Galvarino, also written by Vega and directed by González, was staged in 2012 and focuses on a Mapuche family from the southern part of Chile who awaits the return of Galvarino, the son and brother who has been in exile in Russia for more than three decades. Unbeknownst to them, he was murdered in Russia shortly before his departure by a group of neo-Nazis. The plot of the play was drawn from real events: it is based on the testimony of the man's sister, who also happens to be González's aunt. In this way, the niece of the murdered man uses her role as a theatre director to bring to light this tragic story from the early 1990s and, in doing so, connects family memory to the larger issues of racism and violence enacted upon indigenous bodies on a global scale.

ÑUKE. *Una mirada íntima hacia la resistencia mapuche* [MOTHER. An Intimate Look at the Mapuche Resistance] was written by David Arancibia Urzúa and directed by González in 2016. The production was staged inside a *ruka* (a traditional Mapuche house) that was constructed in front of Mapocho Station in Santiago's historic city center. In the play, a mother, Carmen, must deal with the consequences of her son's arrest. The site-specific performance forces the audience to reconsider the ways violence against Mapuche people in the southern part of Chile invades their homes, intertwining the personal and the political in ways the urban Chilean citizen may not have previously considered. The setting further complicates the relationship between the urban and the rural by bringing the two together in the site of the communally built home/theatre space. The play merges testimony, documentary theatre, architecture, and storytelling to craft a critique of the use of police force and brutality against Mapuche people in their everyday lives.

Similarly, *Trewa. Estado–Nación o el espectro de la traición* [Dog. Nation-State or the Specter of Treason] (2019) forces the audience to confront the ways that the government has supported state-sanctioned violence against the Mapuche community in southern Chile. Written and directed by González, the play is based on real-life events that include the controversial circumstances surrounding the death of Macarena Valdés, an indigenous woman and environmental activist who was protesting the construction of a hydropower dam on the Tranguil River in 2016. Although authorities claim she committed suicide, activists maintain that she was murdered. The play also brings attention to a case where a police sergeant fired more than eighty pellets into the back of Brandon Hernández Huentecol, a seventeen-year-old Mapuche man who was defending his thirteen-year-old brother from the police. Through her work, González puts a spotlight on these stories of gross abuse and injustice and aims to generate a collective memory about them as part of the larger Mapuche efforts to enact political and social change.

González's collaborations also extend beyond KIMVN Teatro. For example, in 2015 she directed *Yo te parí mujer* [I Gave Birth to You, Woman], which she wrote with Karime Letnic Vallejos and Lorena Herrera Phillips. The play tells the true story of two lesbian women who navigated love, motherhood, and their sexual identities in the

Chile of the 1990s. She also collaborated with Violeta Gal-Rodriguez of L'Insoumise, a French performance group, on the creation of *La Memoire Bafouée* [Flouted Memory], which was developed in 2021. The performance piece merges theatre, video, music, and 3D animation to examine the effects of Chilean exile on the subsequent generations.

González joins the ranks of other contemporary Mapuche artists who are using theatre, dance, and performance as mechanisms for presenting an alternative version of Chilean history to the public. Along with KIMVN Teatro, her works present the lives and culture of the Mapuche people in a way that speaks to their cultural resistance, survival, and pride. As González explains, "We are a theatre that seeks an origin that exists before the conception of the Nation-State. We are a theatre that is rooted in the true identity of the citizens of this territory."[3]

Jimmy A. Noriega

Notes

1 Paula González, interview with author, February 27, 2021.
2 "Quienes somos," KIMVN Teatro, accessed January 8, 2021. http://kimvnteatro.cl
3 Paula González, interview with author, February 27, 2021.

Major works

La Memoire Bafouée [Flouted Memory] (2021)
Trewa. Estado–Nación o el espectro de la traición [Dog. Nation-State or the Specter of Treason] (2019)
UL KIMVN [Song of Wisdom] (2018)
Ñiami Tañi Pixan [His Soul Disappeared] (2017)
ÑUKE. *Una mirada íntima hacia la resistencia mapuche* [MOTHER. An Intimate Look at the Mapuche Resistance] (2016)
Galvarino (2012)
Territorio descuajado [Dislodged Territory] (2011)
Ñi Pu Tremen [My Ancestors] (2009)

Further reading

Cortés Rojas, Ignacia and Ignacio Pastén. "La escenificación de la violencia estatal en dos obras mapuche recientes: *Malen* de Ricardo Curaqueo y *Trewa. Estado-Nación o espectro de la traición* de Paula González," *Latin American Theatre Review*, 54.2 (Spring 2021): 71–95.
González Seguel, Paula, ed. *Dramaturgias de la Resistencia: Teatro Documental KIMVN MARRY XIPNTV*. Ñuñoa, Santiago Chile: Pehuén, 2018.

Gutiérrez, Pía. "Revelaciones de archivo: representación y autorrepresentación del pueblo Mapuche en algunas manifestaciones teatrales chilenas a partir de 1940," *Palimpsesto*, 7.11 (January–June, 2017): 191–205.

"Paula González, Directora Mapuche: 'Uso El Teatro Para Visibilizar y Denunciar La Violencia Hacia Nuestro Pueblo.'" Cátedra Indégena. Accessed March 13, 2021. www.uchileindigena.cl/paula-gonzalez-directora-mapuche-uso-el-teatro-para-visibilizar-y-denunciar/

LAGARTIJAS TIRADAS AL SOL (MEXICO CITY, MEXICO, 2003–)

Lagartijas Tiradas al Sol [Lizards Lying in the Sun] was founded in Mexico City in 2003 by Luisa Pardo and Lázaro Gabino Rodríguez, theatre students at the National Autonomous University of Mexico's University Theater Center. The collective has grown to include additional actors—like Francisco "Paco" Barreiro and Mariana Villegas—videographers, visual artists, and crew members. While Lagartijas is firmly rooted in theatre, its members are also active in other artistic fields and have produced, written, and appeared in films, performance installations, and operas. Their model is truly collective—any piece that is produced under the auspices of the group may have more or less involvement by any particular member, but all of them contribute what they can and share credit. Therefore, even unipersonal pieces like Rodríguez's moving play about the death of his mother, *Montserrat* (2013), or Pardo's staged lecture, *Veracruz* (2016), are produced by the group and promoted as belonging to the collective's *oeuvre*.

Lagartijas are known mainly for their roguish use of fiction and reality within their documentary plays. Almost every production since their earliest projects has had some basis in reality. These so-called realities are varied. Some are rooted in personal experience, like their plays about the death of Pardo's mother, *Pía* (2003) or a romantic break-up, *Catalina* (2009). Others focus on national history, for instance, the history of narcotrafficking in Mexico presented in *It Is Written in Their Fields* (2014), or a look at the guerrilla movements of the 1960s and 1970s in *The Sound of Fire* (2010). In their work, Lagartijas use traditional documentary techniques to signal to audiences that what they are seeing is, in some way, real. Nevertheless, as the collective's aesthetic has evolved over the years, their work has begun to challenge the very possibility of recreating or representing what is real. For example, in *Montserrat*, Rodríguez plays himself but makes impossible and unverifiable claims about the veracity of his mother's death certificate and about tracking her down and meeting her years after her reported death. The stage itself becomes a laboratory, a site for investigating the possibilities of theatre. The integration of personal stories and imagined or dreamed experiences into more traditional documentary evidence becomes key in the search for how theatre is related to reality. Lagartijas's central line of questioning has indelibly marked the documentary genre in Latin American theatre.

Daniel Vázquez Touriño argues that Lagartijas no longer invite the spectator to a mimetic representation of reality, but rather to witness a justification of the act of gathering itself.[1] The importance of gathering goes beyond the theatre walls and into the streets, where the right to assemble and protest has been contested and repressed in Mexican history, a frequent theme in Lagartijas's work. Indeed, Lagartijas's theatrical works often include explanations of their motivations for creating a particular work, both onstage and as part of an extra-theatrical apparatus that may include print books, audio recordings, or web resources. This self-referentiality, in which the company reflects on the function of theatricality (both inside and out of the theatre) has been central to Lagartijas since the company's foundation. Their obsession with family history resonates with other Latin American theatre projects, like Lola Arias's *My Life After* (2009) and *The Year I Was Born* (2012), Sebastián Rubio's *Project 1980/2000* (2012), and Vivi Tellas's *Archives Project* (2003–2008).

While the documentary mode has been a central element of Mexican theatre since the mid-twentieth century, Lagartijas represents the vanguard of this genre in the twenty-first century. Borrowing from innovative playwrights such as Vicente Leñero and Víctor Hugo Rascón Banda, the collective employs techniques that include projecting historical news footage, presenting archival evidence in the form of legal documents or photographs onstage, and re-enacting both well-known historical and intimate personal scenes. These techniques are also used by fellow Mexican collectives Teatro Línea de Sombra and Teatro Ojo, two important groups that explore documentary practices. Lagartijas, therefore, forms part of an intense interest within Latin American theatre in bringing real and intimate stories to the stage. What is remarkable about Lagartijas, in particular, is their willingness and insistence upon using themselves as the subject of their own documentaries, featuring family documents like letters, diaries, photographs, recordings, and interviews with family members or friends about a particular character. In traditional documentary fashion, their work also incorporates historical documents, for example, the constitution and video footage of important political events. Even as they impersonate the characters whose lives they are recreating through this onstage archive, the audience will also find Barreiro, Pardo, Rodríguez, or Villegas playing themselves. The lines between subject, actor, director, and writer all blur to create a sense that what is happening onstage is real.

Their plays skirt the line of invention and reality, sometimes using falsified documents as evidence for a fantasy, at other times insisting on the veracity of alternatives to official history, through, for example, personal and autobiographical stories that blur national history with individual life experience. Departing from the strict adherence of the verbatim in documentary theatre tradition, in which a play's text is based in part or entirely on historical records like court transcripts, Lagartijas freely remix other works of art. In their play *Tijuana* (2016), for example, Gabino Rodríguez portrays a character named Gabino Rodríguez, an actor who voluntarily moves to Tijuana to work in a *maquiladora* for minimum wage. The play is based on the Colombian journalist Andrés Felipe Solano's book *Six Months on Minimum Wage*.

Lagartijas join other Mexican collectives like Colectivo Campo de Ruinas, La Comuna, Microscopía Teatro, Murmurante Laboratorio Escénico, and Teatro Para el Fin del Mundo, who seek new relationships with reality and how it is portrayed onstage. Lagartijas Tiradas al Sol have blazed the trail for onstage grappling with the significant questions of our time, and their growing legacy is undeniable.

Julie Ann Ward

Note

1 Daniel Vázquez Touriño, *Insignificantes en diálogo con el público* (Madrid: Editorial Verbum, 2020), 46.

Major works

Tiburón (2020)
Tijuana (2016)
Santiago Amoukalli (2016)
Está escrita en sus campos [It is Written in Their Fields] (2014)
Montserrat (2013)
The Sound of Fire (2010)
Assault on Clear Water (2006)

Published works

Lagartijas Tiradas al Sol. "El rumor del incendio." *El rumor del momento*. Mexico City: Conejo Blanco, 2010, 95–131.

Further reading

Prieto Nadal, A. "*La democracia en México*, Un proyecto de Lagartijas Tiradas Al Sol." *Culturamas*, October 18, 2016, www.culturamas.es/blog/2016/10/18/la-democracia-en-mexico-un-proyecto-de-lagartijas-tiradas-al-sol/

Prieto Stambaugh, A. "Memorias inquietas: Testimonio y confesión en el teatro performativo de México y Brasil." In *Corporalidades escénicas: Representaciones del cuerpo en el teatro, la danza y el performance*, edited by Antonio Prieto Stambaugh and Elka Fediuk, 207–232. Xalapa: Universidad Veracruzana, 2016.

Sabugal Paz, P. "Teatro Documental: Entre la realidad y la ficción." *Investigación Teatral* 7, no. 10–11 (2017): 111–129, https://investigacionteatral.uv.mx/index.php/investigacionteatral/article/view/2533/4415

Salvat, R. "Una aproximación al actual teatro de México." *Assaig de teatre: revista de l'Associació d'Investigació i Experimentació Teatral* 62–64 (2008): 426–439. *RACO*, www.raco.cat/index.php/AssaigTeatre/article/view/182661/235 328

Van Ryzin, Jeanne Claire. "Lagartijas Tiradas Al Sol's 'Tijuana'—Enacting Poverty." *Fusebox Festival Blog*, http://schedule.fuseboxfestival.com/blog/lagartijas-tiradas-al-sols-tijuana-enacting-poverty

Ward, J.A. *A Shared Truth: The Theater of Lagartijas Tiradas al Sol*. Pittsburgh: University of Pittsburgh Press, 2019.

Ward, J.A. "Making Reality Sensible: The Mexican Documentary Theatre Tradition, 1968-2013." *Theatre Journal* 69, no. 2 (2017): 197–211.

JOHN LEGUIZAMO (BOGOTÁ, COLOMBIA/NEW YORK CITY 1964–)

John Leguizamo is an actor, comic, playwright, screenwriter, producer, and author. He was born in Bogotá, Colombia and moved to New York City with his family at age four. His experiences growing up in Queens, in particular the Jackson Heights neighborhood, would have a profound impact on the content and style of his comedy and one-man shows. He attended NYU's Tisch School of the Arts but dropped out to begin a career as a stand-up comic; he later gained notoriety on the NYC nightclub circuit. By the mid-1980s he was appearing in small television roles and by the 1990s was acting in major feature-length films. Although audiences primarily know him for his film and television career, Leguizamo is one of the most accomplished and celebrated Latinx writers and solo performers in US theatre. His one-man shows, most of which have been adapted for television, have garnered him a Primetime Emmy Award (1999), Obie Award (1991), and two Drama Desk Awards (1998 and 2011). He has also been nominated for four Tony Awards, ranging from Best Play to Best Actor in a Play, demonstrating his success as a playwright and performer on the commercial stage. In 2018, he was honored with a Special Tony Award.

At age twenty-three, he made his off-Broadway debut in Reinaldo Povod's *La Puta Vida Trilogy*, playing the part of the Alley Boy at the Public Theater in 1987. He was subsequently cast as the replacement for Puck in the production of *A Midsummer Night's Dream*, also at the Public, which would serve as a home for many of his future collaborations and performances. After workshops and productions across New York City, Leguizamo's first solo show, *Mambo Mouth* (1991), premiered off-Broadway at the Orpheum Theatre. In it, he played seven different Latinx characters, each with his or her own monologue, in what would become a trademark of his early career. His next solo endeavor was *Spic-O-Rama* (1993), in which Leguizamo portrayed multiple Latinx characters from the same family, with roles ranging from an adolescent teen to a Desert Storm veteran, Puerto Rican mother and father, and an aspiring actor who dyes his hair blonde and uses blue contacts to mask his Latinx identity.

Freak (1998) cemented Leguizamo's mark on theatre history when he became the first Latinx person to perform a solo show on Broadway. Prior to this, only three other Latinx-penned plays had ever been staged on Broadway: Miguel Piñero's *Short Eyes* (1974), Luis Valdez's *Zoot Suit* (1979), and Reinaldo Povod's *Cuba and His Teddy Bear* (1986). *Freak* is a semi-autobiographical show that draws upon Leguizamo's early childhood and adolescent experiences, including: the abuse he and his mother endured under his father; his relationships with his brother and gay uncle; the friendships and fights he had with people in his neighborhood; his first sexual experience; and his early exposure to theatre, including a memory of watching *A Chorus Line*. David Román, writing about the success of *Freak*, says, "Leguizamo's gifted impersonations, energetic performances, and irreverent comic sensibilities proved enormously appealing to critics and audiences alike."[1] He also notes that "a main reason for Leguizamo's commercial success had to do with *Freak*'s marketing and outreach efforts to Latino audiences."[2] As a result, the show helped to forge new ways of understanding the kinds of approaches that Latinx artists could take to cultivate audiences and craft material for the commercial stage. Leguizamo built upon these lessons and demonstrated his broad appeal with his next solo show, *Sexaholix ... a Love Story*, which played twice on Broadway (2001 and 2003) and again with *Ghetto Klown* (2011), which was based on his memoir *Pimps, Hos, Playa Hatas, and All the Rest of My Hollywood Friends: My Life* (2007).

Latin History for Morons (2018) was Leguizamo's fourth solo venture to make it to Broadway. The show critiques the omission of Latinx figures in US classrooms and, by extension, the impact and legacy of European and US colonization and violence on the Americas. The premise of the play is quite simple: Leguizamo is trying to help his son find a "Latin" hero to write about for his school history project. This sets him on a frantic journey through time as he tries to learn about the histories of indigenous peoples in the Americas, their colonization by Spain, and the subsequent contributions of Latinx people to US history. The show is formatted as a lecture, with the comedian taking on the role of teacher, as he provides a primer for understanding the ways that Latinx cultures and people are erased from our public education system. In many ways, this performance is an embodied work of archeology, with Leguizamo extracting forgotten and unknown figures from history to present them to his audience. His latest piece of theatre, *Kiss My Aztec!* (2019), follows a similar method of exposing and inverting the dominant historical narrative. In this musical comedy, the colonization of Mesoamerica is told from the indigenous perspective and to the sounds of salsa, hip-hop, gospel, and merengue. Leguizamo and Tony Taccone (the director of *Latin History for Morons*) wrote the book of the musical and developed it at the Public Theater with subsequent premieres at Berkeley Repertory Theater and La Jolla Playhouse.

As a playwright, Leguizamo brings to each of his solo endeavors a combination of autobiography and Latinx-centric storytelling that sheds light onto the complexities of what it means to be a person of Latin American descent living in the United States. He does not shy away from ethnic stereotypes, family drama, and secrets, or embarrassing tales about sex and love. Most importantly, his plays draw upon his own experiences of being an outcast at home and in society, and his portrayal of multiple characters reveals the complexity of identity and struggle in the face of adversity. Miriam Chirico identifies Leguizamo's main acting technique as impersonation and speaks of his comic style as founded on the use of mimicry to highlight the multitude of ways in which caricatures may be superimposed on the self. She continues her analysis of his comic style by stating, "while not all Latinos are happy with Leguizamo's stereotypes-as-empowerment method, Leguizamo believes that by showing the humanity beneath each stereotype he may work to dismantle racist attitudes."[3]

As such, his plays operate within a genealogy of Latinx solo performance that seeks to interrogate and dissect the problematic stereotypes placed upon Latinx communities in the US. Brian Herrera, speaking about the comic works of artists like Leguizamo, Culture Clash, and Carmelita Tropicana, explains that they "satirically surrogated familiar 'Latin types' and through charismatic quick-change alchemies deployed humor to confirm the banal artifice of familiar stereotypes and scenarios and show how much bigger, stranger, and funnier real Latinas/os are by comparison."[4] In doing so, Leguizamo, like his contemporaries, portrays multiple and contradictory versions of the Latinx figure as a way of exposing and upending the racial and gender stereotypes that have permeated film, television, and theatre for decades. The result is not only an expanded repertoire of Latinx characters, but also a new way of imagining the Latinx diaspora and its experience in the United States.

Jimmy A. Noriega

Notes

1 David Román, *Performance in America: Contemporary US Culture and the Performing Arts* (Durham, NC: Duke University Press, 2005), 115.
2 Ibid., 115–116.
3 Miriam Chirico, "Performed Authenticity: Narrating the Self in the Comic Monologues of David Sedaris, John Leguizamo, and Spalding Gray," *Studies in American Humor*, vol. 2, no. 1 (2016), 36.
4 Brian Herrera, *Latin Numbers: Playing Latino in Twentieth-Century U.S. Popular Performance* (Ann Arbor: University of Michigan Press, 2015), 145.

Major works

Kiss My Aztec! (2019)
Latin History for Morons (2018)
Ghetto Klown (2011)
Sexaholix ... a Love Story (2001)
Freak (1998)
Spic-O-Rama (1993)
Mambo Mouth (1991)

Published works

Ghetto Klown: A Graphic Novel. Illustrated by Christa Cassano and Shamus Beyale. Abrams Comicarts, 2015.
The Works of John Leguizamo: Freak, Spic-o-Rama, Mambo Mouth, and Sexaholix. HarperCollins, 2009.
Pimps, Hos, Playa Hatas, and All the Rest of My Hollywood Friends: My Life. HarperCollins, 2007.
Freak: A Semi-Demi-Quasi-Pseudo Autobiography. Riverhead Books, 1997.

Further reading

Alzate, Gastón Adolfo. "When the Subaltern Is Politically Incorrect: A Cultural Analysis of the Performance Art of John Leguizamo." In *The State of Latino Theater in the United States*, edited by Luis A. Ramos-García, 131–151. New York: Routledge, 2002.

Chirico, Miriam. "Laughter and Ethnicity in John Leguizamo's One-Man Worlds," *Latin American Theatre Review*, vol. 36, no. 1 (2002): 29–50.

Cooper, Evan. "Looking at the Latin 'Freak': Audience Reception of John Leguizamo's Culturally Intimate Humor," *Latino Studies*, vol. 6 (2008): 436–455.

CONCHI LEÓN (YUCATÁN, MEXICO, 1973–)

María Concepción León Mora, popularly known as Conchi León, is a playwright, director, actor, and community activist. Born in Mérida, Yucatán, León's first forays into theatre came at an early age. By 1999, she was recognized as one of the leading voices of her generation. She has written over sixty pieces, though many unpublished, has directed and performed in countless more. Among many invitations to participate in international spaces, León was chosen for the selective dramaturgy seminar at the Royal Court of London in 2009, as artist-in-residence at the Lark Play Development Center in New York in 2014, and to represent Latin America in the 2016 "Pen World International Voices Festival." Within Mexico, León was acknowledged in 2011 for her social work via theatre by Yucatán's Commission for Human Rights, and in 2018 was invited to join the prestigious National System of Artist Creators CONACULTA-FONCA and received the Héctor Herrera "Cholo" medal from the Mérida City Council for her theatre contributions.

A common thread throughout León's pieces is the art of storytelling, culminating in her particular style of testimonial theatre. She defines her work as such because the origins of her pieces reside in the stories she absorbs from her own life and from those who inspire her creations. Yet, as recounted memories are not linear, León's work weaves together fragments, pasts, presents, and futures. Balancing artistic interpretation with collected testimonies, León's writing and directing decisions integrate musical interludes, competing narratives, and ritual practice, among other techniques. The result is heartbreakingly beautiful depictions of the human condition.

In 2005, after working alone for more than a decade, León founded the theatre company Sa'as Tun. With core members, Oswaldo Ferrer (actor and producer), Addy Teyer (actor and producer), Lourdes León (actor), Esaú Corona (lighting designer), Susi Estrada (actor), and Salomé Senores (actor), Sa'as Tun has developed a unique theatre semiotics rooted in relating Mayan mysticism and memory through performative gesture. Deploying an anthropological approach, the group's pieces conjoin oral histories, testimonies, and personal reflections. León and Sa'as Tun are perhaps most well-known for the piece, *Mestiza Power* (2005), which relates the lived experiences of Mayan mestiza women in her home state of Yucatán. In this region, the term mestiza does not reference the intermingling of colonizer and indigenous blood but denotes indigenous women who present themselves as such through dress, speech, and other practices. León and her company find constant inspiration in their surroundings, Mayan history, language, and people, all of which motivate their use of theatre to resist commercial trends that dismiss or erase the indigenous body. Despite their prolific list of productions, León and Sa'as Tun's interest in the Yucatán Peninsula commonly results in being dismissed as "regional" theatre. Though their work has much broader ramifications, this general disregard has led to a woefully limited number of critical approximations.

Mestiza Power launched León onto national and international stages, as her depiction of the fictional character "Soco Coyac" captivated audiences. This character emerged out of an ordinary event. Walking through town, León came across a Mayan mestiza woman selling fruit, dressed in the traditional huipil, wearing a pair of Ray-Ban sunglasses. León describes this moment as the "irradiant image" that transformed her theatre trajectory. This woman became the detonator not just for her professional success, but also for broadening popular conceptions of Mayan female indigeneity through theatre. According to León, she bought fruit from this woman and asked her about her sunglasses. The woman proceeded to disclose personal stories of intrafamilial abuse, resonating deeply with the violence that León witnessed in her own home. Beyond her conversations with the real-life "Soco Coyac," León spoke with numerous women in order to faithfully bring their stories, lexicon, emotions, and traditions to the stage in *Mestiza Power*. Organized in two parts, the piece is performed by three actresses, who in the first part, perform the roles of various mestizas. They become a chorus of voices echoing and reaffirming one another's experiences. The second part is comprised of three individual monologues of pain and resiliency, including that of Soco Coyac, culminating in a cleansing ritual.

This act of creating space for complex indigenous female characters is of prime importance for León. In March 2020, she was cast in *Between Pancho Villa and a Naked Woman*, directed by Ana Francis

Mor. León appeared on stage for less than five minutes, interpreting Doña Micaela Arango, a stout, taciturn, mestiza woman. León has confessed on multiple occasions that these are the roles she is most often offered as an actress, caricatures that cement stereotypes of indigenous, overweight, and dark-skinned women as unappealing and lacking in intelligence. These one-dimensional depictions of mestiza femininity reinforce prejudices that further emphasize a divide between Mexico City, perceived as a site of cultural capital, and the rest of Mexico, often considered lacking any worthwhile creations. As a strategic act of defiance, León depicts the mestiza woman as she is: a complicated figure of wonderment and beauty. Pieces such as *Las creyentes* [The Believers] (2006), *Santificarás las fiestas* [You Will Sanctify the Festivals] (2008), *Las Huiras de la Sierra Papakal* [The Escapes from Papakal Mountain] (2009), *Del Manantial del corazón* [From the Spring of the Heart] (2016), *La Tia Mariela* [Aunt Mariela] (2017), among countless others, do just that.

Beyond depictions of the Mayan community, León's testimonial theatre has led her to contemplate broader questions about human rights and forgotten populations. As director of the Cultural Center for Yucatecan Youth (1994–2003), León led workshops for diverse youth populations, including the deaf. From these experiences, León recognized that there was no singular approach to creating theatre, but rather, her practice is determined by the space, resources, and participants themselves. By fitting the needs of her students, she creates space for a kind of dramaturgy of urgency. Pieces such as *De Coraza* [Of Shielded Brass] (2017), in which women reflect on the crimes they committed and life after prison, and *La Espera* [The Wait] (2017), about how three imprisoned men, abandoned by their loved ones, found new life and comradery via theatre, are further examples of this approach. These plays emerged out of León's workshops with incarcerated populations within the Mexico City prison, Santa Martha Acatitla. Inside this space, she heard devastating stories of abuse, false accusations and lives cut short, deprived of dignity and hope. From these stories, she penned and staged the aforementioned works, tender depictions of those stigmatized by being imprisoned.

Starting with her time at the Cultural Center, León has constantly been encouraged to document the creative processes behind her workshops and testimonial pieces. *La Nostalgia de los sentidos. Manual de dramaturgia testimonial* [Nostalgia of the Senses. Manual of Testimonial Dramaturgy] (2019) is a personal reflection about her own life as much as it is an instructive tool for theatre practitioners. Detailing her methodology, León firmly asserts that her work emerges from conversations, not interviews. She explains, "I like to listen to people: it surprises me how in a single sentence they can define the politics of the country, the pain of a people, the cruelty of love, or the hatred between brothers."[1] From this attentiveness, she develops a relationship with her interlocutors, fostering intimacy over time. As a gesture of acknowledging the speaker's privacy, León always works alone, does not rush conversations and does not judge. She also generally does not record anything; her testimonial theatre is crafted from the notes she takes afterwards and from memory. In effect, even having written her instructional manual, León's body is a walking archive of Yucatán and mestiza secrets, only a fraction of which are shared with the world through her artistic contributions.

Christina Baker

Note

1 Conchi León, "From my Universal Village: The Winged Word," in *Theatre and Cartographies of Power: Repositioning the Latina/o Americas*, eds. Jimmy Noriega and Analola Santana (Carbondale: Southern Illinois University Press, 2018), 147.

Major works

Las mujeres de Emiliano [The Women of Emiliano] (2020)
La Espera [The Wait] (2017)
Cachorro de león [The Lion's Pup] (2016)
Todo lo que encontré en el agua [Everything I Found in the Water] (2013)
La ropa sucia se lava en casa [Dirty Clothes Are Washed at Home] (2009)
Santificarás las fiestas [You Will Sanctify the Festivals] (2008)
Las creyentes [The Believers] (2006)
Mestiza Power (2005)

Published works

La nostalgia de los sentidos. Manual de dramaturgia testimonial. Mexico City: Editorial Trópico de Escorpio, 2019.
Mestiza Power. Translated by Virginia Grise. South Gate: No Passport Press, 2018.
Todo lo que encontré en el agua. Mexico City: Paso de gato, 2013.

Further reading

Azor Hernández, Ileana. "Sueños que danzan en el agua. Mestizas y mayas en el teatro de Conchi León." *Latin American Theatre Review*, 44.2 (Spring 2011): 17–34.

Baez Ayala, Susana Leticia and Patricia Andrea Beltrán Henríquez. "*Mestiza Power* de Conchi León, escritora sin fronteras." *Anagnórisis: Revista de investigación teatral*, 9 (June 2014): 102–129.

Mijares, Enrique. "Mestiza de poder. Review of *La nostaligia de los sentidos. Manual de dramaturgia testimonial.*" *Investigación Teatral*, 11.18 (October–March 2020): 227–233.

Noriega, Jimmy A. *Staging Presence/Embodying Absence: Performance and Protest in the Americas*. Cornell University, PhD dissertation, 2011.

JOSEFINA LÓPEZ (SAN LUIS POTOSÍ, MÉXICO/LOS ANGELES, 1969–)

While Josefina López's most famous work to date is co-writing the movie script for *Real Women Have Curves* (2002, based on her eponymous play), the theatre has been her primary area for over thirty years. At age five she moved with her family from Mexico to Boyle Heights, Los Angeles, California, where she continues to pursue her arts and activism. She lived undocumented until age seventeen when she received official documentation to live in the US. That same year, López graduated from Los Angeles Performing Arts School and began working in the theatre. Inspired by Teatro Campesino and in a quest to rectify the lack of strong female roles showing experiences like her own, she began her mission to create them through her own writing. López attended Columbia College in Chicago for her undergraduate degree and completed an MFA in screenwriting at UCLA. Her work in activism, advocacy for people of color and women through representation in theatre, media, and the arts continues. Her plays have been staged across the nation and overseas both by professional and amateur groups and she is called upon to speak at campuses around the country.

López's most important contribution to Latinx theatre beyond the body of her work is creating a space for the intersectional voices of Latinas in the theatre, and continually mentoring writers, artists, and actors through her financially accessible workshops at Casa 0101, founded in 2000. Casa 0101 was first conceived as a workshop facility for amateur filmmakers. Functioning in a former bridal shop storefront, Casa soon switched gears and began working instead with theatre, teaching area residents all areas of production: from writing, to set building, costume design, and performance. In 2011, Casa moved a block away from its original location to a building with a ninety-nine-seat theatre space, an art gallery, and a classroom. Under López's vision, the theatre continues to offer access to the arts for neighbors in East LA, providing "Pay as You Can" ticketing for some shows, ongoing workshops, and free art classes for local youth.

As a playwright, a major theme that dominates López's early work is the coming-of-age story of young Latinas living between their culture of heritage and the expectations of US life. *Simply Maria, or The American Dream* (1987) was written before López graduated from LA's Performance Arts high school. She saw Teatro Campesino's *I Don't Have to Show You No Stinking Badges* at the Los Angeles Theater Center and felt inspired by it and compelled to tell a story from her own perspective. The two-part title forefronts the dual paths the young protagonist faces in her life as she heads toward adulthood and prefaces her decision to follow her own dreams. Likewise, *Real Women Have Curves* examines young Ana's difficulties navigating her life choices between following the traditions of her past or pursuing her desire to study and become a writer. *Drunk Girl* (2015), a set of vignettes decrying cases of sexual aggression, also features young Latinx women coming of age (alongside other age groups). These characters are unsure of how to proceed with claims of sexual assault against them, believing that their poverty and ethnicity will work against the credibility of their stories. Another coming-of-age story is that of Dahlia in *Boyle Heights* (2004), who like Ana from *Real Women Have Curves*, aspires to become a writer and pursue her education despite pressures from her family to conform to tradition. *Hungry Woman in Paris* (2009 novel, 2013 stage adaptation) deals with an adult woman who, like the younger characters in the above-mentioned plays, heads out on a trip for self-discovery. While not a coming-of-age story in the traditional sense, *Hungry Woman* certainly follows a similar path as Canela discovers herself through her time in Paris. Unlike the younger characters in the previously mentioned plays, Canela searches for her true vocation by traveling to Paris and studying cuisine at a prestigious cooking school. Similarly to *Simply María* and *Real Women Have Curves*, this play contains autobiographical elements to López's real life, as she herself studied cooking in Paris.

Criticism of US immigration policy and perceptions of others prevails in many of her works, but particularly in *Detained in the Desert* (2008) where López sets two characters in the desert: a wrongfully detained Latina and a radical conservative talk show host who has been kidnapped. Ironically, the two end up stranded in the desert together, forced to depend on each other in order to survive. López's criticism of immigration policy comes through in other plays, such as *Drunk Girl* when a character dreads coming forth with allegations of sexual assault for fear of being deported, or *Real Women Have Curves*, where the characters suffer the heat of a sweatshop because opening the doors and windows could expose then to the *migra*. Even early in her work, in *Simply María*, López compares the difference between white immigrants entering the US parading proudly past the Statue of Liberty with that of María's family, who dodges the *migra* in the shadows of the statue just to get in.

The former scene, an example of López's critique of US immigration policy, is also an example of how she uses dark humor to dispel, question, and underline social justice issues and harmful stereotypes of Latinxs. *Simply María* contains many such scenes, including but not limited to the dream scene where the young protagonist is giving birth to not one, not two, but more than a dozen babies—which pop out of her body and fly across the stage. The scene is narrated by a talk show host voice over who proclaims that María, like other Mexican women, is a "world renowned reproducing machine."[1] While horrifying, the scene evokes both laughter and dismay about the pervasive stereotypes surrounding Mexican women and procreation. Humor also prevails in *Confessions of Women from East LA* (1997), a series of nine monologues featuring a broad array of characters portraying a multitude of experiences of different Latinx women around the city. This play, written in protest of California's Proposition 187, slides somewhat into a political advertisement against that proposition. Likewise, *Drunk Girl* employs humor in a series of vignettes where characters relay their experiences of sexual assault and rape. Similar to *Confessions*, *Drunk Girl* sounds at some points more like a public service announcement about gender violence than a play. In its final scene, all of the characters in *Drunk Girl* come to the stage, dancing and singing "Let's have sex!" López uses humor in both works to showcase the issues—anti-immigration sentiment and sexual violence. These controversial topics, immigration and sexual violence, are not normally treated with comedy.

López employs humor in her voice precisely to add an edge of critique to draw her audiences' attention to her social criticism. Humor, in fact, is a common thread that ties all López's work together, making her spectators both laugh and think. López continues to bring her community intellectual and artistic fodder, both through her theatrical and artistic endeavors. Her activity, both as an activist and an artist, continues to nurture her community and the entire country, as her plays are staged both in the US and around the world, and ensure that her audiences do not forget the travails of young Latinx people coming of age.

Michelle Warren

Note

1 Josefina López, *Simply María* (1st electronic edn, Alexander Street Press, 2006), 37.

Major works

Drunk Girl (2015)
Hungry Woman (2013)
Detained in the Desert (2008)
Boyle Heights (2004)
Confessions of Women from East LA (1997)
Real Women Have Curves (1990)
Simply María; Or, The American Dream (1987)

Published works

Detained in the Desert & Other Plays. WPR Books, 2011.
Real Women Have Curves & Other Plays. WPR Books, 2011.
Hungry Woman in Paris. Grand Central Pub, 2009.

Further reading

Boffone, Trevor. " 'You Have to Feel It to Heal It': Healing Trauma and Finding the Creative Voice with Josefina López." *Label Me Latina/O* 7 (2017): 1–9.
Boffone, Trevor. "A 'Wild Zone' of Her Own: Locating the Chicana Experience in the Theatre Works of Josefina López." *Gender Forum: An Internet Journal of Gender Studies* 48 (2014): 32–47.
Jacobs, Elizabeth. "Undocumented Acts: Migration, Community and Audience in Two Chicana Plays." *Comparative American Studies: An International Journal* 14.3–4 (2016): 277–288.
Milleret, Margo. "Girls Growing Up, Cultural Norms Breaking Down in Two Plays by Josefina López." *Gestos: Teoria y Practica Del Teatro Hispánico* 13.26 (1998): 109–125.
Narbona Carrión, María Dolores. "The Conflict Between the American Dream and Chicano Traditions: Josefina López's Simply María or The American Dream." In *Critical Essays on Chicano Studies*, edited by Ramón Espejo et al., 179–190. New York: Peter Lang Publishing, 2007.

EDUARDO MACHADO (HAVANA, CUBA/NEW YORK CITY, 1953–)

Eduardo Machado is a playwright and director based in New York. He was born in Havana, Cuba and first came to the United States as a child on a visa obtained through Operation Pedro Pan, a program sponsored by the Catholic Welfare Bureau which relocated Cuban children to the US between 1960 and 1962, sometimes placing them with relatives, sometimes placing them in foster care. He grew up near Los Angeles and studied playwriting with María Irene Fornés at New York's International Arts Relations (INTAR) theatre, which he later led as the artistic director between 2004 and 2010. Machado directed the playwriting program at Columbia University from 1997 to 2007, and he currently teaches at the NYU Tisch School of the Arts, where he has been a professor since 2007. His plays have been produced by major professional theatres in the United States, including Seattle Repertory Theatre, Goodman Theatre, Hartford Stage, Actors Theatre of Louisville, the Mark Taper Forum, Long Wharf Theatre, Hampstead Theatre in London, INTAR Theatre, Theater for the New City, and Repertorio Español.

Machado's playwriting is singular for its deeply personal and raw exploration of memory, family stories, and lived experiences. That is not to say that his plays are strictly autobiographical either, as he did not witness himself many of the events depicted in his plays. For instance, while assisting Fornés with the Hispanic Playwrights in Residency Program in 1981, Machado drafted parts of what would become three of his *Floating Island Plays*, a four-play cycle and family saga spanning from 1920s Guanabacoa, Cuba to 1980s Woodland Hills, California, which include *The Modern Ladies of Guanabacoa* (1984), *Fabiola* (1985), *In the Eye of the Hurricane* (1989), and *Broken Eggs* (1984). Whereas *Broken Eggs* is based on Machado's sister's wedding and his experiences, *Fabiola* is inspired by a family story—one of Machado's uncles killed himself after losing his wife, Fabiola, in childbirth. Much of the other details—Fabiola's corpse disappearing or reappearing or the incestuous relationship between Fabiola's husband and his brother—mine deeper meanings that transcend the personal through poetic license or hyperbole.

Incest carries a certain shock value on a literal level, and yet, like so many themes in Machado's work, remains open to figurative meanings. It can be read as an expression of narcissism and self-isolation. Yet through incest, Machado's plays touch on a frequent theme in literary and theatrical works by Cuban authors dating back, at least, to Cirilo Villaverde's *Cecilia Valdés* (1839, 1882). Other examples of works that evoke incestuous desire in theatre specifically include Virgilio Piñera's *Electra Garrigó* (1941) and José Triana's *Night of the Assassins* (1965). They all deploy this theme in allegorical ways to comment on residual ideologies of colonialism and the bourgeois family.

Machado has written that he approaches playwriting as a kind of therapy to expunge his anger and work through pain. Often cynical in tone, Machado's deceptively realist linear dramas, attend to the trauma of loss, revolution, displacement, and estrangement that mark the history of Cuba and its diaspora in the United States. This is especially the case in the *Floating Island Plays* and his most celebrated Cuba special period plays—*Havana is Waiting* (2001), *The Cook* (2003), and *Kissing Fidel* (2005)—as they dramatize how the aftermath of seismic political shifts and their resulting social divisions play out on the personal, sexual, and familial levels. Although Machado has also written plays about other subjects, most notably *Stevie Wants to Play the Blues* (1990), his better-known plays deal with Cuba in some way.

A major shift in Machado's relationship in writing about Cuba took place as a result of being the first Cuban American playwright to tour a play in Cuba with Repertorio Español's Spanish-language production of *Revoltillo* (*Broken Eggs*) in 1998. The tour afforded him a chance to return to Cuba for the first time since 1961 and gave him contemporary experiences in Cuba to write about, as depicted in *Havana is Waiting* and *The Cook*.

Ricardo Ortiz calls Machado's style "promiscuous."[1] His rhetoric of emotions and extreme situations may flirt with melodrama, or a number of other styles as inspirations, like theatre of the absurd, but his texts remain faithful only to their therapeutic slant, a working through of unresolved issues. The translation from autobiography or memoir to theatrical or literary terms through compression of dramatic action, exaggeration, antithesis, or allusion allows Machado's characters to transcend their particular history in the personal or familial memory of the playwright to take on figurative or allegorical meanings.

Several critics have considered how time functions in non-realist ways in Machado's plays. Kimberly del Busto Ramírez points out how the longing for lost space creates a duality for the exiled characters in how they experience time. Their life in exile is split off from their life in Cuba which has been suspended in time, making exiles feel like they exist in multiple dimensions at once.[2] Del Busto Ramírez ponders that the experience of *destierro* (exile, literally unearthed/uprooted) for Pedro Pan characters also concerns a *destiempo* by means of lost time and a lost childhood, placing them out of sync with time in the world of the play.[3] In *Fabiola*, Machado plays with time as it relates to history. The play recounts several years in the life of a family mourning and haunted by the title character, while the 1950s Revolution and the Bay of Pigs invasion take place in the backdrop. During this time span, Fabiola's corpse first disappears from the mausoleum and is later discovered in another family's vault unchanged, free from decomposition. Ortiz points out that her body's refusal to mark natural time points to a splitting of time and a difficulty in narrating history when two irreconcilable perspectives—revolution and exile—counter one another.

Patricia Ybarra connects Fabiola's suspension in time to another kind of liminal state embodied by the characters in *Kissing Fidel*, which enacts a temporal impasse endemic to the failures of late-capitalism, as a kind of "motion without forward movement."[4] Set during the height of the 1994 *balsero* crisis, all the action of the play takes place at a Miami funeral home the night before the funeral of Cusa, the family matriarch. Coincidently, one of the family's cousins, Ismael, arrives directly to the funeral parlor from his risky journey from Cuba on a raft to cross paths with Oscar, who tells his family that he is on his way to Cuba to kiss and forgive Fidel, a transgressive proclamation that stokes their temper. Coupled with a number of incestuous sexual transgressions between Oscar, his cousins, and his aunt, Ybarra reads the multiple layers of in-betweenness as a queer futurity in search of new possibilities signaled by Oscar's proposal to kiss Fidel.[5]

Ruins, a major motif in Cuban literature during the Special Period, is also key to understanding Machado's dramaturgy. As Solimar Otero has written about the trope of the ruins of Havana in various forms of cultural production, ruins as a representation of a complex and layered past open up the possibility of connecting with Cuba in new ways, including "a possibility of creating catharsis that frees the subject of a coerced responsibility to nation, past and family."[6] Throughout Machado's *oeuvre*, we see trauma fester, relationships deteriorate, and characters struggle to overcome insurmountable divides rippling out from the Revolution, exile and their codependence in antagonism. The ruination that unfolds is often not a sign of tragedy, but just as sex in Machado's plays can embody pleasure in transgressive behavior, the revelation of secrets and the power structures they guard is also pleasurable, as it is liberatory and signals the potential for new beginnings.

Eric Mayer-García

Notes

1 Ricardo L. Ortiz, *Cultural Erotics in Cuban America* (Minneapolis: University of Minnesota Press, 2007), 173.
2 Kimberly del Busto Ramírez, "The Lost Apple Plays: Performing Operation Pedro Pan" (Ph.D. diss., City University of New York, 2009), 111.
3 Ibid., 115.
4 Patricia A. Ybarra, *Latinx Theater in the Times of Neoliberalism* (Evanston: Northwestern University Press, 2018), 78.
5 Ibid., 85–87.

6 Solimar Otero, "The Ruins of Havana: Representations of Memory, Religion, and Gender," *Atlantic Studies* 9.2 (2012): 146.

Major works

Kissing Fidel (2005)
The Cook (2003)
Havana is Waiting (2001)
Crocodile Eyes (1998)
In the Eye of the Hurricane (1991)
Don Juan in New York City (1988)
Fabiola (1986)
Broken Eggs (1984)
The Modern Ladies of Guanabacoa (1983)
Rosario and the Gypsies (1982)

Published works

Havana is Waiting and Other Plays. New York: Theatre Communications Group, 2011.
Havana Journal. New York: Samuel French, 2011.
Once Removed. Alexandria, VA: Alexander Street Press, 2006.
The Floating Island Plays. New York: Theatre Communications Group, 1991.

Further reading

Brantley, Ben. "Eduardo Machado: Creator of a Paradise Lost," *New York Times Magazine*, October 23, 1994, 38.
Del Rio, Eduardo R. *One Island, Many Voices: Conversations with Cuban-American Writers*. Tucson: University of Arizona Press, 2008.
Machado, Eduardo and Michael Domitrovich. *Tastes Like Cuba: An Exile's Hunger for Home*. New York: Gotham, 2007.
Ortiz, Ricardo. "Fables of (Cuban) Exile: Special Periods and Queer Moments in Eduardo Machado's *Floating Island Plays*." *Modern Drama* 48.1 (2005): 132–162.
Pascual Soler, Nieves. "False Memories, False Foods: Eating, Cooking, Remembering in Tastes like Cuba by Eduardo Machado." In *Memory Frictions in Contemporary Literature*, edited by Martínez-Alfaro, M. and Pellicer-Ortín S., 121–139. New York: Palgrave Macmillan, 2017

ROSA LUISA MÁRQUEZ (SAN JUAN, PUERTO RICO, 1947–)

Rosa Luisa Márquez is a director, performer, playwright, dramaturg, and teacher of theatrical arts whose overlapping creative roles often find her simultaneously devising, directing, and appearing in the productions generated from her educational workshops and experimentations. Márquez's artistic philosophy that actors and spectators are active collaborators—co-creating communal understandings through interplays of text, music, environment, costumes, and props—produces spontaneous, synergistic, interactive performances. Her process involves a rehearsal period of intensive game-based exploration, culminating in a live public encounter to provoke reflection on common conditions and inspire change. Márquez's work endeavors to adapt and enact popular scripts and scenarios in ways that are universal yet unique to the Puerto Rican experience.

Born in the *barrio* of Santurce, San Juan, Puerto Rico in 1947, Márquez began creating theatre in Sunday school sessions around the age of eight. Throughout her youth, she attended dramatic performances, musicals, and mime, and was impressed when actors broke the fourth wall and infiltrated the audience area. Studying theatre in Puerto Rico during the Vietnam War era instilled in Márquez an urgent need to problem-solve and confront colonialism by joining forces with others in public arenas instead of "traditional [theatre] spaces [that] limit the possibilities of democratic exchange."[1] Márquez obtained a BA in Theatre from the University of Puerto Rico (UPR)-Río Piedras and an MA in Educational Theatre from New York University before founding the Amanú theatre troupe in 1971. She continued participating in theatre-in-education initiatives while earning a PhD at Michigan State University. Márquez developed her technique with mentors Peter Schumann of Bread and Puppet Theatre, Augusto Boal of Theatre of the Oppressed and Argentine dramatist Osvaldo Dragún. She also launched a long-time collaborative partnership with the artist Antonio Martorell with whom she co-founded the itinerant troupe Teatreros Ambulantes de Cayey.

Through such transnational alliances, Márquez accumulated a repertoire of theatrical play exercises to stimulate students and communities to "solve problems, create, and loosen up" while conceiving real and ideal images of "shared problems."[2] She directed collective reflections on public perceptions of body image and physical health with *Sí-Dá* (1987–1989), an informative piece about AIDS staged for healthcare workers and the greater community, and *La mujer ideal* [The Ideal Woman] (1987), a satire of stereotypes associated with the obsession of women who starve themselves thin because of the heteromasculine gaze, performed as mealtime *edutainment* in a college dining commons.

Schumann's influence reinforced Márquez's emphasis on process over product. Together they created *La pasión y muerte de Adolfina*

Villanueva [The Passion and Death of Adolfina Villanueva] (1989) as a collaboration between Bread and Puppet Theatre and Teatreros Ambulantes de Cayey. On the grounds of the UPR campus, an outdoor audience followed musicians, stilt walkers, puppeteers, and colossal puppets conveying the story of the Afro-Puerto Rican mother who was murdered by police while expropriating her family's residence. The dramatization of this historical incident of discriminatory oppression concludes when a puppet representing the island's "progress" via forceful gentrification of communities is obliterated in a spectacular fire. This pseudo-catharsis is punctuated by urgent irresolution: performers caution spectators "we are all in the same boat" while marching en masse inside a paper ship.

Influenced by Boal's "Image Theatre" techniques and Martorell's visual artwork, Teatreros Ambulantes de Cayey mounted multiple productions of the non-verbal piece *Foto-estáticas* [Still Photos] (1985–1993, 2002). Márquez composed live, aural language as a percussionist/noisemaker to score performers' movements with found objects and instruments. Audience members help create the cast's paper costumes before the action begins. Once a photographer snaps pictures, the garments are destroyed as an ongoing wedding photo tableau exposes a lifelong portrait of a Puerto Rican family enduring typical triumphs with trials and tribulations like unemployment, military enlistments, and domestic violence. Chance interactions ensured the performance was never the same: a signature characteristic of Márquez's work.

Márquez also remounted several incarnations of Dragún's *Historias para ser contadas* [Stories to be Told] (1988–1990, 2001), collaborating with Dragún, Martorell, and UPR student group Teatro Rodante. A metatheatrical pastiche of dramatic modes, traditions, and techniques including commedia dell'arte, Sophoclean and Shakespearean tragedies, Brechtian *verfremdungseffekt*, and absurdism, audience and performers merge into an "impossible community that can actively reflect on the dehumanization of the stories' contents."[3] Márquez documented her process of creating *Historias* in an illustrated published volume she co-authored with Dragún.

Márquez's commitment to community-based Latin American popular theatre intensified when she became a board member and teacher for the International School of Latin American and Caribbean Theatre (EITALC). Through EITALC, she convened with other dramatic artists, critics, and theorists across the Americas, helping to enhance perspectives on producing theatre as colonized nations and territories. Márquez also forged ongoing collaborations with Ecuadorian theatre collective Grupo de Teatro Malayerba and Peruvian company

Grupo Cultural Yuyachkani, arranging interchanges with both groups through workshops, training, and tours for students and professionals both in Puerto Rico and abroad.

With Malayerba, Márquez created a distinctively Puerto Rican version of Arístides Vargas's *Jardín de pulpos* [Octopus's Garden] (1996). The performance pointed to Puerto Rico's past and present while associating the persecution of other oppressed populations across Latin America. Márquez incorporated traditional Afro-Puerto Rican myth, rhythm, and dance elements alongside Beatles' tunes in the Ecuadorian script. She also directed the actors to attend a ritual island carnival of masks as part of their creative process, challenging them to bring back artifacts to incorporate into the production.

With Yuyachkani's Miguel Rubio, Márquez conducted developmental workshops with her cast for her masterpiece *Godó* (1997), a politically charged production of Samuel Beckett's *Waiting for Godot*. The play's representation of a stagnant, directionless limbo characterizes the perpetual waiting and subjugation that marks Puerto Rico's colonial condition. Beckett's characters are reimagined to represent the island's vulnerable homeless population. The audience was seated onstage, flipping the house so that the 2000 vacant, dilapidated seats of the University of Puerto Rico's underfunded university theatre—a space *waiting* for a long-promised restoration—became the backdrop. The aisle served as the play's road, carpeting the way into a void, and Beckett's tree is reimagined as a scrap metal structure, suggesting the increasingly bleak, dehumanizing industrial landscape imposed by the US upon the island. *Godó* is the consummate example of how Márquez reinterprets a universal text to reveal the unchanging realities of the commonwealth; her clever strategy of role-switching in Act Two leads us to consider possibilities for dismantling hegemonic structures.

The Puerto Rican Circle of Theater Critics designated *Jardín de pulpos* the Best Production of 1996 and *Godó* the Best Production of 1997. Márquez was presented with the Lifetime Achievement in the Performing Arts Award at Teatro Avante's 2018 International Hispanic Theatre Festival in Miami, where she also presented her production of *Hij@os de Bernarda* [Children of Bernarda]. Márquez's musical, dance-movement adaptation of García Lorca's *The House of Bernarda Alba* exposed the cruel tradition of violence endured by Carribean and Spanish women at the hands of both household oppressors and government dictatorships. Also in 2018, Márquez was awarded the prestigious "El Gallo de La Habana" [The Rooster of Havana] by Cuba's Casa de las Américas to commemorate her significant contributions to the theatre of Latin America and the

Caribbean. Post-retirement, Márquez remains an active director of Puerto Rican popular theatre and defender of free and ongoing artistic expression on the island in response to public budget cuts depriving cultural institutions and devastations caused by Hurricane María and the COVID-19 pandemic.

Kimberly del Busto Ramírez

Notes

1 Rosa Luisa Márquez, "Between Theatre and Performance," trans. Miguel Villafañe, in *Holy Terrors: Latin American Women Perform*, eds. Roselyn Costantino and Diana Taylor (Durham, NC: Duke University Press, 2004), 374.
2 Rosa Luisa Márquez, *Brincos y saltos: el juego como disciplina teatral: un documental de Rosa Luisa Márquez* (Puerto Rico: JKL Films, 2010).
3 Osvaldo Dragún and Rosa Luisa Márquez, *Historias para ser contadas: del texto al montaje teatral* (San Juan: Ediciones Callejón, 2004), 20.

Major works

Hij@s de Bernarda [Children of Bernarda] (2017)
La razón blindada [The Armored Reason] (2006)
Romeos y Julietas [Romeos and Juliets] (2003)
Godó [Waiting for Godot] (1997)
Jardín de pulpos [Octopus's Garden] (1996)
Denuncaacabar [Neverending] (1995)
Si el grano no muere [If a Grain Does Not Die] (1992)
La mujer ideal [The Ideal Woman] (1987)
Foto-estáticas [Still Photos] (1985)
La leyenda del cemí [The Legend of Cemí] (1982)

Further reading

Márquez, Rosa Luisa. *Memorias de una teatrera del Caribe: Conversaciones con Miguel Rubio Zapata*. Puerto Rico: Ediciones Cuicaloca, 2020.
Martínez Tabares, Vivian. "Rosa Luisa Márquez: De Jardín de Pulpos a Godot." *Conjunto* 106 (1997): 38–46.
Perales, Rosalina. "La dirección escénica femenina en Puerto Rico." *Diógenes: Anuario Crítico del Teatro Latinoamericano* (1993–1994): 383–392.
Ríos Ávila, Rubén. "Puerto Rico 1990: Entrevista a Rosa Luisa Márquez." *Diógenes: Anuario Crítico del Teatro Latinoamericano* (1990): 245–250.

LIN-MANUEL MIRANDA (NEW YORK CITY, 1980–)

Award-winning composer, lyricist, playwright, performer, and producer, Lin-Manuel Miranda is one of the most recognized theatre celebrities in the twenty-first century. Known for his Broadway musicals *In the Heights* (2008) and *Hamilton* (2015), Miranda has opened a myriad of possibilities for actors of color to be on stage, expanded casting practices, and extended the work of theatre off the stage, into cinema, the streets, and the virtual world with his viral social media presence. Most notably, his work has incited critical conversations about the responsibility, significance, and fraught complexities of narrating Latinx and non-Latinx experiences through and with bodies of color.

Raised near New York City's Washington Heights and influenced by the activism and tenacity of his Puerto Rican parents, Miranda brings a Nuyorican, urban flair to his theatre works. When he first saw Paul Simon's *The Capeman* (1998), the story of redemption about the Puerto Rican gang member Salvador Agron, during his senior year in high school, he was motivated to write his own Latinx musical story. He pursued this dream at Wesleyan College where he studied theatre. It was there that he wrote and staged an eighty-minute version of *In the Heights* as part of a sophomore project. He teamed up with director and Wesleyan alumnus Thomas Kail after graduating in 2002 and then two years later with Quiara Alegría Hudes as book-writer. After several readings and an off-Broadway production, *In the Heights* premiered on Broadway in 2008. This journey of almost ten years resulted in a Grammy for Best Musical Show Album and four Tony Awards, including Best Musical, Best Choreography, Best Orchestration, and Best Score. The musical film of *In the Heights* directed by Jon M. Chu with screenplay by Hudes premiered June 11, 2021 on the silver screen.

During the run of *In the Heights*, Arthur Laurents and Stephen Sondheim recruited Miranda to translate some of the dialogue and lyrics into Spanish for the Broadway revival of *West Side Story* (2009) at the Palace Theatre. After the success of *In the Heights*, Miranda performed *The Hamilton Mixtape* as part of the White House Evening of Poetry, Music, and Spoken Word on May 12, 2009, the seeds of what would become the record-setting musical *Hamilton*. Before *Hamilton* came to full fruition, Miranda co-wrote music and lyrics for *Bring It On: the Musical*, which had an Atlanta, GA production, national tour, and limited 2012 Broadway run. He also performed in the *Encores!* series productions of *Merrily We Roll Along* (2012) and *tick, tick … BOOM!* (2014).

Since its off-Broadway debut at the New York Public Theater in early 2015, the same year he received the prestigious MacArthur "Genius" Fellowship, *Hamilton* became a national phenomenon, achieving staggering levels of critical and commercial success. In a matter of months, *Hamilton* went from off-Broadway to Broadway, becoming one of the highest-grossing musicals in the industry and garnering a wide range of accolades from winning eleven Tony Awards to receiving the 2016 Pulitzer Prize in Drama to gaining international success with the London production and winning seven Olivier Awards. Along with receiving theatrical accolades, the musical has proliferated a plethora of resources: the cast recording; *The Revolution*, a libretto with annotations and essays; *The Hamilton Mixtape*, a spin-off album performed by a variety of R&B, hip hop and pop artists; and *Great Performances: Hamilton's America*, a PBS documentary chronicling the creation and reception of the musical to name a few.

Before the hit musical *Hamilton*, there was *In the Heights*, his first Broadway musical, about residents who live in Washington Heights, a New York City neighborhood historically populated by Dominicans, other Latinxs and immigrant communities. Written during a period of increased anti-immigrant rhetoric and zero-tolerance immigration neoliberal policies, *In the Heights* sheds light on the lives of mostly first- and second-generation immigrants trying to overcome the barriers that arise from gentrification. Usnavi, a Dominican immigrant and bodega owner (originally played by Miranda), plays the protagonist role of narrator. He dreams of returning to his native home of the Dominican Republic, which he left as an infant, but the bodega he inherited from his parents has anchored him in New York City. Neighbors who chase their dreams come in and out of Usnavi's bodega. Vanessa, Usnavi's love interest, is desperately saving enough money to move downtown in the West Village. Neighbors celebrate and set high expectations of Nina's success of getting into Stanford and being the first in the family to go to college. Her proud Puerto Rican parents, Kevin and Camila Rosario, have no other choice but to sell their taxi cab company to pay their daughter's college tuition.

Amidst the financial pressures, noisy traffic, and oppressive New York City heat, there is a moment of relief when Abuela Claudia, the matriarch of the block who immigrated from Cuba, wins the lottery, giving neighbors a glimpse of hope as they imagine life outside of the barrio. Before she passes, Abuela Claudia gives most of her winnings to Usnavi, who was already planning on selling the bodega and leaving the barrio. Here economic mobility relies solely on the unrealistic winning of a lottery ticket as a way out of poverty, but that amount of money can't save the neighborhood from gentrification. Usnavi decides to stay in the neighborhood when his fifteen-year-old cousin Sonny contracts Graffiti Peter, a local artist, to paint a memorial mural of Abuela Claudia on the bodega gates. Usnavi realizes that despite all the challenges, Washington Heights is his home.

Miranda affirms a Latinx sense of belonging when along with Cuban-American musical director Alex Lacamoire they create a New York City Afro-Latinx soundscape. For *In the Heights*, they seamlessly fuse traditional musical theatre ballads with a range of Afro-diasporic musical genres, including hip hop, popular Latin rhythms such as salsa, merengue, and samba, as well as Motown-inspired soul and R&B. This musical "resonates as simultaneously Latin and Broadway, not merely Latin on Broadway."[1] Miranda further elevates the Afro- and Latinx-diasporic musical texture of *In the Heights* by deftly blending English and Spanish in the lyrics and dialogue. Characters sometimes speak English, Spanish, or Spanglish. Other times they code-switch, use word substitution or translate from Spanish to English or vice versa. Language serves to signal cultural differences as well as bridge cultures across differences.

Similar to *In the Heights*, Miranda marries the conventions of Broadway musicals and the formal structures of hip-hop, rap, and R&B to the story of a less popular Founding Father, Alexander Hamilton, the man on the ten-dollar bill. With a virtuous cast of color embodying Alexander Hamilton and other white founding fathers, Miranda positions people of color as history and law-makers instead of being on the other side of the judicial paradigm—behind bars as prisoners, drug dealers, gangsters, or enslaved people. While the show refers to slavery, scholars have argued that the voices of enslaved people remain audibly silent. Performers of color detach from the narrative of slavery thus denying the existence of enslaved Black bodies. By telling the story of the founding fathers, actors of color bring the white body to life, absolving them from the racial terror they inflicted on Black people. This historical obscuration in *Hamilton* reveals how diversity feeds the neoliberal machine of decorative representation, which does not equate to creating an inclusive narrative where audience hear the experiences of Black people.

In addition to bringing an Afro-diasporic music tradition to the Broadway stage, Miranda forges new casting opportunities for Latinx performers and other performers of color. *Hamilton* is a game-changer for pushing back Broadway's exclusionary casting practices. Miranda's character description places race and ethnicity at the center of the storytelling. In the casting call, Miranda describes Alexander Hamilton as a "non-white, 30s, tenor-baritone. An earnest, ambitious hothead, a man possessed. Speaks his mind, no matter the cost. Must be able to rap VERY well. Eminem meets Sweeney Todd."[2] Miranda's nontraditional casting approach thus pushes against a homogenous notion of America's origins inciting difficult conversations about race and representation in America.

In addition to captivating many audiences with Miranda's racially and ethnically diverse casting approach, he transformed the way audiences engage and consume Broadway musicals inside and outside of the theatre. As Trevor Boffone explains, instead of waiting for people to come to the theatre, Miranda took the theatre into the streets using the tactics of Latinx theatre and hip hop. Similar to the tactics of El Teatro Campesino, poets from the Nuyorican movement, and hip-hop practitioners, Miranda captivated his audience by pioneering "a new era of accessibility in commercial theatre," which Boffone terms as an "aesthetic of accessibility."[3] Miranda created a daily lottery for *Hamilton* available for only $10. To promote the lottery, members of *Hamilton* would put on five-minute performances every day outside the Richard Rogers Theater, attracting hundreds of people to gather. These outside-of-the-theatre performances quickly went viral, creating a social media presence that helped to feed the *Hamilton* publicity campaign. The lottery became so popular that a digital lottery was created to manage the large crowds. On the first day, the digital lottery crashed with 50,000 entries, but Miranda continued the show by dropping a digital *Ham4Ham* performance on YouTube. Offering options for spectators to see *Hamilton* besides paying the astronomically priced tickets changed the theatrical experience. Whether using theatre to tell the story from a Latinx perspective or the point of view of the founding fathers through bodies of color, Miranda reveals the boundless possibilities and challenges of working in and outside the boundaries of theatre and Broadway.

Patricia Herrera

Notes

1 Brian Herrera, "Miranda's Manifesto," *Theater* 47.2 (May 2017): 27.
2 "Breakdown for *Hamilton*, EPA Day 1 of 3," *Backstage*, www.backstage.com/casting/hamilton-epa-308036/ (accessed April 18, 2021).
3 Trevor Boffone, "Ham4Ham: Taking *Hamilton* to the Streets," *HowlRound Theatre Commons*, March 18, 2016, https://howlround.com/ham4ham (accessed May 1, 2021).

Major works

Free Love Supreme (2019), Founding Member and Producer
Hamilton (2015), Creator, Composer, Lyricist, and Original Broadway Star
21 Chump Street (2014), Creator, Composer, and Lyricist
Bring it On The Musical (2012), Co-Composer and Co-Lyricist
In the Heights (2008), Creator, Composer, and Lyricist

Published works

In the Heights: Finding Home, Co-author with Quiara Alegría Hudes and Jeremy McCarter. New York: Random House, 2021.
Gmorning, Gnight!: Little Pep Talks for Me & You. New York: Random House, 2018.
Hamilton: The Revolution. Co-author with Jeremy McCarter. New York: Grand Central Publishing, 2016.

Further reading

Cázares, Gabriela. "Resisting Gentrification in Quiara Alegría Hudes and Lin-Manuel Miranda's 'In the Heights' and Ernesto Quiñonez's 'Bodega Dreams'." *American Studies* 56.2 (2017): 89–107.
Galella, Donatella. "Being in 'The Room Where It Happens': *Hamilton*, Obama, and Nationalist Neoliberal Multicultural Inclusion." *Theatre Survey* 59.3 (2018): 363–385.
Herrera, Patricia. "Reckoning. With America's Racial Past, Present, and Future in *Hamilton*." In *Historians on Hamilton: How a Blockbuster Musical is Restaging America's Past*, edited by Renee C. Romano and Claire Bond Potter, 260–276. New Jersey and London: Rutgers University Press, 2018.
Monteiro, Lyra D. "Race-Conscious Casting and the Erasure of the Black Past in Lin-Manuel Miranda's Hamilton." *Public Historian* 38 (2016): 89–98.
Nathans, Heather. "Crooked Histories: Re-Presenting Race, Slavery, and Alexander Hamilton Onstage." *Journal of the Early Republic* 37.2 (2017): 271–278.
Ybarra, Patricia A. *Latinx Theater in the Times of Neoliberalism*. Evanston: Northwestern University Press, 2018.

CHERRÍE MORAGA (WHITTIER, CALIFORNIA, 1952–)

Chicanx, poet, essayist, playwright, director, theorist, and cultural activist Cherríe Moraga's contribution to theatre is situated as an extension of the Chicano and Feminist Movements. In 1981, along with Barbara Smith and Audre Lorde, Moraga co-founded Kitchen Table/Women of Color Press, a collective venue for women of color writers to publish their work. That year, Moraga and Gloria Anzaldúa published *This Bridge Called my Back: The Writings of Radical*

Women of Color, one of the most influential anthologies. As a founder of Chicanx literary and theoretical tradition, Moraga paved the way for the creation of Chicanx/Latinx Studies, becoming a major influence for many playwrights, artists, and directors. Her accolades as a playwright include Fund for the New American Play Awards, NEA's Playwrights' Fellowship, Drama-logue, Critics Circle, and Pen West Awards. She also received the prestigious 2007 United States Artist Rockefeller Fellowship for Literature (Drama), the American Studies Association Lifetime Achievement Award, and the Lambda Foundation's "Pioneer" award in 2013, among other honors. For over twenty years, Moraga served as Artist in Residence in the Department of Theater and Performance Studies at Stanford University, where she mentored a generation of writers and playwrights like Karen Zacarías, Irma Mayorga, Adelina Anthony, and Netflix's *Gentefied* co-creator Linda Yvette Chávez. In 2017 she began her tenure as Professor in the Department of English at the University of California, Santa Barbara, where she co-founded, along with artist Celia Herrera Rodríguez, Las Maestras Center for Chicana and Indigenous Thought and Art Practice. Most recently, Moraga published a memoir, *Native Country of the Heart* (2019), where she explores her mother Elvira's life along with her own coming out and the difficulty of caring for a parent with Alzheimer's.

As the daughter of a Chicana and an Anglo father, Moraga places women, Chicanx, and queer communities front and center. She grew up surrounded and influenced by her mother's family, immersed in their cultural traditions, bilingualism, and Catholic customs in both California and Mexico. Thus, Moraga's *oeuvre* gives voice to bilingual communities, second-generation Chicanx, making those silenced or marginalized visible. This focus on (in)visibility, already manifested in her groundbreaking text with Anzaldúa, centers on the importance of including race-related subjectivities through their concept of *theory in the flesh*, meaning to theorize from the "physical realities we inhabit, our firsthand knowledge, and our bodies as discursive sites of knowledge construction that is created from a need to challenge and inscribe dominant discourses."[1] Moraga's theatre, then, puts this theory into practice through a series of methods and themes that include a combination of prose and poetry: visualizing the Chicanx lesbian experience through sexuality and desire as well as problematizing the mestiza consciousness.

Her primary mentor was Cuban American playwright and director María Irene Fornés, with whom she trained during a six-month residency at International Arts Relations (INTAR). Under Fornés's mentorship, Moraga created strong and defiant female-centric plays, with characters defined not only by gender, class, sexuality, and race, but also by their inner struggle. During this time, Moraga wrote *Giving up the Ghost* (1987), one of the first plays to stage Chicanx lesbian characters. The play follows the character of Marisa from her younger self as Corky, to her later relationship with her lover, Amalia. Though monologues, poetry, prose, and flashbacks, the characters explore how their Chicanx community and family shapes their sexual identities, and in turn, offer a critique of patriarchal oppression. This same theme is also salient in *Shadow of a Man* (1990), directed by María Irene Fornés. The characters' lives are marked by conflict due to a family secret. Confrontation ensues between a mother abiding by patriarchal codes of morality and her daughters, who defy male privilege, domestic and sexual abuse, together with religious ideologies. Moraga employs the traditional mode of Chicano family drama predominant in the 1970s and 1980s, often used by Chicanx playwrights of the time, to explore gender differences based on dated notions of womanhood and sexuality.

Following the successes of *Shadow of a Man* and *Giving up the Ghost*, Moraga turned to social, environmental, and political struggles of Chicanx farmworkers in *Heroes and Saints* (1990). Moraga addresses their plight during the 1960s, heavily influenced by Teatro Campesino's *actos* and Luis Valdez's *The Shrunken Head of Pancho Villa*. Nevertheless, this play is grounded in feminist theatre-practices as "an opportunity to re-(en)vision Mexican and Xicano history from a Xicana Indígena and feminist perspective."[2] In *Heroes and Saints*, the central Chicana character, Cerezita, is bodiless because of pesticides found in her community. Despite her disability, Cerezita rallies her people to fight against social, cultural, and economic disparities that oppress them, evoking other Chicanx, indigenous, and Latin American land rebellions. Through Cerezita, Moraga emphasizes a female, Chicanx, and indigenous perspective that was lacking in the Chicanx theatre and the Chicano movement in general. The play influenced the evolution of Chicanx theatre for its critique of Teatro Campesino's male-centered vision. Moraga represents real-life events in the fields by giving agency to Chicanx women, condemning institutional racism and sexism in Chicanx households and farmworker communities.

Of particular importance in her plays is how she foregrounds language and character development, allowing readers and spectators alike to imagine their position in the world. These characteristics are made evident in *A Hungry Woman: A Mexican Medea* (1995), where in a dystopian future, imagined nations, like the Chicano homeland, Aztlán, secede from the United States establishing political, cultural, and economic sovereignty. However, the queer characters, Medea, her grandmother, Mamá Sal, and Medea's lover, Luna, are exiled from Aztlán. Medea's impending divorce from Jasón, a custody battle for their son, Chac-Mool, and her refusal to "give-up" her queer identity, force her into self-destruction. Medea's story unfolds through flashbacks guided by her son's ghost, who makes her relive how she poisoned him, eventually leading her to commit suicide. Even though the play takes place in a dystopian future, it is grounded on a contemporary context of racism, sexism, and homophobia.

A Hungry Woman fuses the well-known myth of La Llorona ("Wailing woman") and Medea, two scorned women who murdered their own children, to center on the obstacles that society imposes on a woman loving another woman. Destabilizing Medea and La Llorona through queer Chicanx and indigenous lenses recasts meaning making in the Chicanx imaginary, culturally anchored to history, culture, and language. She reframes and queers traditional depictions of womanhood/motherhood and stages a more representative cross-section of the Chicanx collective body. All of Moraga's characters make their words "flesh," inhabiting multiple worlds, other ways of knowing and being, including multilingual realities.

Articulating multilingual and multiethnic realities are crucial to Moraga, "Everything I write, even essays, really has an oral quality."[3] Moraga's characters navigate a pastiche of languages in *Heart of the Earth: A Popol Vuh Story* (1994), *Circle in the Dirt* (1995), and *Watsonville: Some Place Not Here* (1996). In *Heart*, Moraga dramatizes the Quiché Maya creation story through two Chicano soccer-playing teens that become Mayan gods. Moraga's characters inhabit Quiché Maya, Spanish, English, Spanglish, and Southwestern Spanish. She reaffirms her vision of staging and representing silenced, invisible Chicanx and indigenous linguistic realities of multilingual self-expression. *Circle* and *Watsonville* explore solidarity across identities, focusing on two California communities, the former in East Palo Alto, CA, and the latter, echoing *Heroes and Saints*, a cannery strike in Watsonville, CA. Both plays were developed through interviews and oral histories conducted with local residents, depicting racially, ethnically, and linguistically diverse characters. These plays stage solidarity across diverse identities, recognizing a complex relationship between marginalized characters and their fight against the dominant cultures.

Moraga's plays in the last decade, such as *Digging up the Dirt* (2010), *New Fire: To Put Things Right Again* (2012), and *The Mathematics of Love* (2017), expand on her major themes: queer Chicanx identities, indigenous women's issues, and the dominance of patriarchal oppression. In *Digging up the Dirt* (co-directed with Adelina Anthony), Moraga weaves together two stories: the murder of Sirena by Josefa, her female personal assistant and fan; and the murder of mestiza lesbian artist Amada by her son, Heyoka. Like *A Hungry Woman*, this play stages queer love and dynamics of power, and redefines family, love, and community. *New Fire* (directed by Moraga) prioritizes Chicanx and indigenous women's experience, mind and body, "to wonder of the place of the sacred in our lives and its correspondence to human acts of violence."[4] In 2017, Moraga (with Ricardo A. Bracho) wrote and premiered *The Mathematics of Love* at Brava Theater, San Francisco. In the play, an eighty-five-year-old Mexican American woman with Alzheimer's named "Peaches" meets MalinXe (La Malinche), complicating a temporal chronology that combines the past and the present, exploring how Chicanx, indigenous, and queer women live in the world by providing avenues for audiences to liberate their selves from patriarchal oppression.

Cherríe Moraga is a trailblazer for Chicanx/Latinx artists through her work as a playwright and director. She writes about and for those rarely staged in mainstream theatre— Chicanx, indigenous, and queer families—challenging spectators to look beyond single Chicanx stories. Moraga practices the Chicanx/Latinx theatre imperative: to write stories challenging what is taboo and silenced. Her work illuminates Chicanx communities, experiences, and histories, and inspires others to interrogate past and present to reimagine a better future.

Melissa Huerta

Notes

1 Cherríe L. Moraga and Gloria E. Anzaldúa, eds., *This Bridge Called my Back*, 3rd edition. Berkeley: Third Woman Press, 2002, 23.
2 Cherríe L. Moraga, *A Xicana Codex of Changing Consciousness*. Durham, NC: Duke University Press, 2011, 36.
3 Adelina Anthony and Cherríe Moraga, "Cherríe Moraga." *Bomb* 98 (2007): 61.
4 Cherríe Moraga, "New Fire-To Put Things Right Again." Cherríe Moraga. Accessed April 20, 2021. https://cherriemoraga.com/index.php/theater-2/133-new-fire

Major works

The Mathematics of Love (2017)
New Fire: To Put Things Right Again (2012)

Digging up the Dirt: Prison Correspondence Poet to Pervert (2010)
Watsonville: Some Place Not Here (1996)
Hungry Woman: A Mexican Medea (1995)
Circle in the Dirt (1995)
Heroes and Saints (1990)
Shadow of a Man (1990)
Giving up the Ghost (1987)

Published works

The Hungry Woman: A Mexican Medea & The Heart of the Earth: A Popol Vuh Story. Albuquerque: West End Press, 2001.
Watsonville: Some Place Not Here. Albuquerque: West End Press, 1996.
Circle in the Dirt: El Pueblo de East Palo Alto. Albuquerque: West End Press, 1995.
Heroes and Saints & Other Plays. Albuquerque: West End Press, 1994.

Further reading

Duran, Maria J. "Bodies that should Matter: Chicana/o Farmworkers, Slow Violence, and the Politics of Visibility in Cherríe Moraga's Heroes and Saints." *Aztlán* 42, no. 1 (2017): 45–71.
Garland, Leah. *Contemporary Latina/o Performing Arts of Moraga, Tropicana, Fusco, and Bustamante.* New York: Peter Lang, 2009.
Huerta, Jorge. *Chicano Drama: Performance, Society, and Myth.* Cambridge: Cambridge University Press, 2000.
Jacobs, Elizabeth. "*Shadow of a Man*: A Chicana/Latina Drama as Embodied Feminist Practice." *New Theatre Quarterly* 31, no. 1 (2015): 49–58.
López, Tiffany Ana. "The Staging of Violence Against and Amongst Chicanas in *Digging Up the Dirt* by Cherríe Moraga (2010): Performance Review." *Chicana/Latina Studies* 10, no. 1 (Fall 2010): 108–113.
Martin-Baron, Michelle R. "Mythical Enjambment in the Hungry Woman: Nation, Desire, and Cherríe Moraga's Utopic Turn." *Women & Performance: A Journal of Feminist Theory*, 28, no. 3 (2018): 239–258.
Yarbro-Bejarano, Yvonne. *The Wounded Heart: Writing on Cherríe Moraga.* Austin: University of Texas Press, 2001.

GUSTAVO OTT (CARACAS, VENEZUELA/ WASHINGTON, DC, 1963–)

With nearly fifty published plays, and works that are translated into fourteen languages, Gustavo Ott certainly ranks among the most prolific figures of contemporary Venezuelan theatre. Ott is a playwright, director, and novelist, mentored within a literary tradition of playwrights Rodolfo Santana and Ignacio Cabrujas, a theatre concerned with the morality of the middle class. Yet his plays delve into even more sinister dimensions, where characters become deeply ensnared by self-obsession, crime, the machinations of power, and other pathologies of the human experience. Rich with dialogue, and always driven by moral tensions, Ott's plays take audiences to the brink of the dystopic, yet never relinquish the possibility of greater human understanding in times of crisis.

Ott is perhaps most well-known for a genre of works he called "the Latin American macabre," which forged his reputation as a serious playwright following a brief stint as a career journalist. No doubt, Ott's training in journalism heightened his sensibility for real stories. Like a detective, he carries a discipline of historical research and interview technique into his creative process, allowing him to develop more detailed layers of complexity in his works. Ott also follows his own curiosities through stories, at times with a touch of humor, into a maze of bizarre, almost surreal or "noir," real-life situations to probe the nature of political and ultimately moral decline. In *Tres esqueletos y medio* [Three and a Half Skeletons] (1998), a play about three women archeologists who dig up unknown skeletal remains, Ott unearths the untold story of the (pre-Chávez) US-supported neoliberal "model nation," in which state-sanctioned massacres and colonial histories of violence were silenced and disappeared by the aspirations of progress.

Ott developed his love of writing as a young person growing up between the neighborhood of El Paraíso in Caracas and the small rural town of El Tocuyo in the foothills of the Andes. In these perennial journeys, he adopted a different name for himself in each location, which later became a device for his storytelling. In a sense, the very landscape became characters. He studied in London in the mid-1980s and committed further to playwriting at the International Writing Program in Iowa in 1993. However, in all his world travels, he has maintained a foothold in Caracas, and for a time dedicated himself to directing and producing, engaging more with audiences in practice in a theatre he founded called Teatro San Martín from the late 1990s to the mid-2010s on the west side of Caracas. Now, from his home in the wooded suburbs of Virginia, Ott continues to draw together people and places, dedicating himself further to his writing. He moves nimbly between languages, as he navigates from commissions across the United States and Europe. Indeed, his work is now as widely recognized and produced outside of Venezuela as within.

Perhaps because of his expanded audiences, Ott tends toward a universalism of human experience, one less grounded in colloquialisms and more emblematic of a broadly construed "modern Latin American" subject. His settings are often in ambiguous locations: a customs office somewhere in Latin America, such as in his hit play, *Passport* (1988), with less by way of stage notes to locate that space in a particular place and time. Indeed, as commissions, speaking engagements, and interlocutors expanded to international audiences, the tendency in Ott's plays has been to produce a certain "limbo of location" in more controlled, often domestic, or office settings, where the action is compelled by heightened tension among the relationships of his characters.

In the spring of 2014, amidst a wave of US-supported violence seeking to overturn the socialist state, Gustavo Ott's theatre, El Teatro San Martín, was nearly empty, and yet the show went on. Ott's award-winning play *Lírica* [Poetry] (2010), the story of two schoolchildren seeking a connection across their parents' political differences through their passion for the creative arts, was timely given that this night was besieged by intolerance. The play, and his ongoing dedication to El Teatro San Martín, speaks to Ott's concerns over the last twenty years to maintain a space open for dialogue as venues, audiences, and the conditions of producing theatre in the country have dramatically changed.

While much of his work is inspired from real-life events, Ott also has curiously veered away from the polemics of representation within Venezuela, and about Venezuela within the United States. In this way, one could say that Ott occupies the somewhat rarified position of a centrist concerning Venezuela. Yet, it is also clear that after forty years of his career, and notably in his more recent novels, Ott is now drawn to a new emergence of the poetic, finding deeper and even more beautiful words about existential matters, where, for him, the ideas of love, country, and politics are paled in a search for new meaning and new hope.

While Gustavo Ott's legacy is cast much wider than Venezuelan national borders, other highly respected and established figures such as Román Chalbaud (1931–), various popular arts collectives throughout the country, and more emerging director/playwrights like Jericó Montilla have brought tremendous vitality to Venezuelan theatre within the country today. Nevertheless, Ott continues to seek dialogue within the constraints of literary production in the north, ultimately asking mainstream audiences to join him in a more philosophical reflection on the nature of human conflict.

Angela Marino

Major works

Todas las películas hablan de mí [All the Movies are about Me] (2020)

Brutality (2016)
Lírica (2010)
Momia en el closet [Mummy in the Closet] (2008)
Tu ternura molotov [Your Molotov Kisses] (2002)
Dos amores y un bicho [Two Loves and a Creature] (2001)
80 dientes, 4 metros y 200 kilos [80 Teeth, 4 Feet and 500 Pounds] (1996)
Divorciadas, evangélicas y vegetarianas [Divorcées, Evangelicals, and Vegetarians] (1989)
Passport (1988)
Pavlov: 2 segundos antes del crimen [Pavlov: 2 Seconds Before the Crime] (1986)

Published works

"Passport" in *Spectacular Bodies, Dangerous Borders: Three New Latin American Plays*. Ed. Ana Elena Puga. Translated by Ana Elena Puga and Heather K. McKay. Lawrence: LATR Books, 2011.
Divorciadas, evangélicas y vegetarianas; Quiéreme mucho; El siglo de las luces. Madrid: La Avispa, 2000.
Teatro 5. Caracas: Textoteatro Ediciones, 1989.
80 dientes, 4 metros y 200 kilos. Madrid: Agencia Española de Cooperación Internacional, Ediciones de Cultura Hispánica, 1999.

Further reading

Falska, Maria. "Juegos temporales en el teatro de Gustavo Ott." *Itinerarios* 29 (2019): 335–352.
Neville, Paula and Nidia Burgos. "Una lectura de 80 dientes, 4 metros y 200 kilos de Gustavo Ott." In *Modernización/ Identidad: Tensiones de una disyuntiva constante en la historia y literatura iberoamericana*, edited by Nidia Burgos, 135–151. Buenos Aires: Editorial de la Universidad Nacional del Sur, 2006.
Ott, Gustavo. "A Personal Map/Living Hieroglyphs." In *Theatre and Cartographies of Power: Repositioning the Latina/o Americas*, edited by Jimmy Noriega and Analola Santana, 62–70. Carbondale: University of Southern Illinois Press, 2018.
Rodríguez Velázquez, Ocdilys. "Claves de la dramaturgia de Gustavo Ott." In *Análisis de la Dramaturgia Venezolana Actual*, edited by José García Barrientos, 139–154. Madrid: Ediciones Antígona, 2017.

DOLORES PRIDA (CAIBARIÉN, CUBA/ NEW YORK CITY, 1943–2013)

Cuban American playwright, poet, translator, journalist, and magazine editor Dolores Prida imparted feminist and anti-racist wisdom to her theatre audiences as well as to the readers of "Dolores Dice" ("Dolores Says"), the advice column she wrote for *Latina* magazine. Born in

Caibarién, Cuba, Dolores Obdulia Prida's theatrical works also draw from her experience as one of the many refugees and exiles who came to the United States shortly after the Cuban Revolution of 1959. Prida recounts this experience in her one-act play, *Coser y Cantar* [Sewing and Singing] (1981), in which the Spanish-speaking character of a bilingual duo compares the dirty glass partition at the Havana airport to the wall of a fish tank that separated families who wanted to touch each other one last time before departure. Traveling with her mother and two younger sisters, Prida reunited with her father in Miami in 1961 and then moved to New York City, where she would live for the rest of her life.

Prida's plays explore the trauma of geographical and cultural dislocation, the struggle to preserve a linguistic and cultural heritage in a hostile and discriminatory society, and the clash between traditional Cuban gender norms and progressive feminist politics in the US. Prida was able to address these conflicts and the potential for transformative change with humor, bilingual poetics, and a deep reverence for the matrilineal and communal bonds that can create a home in a rapidly changing urban landscape. A resident of New York City until she passed away from cardiac arrest in 2013, Prida's plays and prose journalism also imagine individual and collective ways to combat the stresses and anxieties of city life, particularly for immigrant women of color with aspirations of upward mobility and economic autonomy. Whether one attends a professional, community, or university production of one of her plays, or reads the online archive of her advice column, Prida offers her audiences and readers survival strategies and ways to overcome disenfranchisement and disaffection, always while celebrating her bicultural sensibilities and efforts to promote Latina empowerment.

Prida's small hometown in northwest Cuba lacked the cultural and theatrical venues that she found more readily when her family had migrated to Queens, New York. There she began to participate in the local Latinx theatre scene with DUO Theater, International Arts Relations (INTAR) Theater, the Repertorio Español, and the Puerto Rican Traveling Theater, founded by Miriam Colón. The DUO Theater produced Prida's first play, *Beautiful Señoritas* (1977), which Alberto Sandoval-Sánchez describes as a musical that "focuses on the process of being born a woman, of being trapped in gender roles in a patriarchal world, of being Latina in the U.S."[1] These themes reappear in all of Prida's subsequent contributions to the Latinx theatrical repertoires that emerged from New York since the 1970s. Prida's combination of humor, music, and bilingual poetics places her works among those from Nuyorican playwrights like Miguel Piñero and Pedro Pietri, or other Cuban American artists such as Eduardo Machado and María Irene Fornés, a foundational figure in Latinx theatre. What sets some of Prida's works apart from the Nuyorican theatre scene is her use of Spanish as the dominant language in the script. Plays like *Pantallas* [Earrings] (1986), *Botánica: Una comedia de milagros* [The Herb Shop: A Comedy About Miracles] (1990), and *Casa Propia* [A Home of Her Own] (1999), are almost entirely in Spanish mixed with some English or Spanglish dialogue. In fact, the stage directions for *Coser y Cantar* state specifically, "This play must NEVER be performed in just one language."[2] These works challenge the English-dominant theatre scene and open the stage to Spanish-speaking and bilingual audiences, whose linguistic sensibilities are often overlooked by mainstream and even off-off-Broadway theatre productions. These audiences can see and hear their own stories in a language that reflects their experiences and cultural imaginaries. One of Prida's most experimental plays, the aforementioned *Coser y Cantar*, pits two actors—Ella and She—in a bilingual struggle over whose culture, language, dreams, and desires will articulate an authentic self. The irony of the play is that both characters embody the bicultural imaginary of the same Latina woman, and the conflict reflects the negotiated disharmony with which many Latinxs have forged their identities. Theatre and performance studies scholar José Esteban Muñoz would later call this push-and-pull a "disidentification," in which "different identity components occupy adjacent spaces and are not comfortably situated in any one discourse of minority subjectivity."[3] Prida continued to produce works in Spanish as a translator of fiction by Dominican American writer, Julia Alvarez, including the novels *¡Yo!* (1998) and *In the Name of Salomé* (2002), and the children's book, *The Secret Footprints* (2002).

One of the other recurrent themes in Prida's work depicts Latina women overcoming personal and economic hardships through communal support and a bicultural imaginary. In her play *Botánica* (1990), Prida portrays the struggle of a young, mixed-race college graduate, Milagros, who comes to terms with the Afro-Caribbean heritage of her matriarchal family based in New York's El Barrio. Milagros, or Millie as she prefers to be called, attempts to distance herself from the *Santería* traditions that her grandmother, Doña Geno, has turned into the family business of the titular herb shop, or *botánica*. Millie lies to her family to prevent them from attending her graduation ceremony at a prestigious university in New Hampshire, presumably

Dartmouth College where Dolores Prida later taught as a visiting professor in 1995. At college, Millie was the victim of racial violence and vowed to erase any signs of her Latina heritage in order to succeed in a career in finance. With the help of her grandmother, mother, and longtime friend, Rubén, as well as the divine intervention of Santa Bárbara, Millie overcomes the shame she feels toward her racial and cultural heritage and reclaims her place among the family of women who always supported her. A similar feminist dynamic appears in Prida's play, *Casa Propia: Ópera sin música en dos actos* [A Home of Her Own: An Opera Without Music in Two Acts] (1999), in which Cuban American Olga and her daughter, Marilis, establish their own sense of belonging through home ownership, despite the discrimination they face from their Italian neighbor and the attempts by Olga's ex-husband to reassert himself as the dominant macho.

These and other plays echo the advice Prida offered the readers of her column, "Dolores Dice," which she wrote for *Latina* magazine starting in 1998. For example, when one reader asked if she should allow her ex-husband to bring his new wife to their daughter's *quinceañera* party, Dolores Dice writes:

> The husband/father who abandons his family to run away with his wife's best friend and contributes nothing to the quinceañera forfeits his right to the first dance with his daughter ... So I say, enjoy your fiesta and you and your daughter do the first dance together—it's your party and you do as you want to.[4]

Whether the drama was taking place on the stage or on the pages of a magazine, Prida's plays and advice column encouraged Latinas to hold on to their traditions but not become immobilized by them. She made clear that Latinas living and striving in the US are not selling out their identities or communities when they reimagine and transform their families, communities, and their multicultural society.

Israel Reyes

Notes

1 Alberto Sandoval Sánchez, *José Can You See?: Latinos On and Off Broadway* (Madison: University of Wisconsin Press, 1999), 153.
2 Dolores Prida, *Coser y Cantar*, in *Beautiful Señoritas and Other Plays*, edited by Judith Weiss (Houston: Arte Público Press, 1991), 49.
3 José Esteban Muñoz, *Disidentifications: Queers of Color and the Performance of Politics* (Minneapolis: University of Minnesota Press, 1999), 32.

4 Dolores Prida, "Dolores Dice ... Quinceañera from Hell," *Latina*, April 23, 2010, www.latina.com/blogs/dolores-dice/dolores-dicequincea-era-hell (accessed January 13, 2021).

Major works

Una Mujer Named María (2000)
Four Guys Named José (2000)
Casa Propia (1999)
Botánica: Una comedia de Milagros (1991)
Coser y Cantar (1981)
Beautiful Señoritas (1977)

Published works

Casa Propia. In *Teatro cubano actual: Dramaturgía escrita en Estados Unidos*. Edited by Alberto Sarraín and Lillian Manzor. Havana: Ediciones Alarcos, 2005.
Beautiful Señoritas and Other Plays. Edited by Judith Weiss. Houston: Arte Público Press, 1991.
Women of the House: Cosmic Feminist Poetry. New York: Ediciones Nuevasangre, 1971.

Further reading

Feliciano, Wilma. "Language and Identity in Three Plays by Dolores Prida." *Latin American Theatre Review* 28.1 (1994): 125–138.
González, Carolina. "Dolores Prida." In *The Oxford Encyclopedia of Latinas and Latinos in the United States, Volume 3*, edited by Suzanne Oboler and Deena J. González, 441. Oxford: Oxford University Press, 2005.
Sandoval-Sánchez, Alberto. "Más allá de un cuarto propio: El montaje de la latinidad en el teatro e Dolores Prida." In *Paradigmas recientes en las artes escénicas Latinas y latinoamericanas: Current Trends in Latino and Latin American Performing Arts*, edited by Beatriz J. Rizk, 187–205. Miami: Ediciones Universal, 2010.
Umpierre, Luz María. "Interview with Dolores Prida." *Latin American Theatre Review* 22.1 (1988): 81–85.

JUAN RADRIGÁN (SANTIAGO DE CHILE, 1937–2016)

The theatrical career of Chilean playwright Juan Radrigán spanned from 1979 to 2016. While he also published short stories, novels, and poetry, Radrigán is primarily known for the more than forty plays he authored. He has earned widespread acclaim for the plays he wrote in the late 1970s and 1980s in defiance of Chile's dictatorship, yet he also wrote many noteworthy plays after the dictatorship, in the 1990s and 2000s. His reputation was built on how he constructed socially marginalized characters who spoke in the vernacular of a barely working (or unemployed) class struggling to survive. He even created elevated laments in a mix of Spanish and the indigenous language of Mapudungun for a Mapuche *Medea*, and peopled a lost town full of dead characters who speak as if they have just emerged from a Bible.[1]

Critics have generally divided Radrigán's career into two periods: during the dictatorship (1973–1990) and after (1990–2016). This duality can be productively complicated by also highlighting a third category of works: plays that are neither in the thick of resistance to dictatorship nor explorations of themes unrelated to dictatorship. Instead they grapple with the long legacy of dictatorship that questions how to grieve for the loss of democratic socialism, how to commemorate the victims of the repression that followed the 1973 military coup, and how to survive, especially as an artist, despite the continued dominance of the neoliberal economic system established under dictatorship. Finally, some of Radrigán's most significant pre- and post-dictatorship works alike consider a wide variety of themes that have no direct connection to dictatorship and little explicit reference to politics: the nature of love, the purpose of artistic creation, and the meaning of human existence. A sense of existential mystery and wonder runs through all of his works.

Taught to read by his mother, who had trained as an elementary school teacher, Radrigán attended school only sporadically yet became an autodidact who read voraciously and wrote poetry and novels while working at a variety of jobs before settling into a career as a textile worker and union leader. Because it was unsafe to return to work as a labor activist during the viciously anti-labor dictatorship, Radrigán turned to bookselling by day and playwriting by night. Though he had never attempted a play before, it struck him as an effective way to directly confront audiences while remaining under the radar of mass-media censorship.

His first theatrical work, the two-hander *Testimony to the Deaths of Sabina* (1979), alludes to political repression only indirectly, as its elderly protagonists, a husband and wife who run a fruit stall, are plunged into a terrifying maze of bureaucracy and risk losing their livelihood because of an unpaid fine that they cannot figure out how to pay. The play was staged by a young director at the time, Gustavo Meza, in a small Santiago theatre, Teatro de los Comediantes. The following year he wrote *Viva Somoza!!!* together with Meza, contributing a darkly humorous vignette in which a young girl dies of malnutrition while her family members squabble about where to position their new television set—a pointed critique of the neoliberal values embraced by the dictatorship.

Radrigán was forty-two years old when his first play was staged but as if to make up for lost time, he produced a dozen plays in the next five years, some short and others full-length. The most prominent of these works was *Finished from the Start* (1981), which has also been translated as *Children of Fate*. First staged in mid-dictatorship, *Finished from the Start* was courageous in its thinly veiled references to those "disappeared" by the military regime: an endless stream of offstage ghostly figures visible only to four onstage characters who dwell in a desolate urban space. The male protagonist, Emilio, is vaguely reminiscent of deposed civilian president Salvador Allende in how he stubbornly stands his ground and refuses to cede to brute force, a principled stance that leads to his murder, similar to Allende's refusal to abandon the Chilean presidential palace in the midst of the military coup on September 11, 1973 leading to his death. *Finished from the Start* was first directed by Nelson Brodt, one of the founding members of Radrigán's theatre company El Telón and later directed by the renowned Alfredo Castro (1999) and adapted for film by director Luis Vera (1986).

Another of Radrigán's most often produced plays is *Las brutas* [The Beasts] (1980), based on the 1974 suicide of three sisters in a remote rural area of northeastern Chile, at the foot of the Andes. While rooted in the harsh realities of eking out subsistence from land and animals, the work has the majesty of a Greek tragedy. The youngest sister, Luciana, brings to mind Iphigenia for how she at first desperately wants to live yet in the end accepts death. Still, the comparison is not entirely apt because there does not seem to be any reward for the sacrifice Luciana makes to fulfill her older sisters' desire to die together rather than relocate to a city in which their existence would be precarious at best. *Las brutas* has been staged around the world and was also adapted for film as *The Quispe Girls* (2013), written and directed by Sebastián Sepúlveda.

Throughout the 1990s and 2000s, Radrigán produced many works that grappled with the legacy of the dictatorship, including *Islas de porfiado amor* [Islands of Stubborn Love] (1993), *El encuentramiento* [The Encounter] (1995), *Esperpentos rabiosamente inmortales* [Enraged Immortal Grotesques] (2002), and *El desaparecido* [The "Disappeared" Man] (2004). Among the most boldly experimental of these works was *El exilio de la mujer desnuda* [The Exile of a Naked Woman] (2001).

The play is structured in three concentric circles of metatheatre, as a play-within-a-play-within-a-play. On one level, two allegorical characters named Man and Woman seem to represent, respectively, all artists and their doomed quest for truth and justice in the face of the political compromises made in post-dictatorship Chile. On a second level, the same actors morph into Jorge and Pilar, the actors rehearsing the parts of Man and Woman. And on a third level, the actor who debuted the role of Jorge, whose name was Jorge Larragaña, broke the fourth wall to address the audience and ask if anyone was interested in renting a room from his mother. Larragaña would then pass out flyers with the actual contact information for the room rental, while the actor playing Pilar (Sandra Lema) would remark that Juan (Radrigán) had shown solidarity by writing the moment into the plot of the play. *Exilio* functions simultaneously as a testament to how difficult it is for artists to survive economically in neoliberal Chile and as a condemnation of the willingness on the part of some to forget, or forgive, the atrocities of the dictatorship.

Radrigán's most popular play is perhaps *Amores de cantina* [Barroom Loves] (2011), which has been seen by tens of thousands of people in many successful productions in Chile, Spain, and the United States, where it debuted in 2011 at the International Hispanic Theatre Festival, presented by Teatro Avante in Miami, Florida. One of only two musicals in his opus (the other is *The Encounter*), *Amores de cantina* is an ironic allegorical portrait of Chile as a bar full of heavy drinkers who like to sing, mostly about loss and love gone wrong. The work's eclectic mix of folkloric music—tango, cumbia, bolero, ranchera, and cueca—was composed by musical director Joselo Osses with contributions from the original cast. Directed by Mariana Muñoz, its Brechtian staging did not pretend to represent a realistic plot. Instead, eight actors and four musicians sat in a semi-circle and sang, occasionally entering the center of the playing area to dance or act out a beat. The plot revolves around Sofía, the victim of a magic spell that impedes her from leaving the bar until someone dies for her. While some critics have read the work as yet another depiction of the marginalized common person, these characters seem far better off than those who loiter in vacant lots in *Finished from the Start* or on the streets talking to garbage cans in *Isabel Banished in Isabel* (1981), or hunker down in soon-to-be demolished shanties in *The Crazy Man and the Sad Woman* (1980). The characters in *Amores de cantina* speak the language of the Chilean streets in combination with poetry that sometimes recalls Federico García Lorca. Their tragedy is not that they are poor but rather that they are paralyzed, stuck in their sorrow about the past. One of the characters, Tomás, openly urges political protest; in hindsight, he presages the antineoliberal protests that have rocked Chile in recent years. Though it is difficult to say to what extent Radrigán's work inspired political protest, there is no doubt that his career as a playwright, as well as the many workshops he led as a playwriting teacher, inspired a younger generation of Chilean playwrights and directors, including Luis Barrales, Martín Balmaceda, Guillermo Calderón, Alfredo Castro, Mariana Muñoz, Rodrigo Pérez, Alexandra von Hummel, and his daughter, who is also a playwright, Flavia Radrigán.

Ana Elena Puga

Note

1 These descriptions allude to the following plays: *Beckett y Godot* [Beckett and Godot] (2004), *Digo siempre adios, y me quedo* [I Always Say Goodbye, then I Stay] (2002), *El encuentramiento* [The Encounter] (1995), *Medea mapuche* [Mapuche Medea] (2000), and *El pueblo del mal amor* [People of Bad Love] (1986).

Major works

Amores de cantina [Barroom Loves] (2011)
Esperpentos, rabiosamente inmortales [Enraged Immortal Grotesques] (2002)
El exilio de la mujer desnuda [The Exile of a Naked Woman] (2001)
Medea Mapuche [Mapuche Medea] (2000)
El encuentramiento [The Encounter] (1995)
Finished from the Start (1981)
The Beasts (1980)
Mad Man Sad Woman (1980)
Isabel Banished in Isabel (1980)

Published works

Children of Fate. Trans. Robert Shaw. London: Oberon Modern Plays, 2014.
Teatro I. Santiago: LOM Ediciones, 2013.
Finished from the Start and Other Plays. Trans. Ana Elena Puga with Mónica Núñez-Parra. Evanston: Northwestern University Press, 2008.
Crónicas del amor furioso. Santiago: Ediciones Frontera Sur, 2004.
Teatro de Juan Radrigán: 11 obras. Santiago: CENECA – Universidad de Minnesota, 1984.

Further reading

Alexandre, Marcos Antônio and Sara Rojo. "Plínio Marcos y Juan Radrigán: Íconos del teatro de Resistencia." *Latin American Theatre Review* 40, no. 2 (Spring 2007): 53–74.

Bravo, Elizondo. "Juan Radrigán, la dictadura y su teatro." In *Resistencia y Poder: Teatro en Chile*, edited by Heidrun Adler and George Woodyard. Madrid: Iberoamericana Vervuert, 2000. 99–112.

Kruger, Loren. "Dispossession and Solidarity in Athol Fugard and Juan Radrigán." *Theatre Research International* 40, no. 3 (2015): 314–331.

Oyarzún, Carola, ed. *Radrigán: Colección Ensayos Críticos*. Santiago: Ediciones Universidad Católica de Chile, 2008. [Includes relevant critical essays by María de la Luz Hurtado, Catherine Boyle, Cristián Opazo, Paola Hernández, Soledad Lagos, and Alfredo Castro.]

Puga, Ana Elena "Juan Radrigán and the Duty to Tell." In *Memory, Allegory, and Testimony: Upstaging Dictatorship*. New York: Routledge, 2008. 194–231.

Santana, Analola. "Desesperanza en el porvenir: reflexiones sobre la puesta en escena de *Amores de Cantina* de Juan Radrigán." *Chasqui: Revista de literatura latinoamericana* 45, no. 2 (November 2016): 150–166.

Vidal, Hernán. "Juan Radrigán y los limites de la imaginación diológica." In *Teatro de Juan Radrigán: 11 obras*. Santiago: CENECA – Universidad de Minnesota, 1984. 5–38.

JESUSA RODRÍGUEZ (MEXICO CITY, 1955–)

Jesusa Rodríguez is a playwright, performance artist, theatre director, social activist, and currently an elected senator for the National Regeneration Movement, MORENA, the political party of Mexican president Andrés Manuel López Obrador. Rodríguez is also one of the most recognized artists of the Mexican political cabaret movement, which broke out in the 1980s with an unusual force, and which is today widely recognized as one of the most significant Latin American contemporary theatre movements. Rodríguez's stage works mix and challenge theatrical categories, *teatro de carpa* (itinerant theatre), *teatro de revista* (Musical Theatre), burlesque, *pastorelas* (Christmas plays), opera, performance art, and stand-up comedy, among others. These genres, in her work, have always been linked to community life and its daily-political realities.

Rodríguez began her theatrical career studying theatre at CUT, the University Theatre Center of the UNAM (National Autonomous University of Mexico) in the late 1970s. Disappointed by the lack of support for new theatrical proposals such as "performance art," she left the university to embark on an alternative adventure. In that exploration Rodríguez was part of the group "Sombras Blancas" (White Shadows) with whom she staged several works; the most successful of which was *Vacío* [Empty] (1980), written by Carmen Boullosa and directed by Julio Castillo (1943–1988). The play dramatized the last moments of the life of the poet Sylvia Plath, staging the ceremony of her suicide in her final routine. The piece was the result of the actresses improvising on Plath's poems, predominantly "Three Women." In addition to representing one of the characters, Rodríguez was the costume designer and choreographer. The actresses used improvisation in the manner of Commedia dell'arte. Since then, this mixture of rigor and freedom has determined Rodríguez's work.

As part of that same dramatic venture, with her partner and current wife the Argentine singer, piano player, and composer Liliana Felipe, Rodríguez opened two cabaret establishments in the early 1980s. Initially El Fracaso [The Failure], and later El Cuervo [The Raven], which they used as a platform to experiment with works that went beyond the traditional definition of theatre. Emulating German cabaret and Mexican Carpa, both from the early twentieth century, Rodríguez gave minor genres a place on stage, where political questioning and frivolous theatre were mixed. At the same time, she incorporated grandiloquent elements of operetta to interrogate the main archetypes of the social imaginary. For this reason, Rodríguez prefers to call it "Mexican farce."

This theatrical work bore fruits that went beyond laughs. Such is the case of *Donna Giovanni* (1983–1987), a tribute to Scottish artist Fiona Alexander, mother of actor Diego Luna. This dramatic piece, staged by the theatre cooperative Grupo Divas A.C., is a revision of Mozart and Da Ponte's opera *Don Giovanni*. The play toured Latin America, the United States, and Europe, receiving recognition for its use of cross-dressing, humor, and interaction between music, word games, and *tableaux vivants*. The play received some negative reviews for the excessive use of nude scenes, and also for the fact that the singers were "actors who sang." However, the idea to set Mozart's opera in a Mexican-religious context, proved very powerful. Nudity is something that Rodríguez continued to claim in her work.

During this time Rodríguez obtained significant recognition, including the Julio Bracho Award, from the Union of Theatre Critics and Chroniclers, bestowed for best play on *Atracciones Fénix* (1986), a Mozartian musical show with prehistoric and post-historical animals produced by our civilization. She also received the Best Actress award for *El Concilio de Amor* [Council of Love] (1988), an adaptation of *Das Liebes-Koncil*, by Oskar Panizza, at the Festival de las Americas in Montreal (1989). The so-called council is staged in a heaven that looks more like a decaying brothel and is summoned by a senile and filthy

God. The result is visually austere, "between baroque and kitsch, akin to the aesthetics of other similar productions by Jesusa."[1] As in the time of Panizza, the play was accused of blasphemy.

This cycle of cabaret administration and avant-garde dramaturgy climaxed in 1990, when Rodríguez and Felipe owned and managed Teatro La Capilla [The Chapel] and a cabaret bar El Hábito [The Habit]. To generate the money to help rebuild the former, Rodríguez and Felipe opened the latter, El Hábito, which over time became an experimental theatre laboratory in which more than 320 cabaret works were produced. While many of these pieces were the result of the cabaret's dramaturgical experimentation, some of them were also performed in conventional theatres. Such is the case of *El fuego* [Fire] (2000) created to represent the Acteal massacre (1997) in which forty-five indigenous people were killed. In the play, despite the gift of knowledge that Prometheus, the god of foresight, gave to all humanity, a new fire is sought to ignite political consciousness. However, the mythical shadows gain ground and the massacre is unleashed, producing a cruel scene of explicit dramatic violence.

Entering the 1990s, there are significant theatrical productions that delve into the iconography of Mexico's past, including pre-Columbian indigenous deities, such as *La gira Mamal de la Coatlicue* [The Coatlicue Mammal Tour] (1990), in which Rodríguez reinterprets the sculpture of the Aztec earth goddess. The result is a half-circus monumental-looking costume that allows the actress to move on stage and even dance at any given moment. Another historical feminine figure is La Malinche, translator of the conqueror Hernán Cortés, *La Malinche en Dios TV* [La Malinche on God TV] (1991). In Jesusa's work, la Malinche is transformed into an interpreter for the Emperor Zedillitzin (former President Ernesto Zedillo) with the US Marines. A third example is Sor Juana Inés de la Cruz, *Sor Juana en Almoloya* (1995), whom Rodríguez imagines as imprisoned in the Almoloya prison. Through satire and humor, in the deconstruction of these female icons Rodríguez highlights the dissident sexualities of women, which have been strategically forgotten by the official culture.

While at El Hábito, Rodríguez received the Guggenheim Fellowship (1990), a Rockefeller Foundation Grant (1994), and an Obie Award for the staging of *A Book of Hours* awarded by *The Village Voice* newspaper in New York (1999). This play focuses on the incarceration of women in Belén, a charitable "home"/prison founded in Mexico in 1683 as a Roman Catholic "sanctuary" for single, indigent women, who were forced to stay until they died once they entered. This was a collaborative performance piece with Ruth Maleczech, director of New York-based Mabou Mines, visual artist Julie Archer, and poet Catherine Sasanov. The play included the music of Liliana Felipe and a silent movement piece by Rodríguez.

In their collaborative pieces Rodríguez and Felipe also made a critical scrutiny of the contradictory rhetoric of the "progressive policies" of the only party in power up to that moment for seventy years, the Revolutionary Institutional Party (PRI), and of the right-wing party PAN which emerged in 2000. From these plays we must highlight *Foximiliano y Martota* (2003), in which former emperor Maximilian of Habsburg, his wife Carlota and President Benito Juárez await "History's judgment." During the play, the historical characters observe a puppet show of "Little Red Riding Hood," where a girl (Marta Sahagún, first lady of México) makes love with an American wolf (George "W" Bush), who ended up killing Vicenta, the grandmother (President Vicente Fox). In addition to Rodríguez and the music of Felipe, the work was a collective creation with Las Reinas Chulas (Nora Huerta, Cecilia Sotres, Marisol Gasé, and Ana Francis Mor), a theatre company which would become the new administrators of El Hábito (renamed El Vicio [Vice]), as well as the center of the cabaret movement.

Rodríguez and Felipe then embarked on a new theatrical proposal that they have called "the massive cabaret." The trigger for this radical change was the disputed presidential election of 2006 and their commitment to the Peaceful Civil Resistance movement which led these cabaret women to organize around 3,600 cultural activities for the millions of people who congregated in the streets and in the Zócalo plaza of the Mexican capital. While it is true that the social component had always existed in the prolific work of Rodríguez, the political had somehow hierarchically superimposed itself on the social. From Rodríguez last creative period before definitively abandoning theatre, we can highlight *El Maiz* [Corn] (2006–2008), a response to the growing threat of the contamination of Mexico's crops by genetically modified seeds. In this work, Rodríguez and Felipe construct a fractured narrative that fluctuates between the world of the supernatural and the present.

Since 2018 Rodríguez has consciously entered partisan political territory. Her theatrical work has been self-limited to an extreme where the notion of art has disappeared. We could say that she has finally found the authentic Mexican farce. Today Rodríguez performs on the political stage of the upper house of the Federal Legislative Power of Mexico.

Gastón A. Alzate

Note

1 Bruno Bert, "Virulencia ligera," *Tiempo Libre*, no. 769 (February 20, 1995): 29.

Major works

Diálogos entre Darwin y Dios [Conversations Between Darwin and God] (2009)
Primero sueño [First Dream] (2002–2007)
El maíz [Corn] (2003)
Boda en Los Pinos [Wedding at Los Pinos] (2001)
Las horas de Belén (with Mabou Mines) [A Book of Hours] (1999)
Sor Juana en Almoloya [Sor Juana in Almoloya] (1995)
Cabaret prehispánico: Cielo de abajo [Prehispanic Cabaret: Sky Below] (1992)
La gira mamal de Coatlicue [The Coatlicue Mammal Tour] (1990)
El concilio de amor [Council of Love] (1987)
Donna Giovanni (1983)

Published works

Derecho de abortar: Pastorela, with Carlos Pascual, *debate feminista* 10.19 (1999): 329–357.
El genesis, debate feminista 8.16 (1997): 401–413.
Sor Juana en Almoloya: Pastorela Virtual, debate feminista 6.12 (1995): 395–411.
La Malinche en Dios TV, debate feminista 2.3 (1991): 308–312.
La gira mamal de la Coatlicue, debate feminista 1.2 (1990): 401–403.

Further reading

Alzate, Gastón A. "El fin de la simulación: comentarios al cabaret masivo de Jesusa Rodríguez y Liliana Felipe." In *Las mujeres y la dramaturgia Mexicana del siglo XX: aproximaciones críticas*, edited by Claudia Gidi and Jacqueline Bixler, 265–299. Mexico City: Ediciones El Milagro/U Veracruzana/U de Sonora/U de Virginia Tech, 2011.
Costantino, Roselyn. "Jesusa Rodríguez: An Inconvenient Woman." *Women & Performance: A Journal of Feminist Theory* 11.2 (2000): 183–212.
Day, Stuart A. "Misa (Neoliberal) en Los Pinos." *Gestos* 17.33 (2002): 111–117.
Franco, Jean. "A Touch of Evil: Jesusa Rodriguez's Subversive Church." *TDR: The Drama Review* 36.2 (1992): 48–61.
Gutiérrez, Laura. "'El derecho de re-hacer': Signifyin(g) Blackness in Contemporary Mexican Political Cabaret." *Arizona Journal of Hispanic Cultural Studies* 16 (2012): 163–176.
Nigro, Kirsten. "Un revuelto de la historia, la memoria y el género: Expresiones de la posmodernidad sobre las tablas mexicanas." *Gestos* 9.17 (1994): 29–41.
Taylor, Diana. "'High Aztec' or Performing Anthro Pop: Jesusa Rodriguez and Liliana Felipe in Cielo de abajo." *TDR: The Drama Review* 37.3 (1993): 142–152.

MARCO ANTONIO RODRÍGUEZ
(NEW YORK CITY, 1971–)

Marco Antonio Rodríguez is a Dominican American actor, director, screenwriter, and playwright. He was born in New York City but learned Spanish as his first language living in the Dominican Republic during the first few years of his life. He pens Spanish and English versions of his major plays, which uniquely positions him to reach a wide audience in the US and abroad. Rodríguez is a graduate of New York City's famous Fiorello H. LaGuardia arts high school and of the theatre program at the State University of New York at Buffalo. In addition, he holds Master of Fine Arts degrees in acting (Southern Methodist University) and in writing for television and film (Stephens College). He spent his formative years as an actor and playwright in Dallas, Texas, where he won the Outstanding New Play award from the Dallas/Fort Worth Theater Critics Forum for *Heaven Forbid(!)* in 2007. Rodríguez returned to his hometown when his Dominican-themed plays began to be produced regularly on Off-Broadway stages. Parallel to his work in the theatre, Rodríguez has developed screenplays and frequently performs in television shows, films, voiceovers, and commercials.

Rodríguez's main contribution has been to bring the story of the Dominican diaspora into mainstream Latinx ensemble theatre production. His dramatic comedies *Ashes of Light* (2011) and *Barceló on the Rocks* (2014) explore the intersections of immigrant identities and race, gender, and sexuality within a frame of dramatic realism. *Ashes of Light* was produced in New York at Teatro LaTea and Lehman College Stages; in Santo Domingo at Teatro Las Máscaras; in Buenos Aires at Teatro La Mueca; and in Chicago at Batey Urbano (Urban Theater Company). *Barceló on the Rocks* was selected among seventy-five entries as the winner of the 2012 MetLife Nuestras Voces Playwriting competition at New York City's Teatro Repertorio Español, where it was produced in 2014. The plays were well received; together, they won nine HOLA (Hispanic Organization of Latin Actors) awards and four ACE (Association of Latin Entertainment Critics of New York) awards in categories including playwriting, direction, acting, and production.

Set in New York City, *Ashes of Light* and *Barceló on the Rocks* constitute landmarks for creating the first fully Dominican American cultural milieu on stage. The setting for *Ashes of Light* is a small Upper West Side studio apartment with a jam-packed kitchen, a large portrait of Pope John Paul II hanging on pink walls, and a bed, while the action in *Barceló on the Rocks* takes place in the living room of a Washington Heights apartment furnished with plastic-covered furniture and decorated with Caribbean artwork, a dried palm, and a portrait of Jesus Christ. Along with these visual scenographic cues, Rodríguez encourages identification with Dominican culture by crafting dialogue that includes four distinct registers of Dominican Spanish and by frequently incorporating music and the preparation of typical Dominican dishes into the dramatic action. In these meticulously constructed domestic spaces, the companion pieces explore contentious relationships between parents and their offspring. Rodríguez links the two plays by creating a family genealogy that encompasses both stories. The protagonists include patriarch Nino Antonio Ortiz, and matriarch, Luz Hortensia Cruz, who migrated to the US in the 1970s. Nino's infidelities break up their marriage. Nino has three sons, including one with Luz. In each work, the impending death of Nino sets the action in motion and family secrets drive the dramatic tension.

Much of Rodríguez's work explores the legacies of Dominican authoritarianism in the diaspora and focuses in particular on the marginalization and silencing of non-normative sexualities in Dominican culture. In *Barceló on the Rocks*, the traumas of political oppression and the repression of his sexual identity haunt Nino, who, facing his mortality and fueled by Barceló rum, is visited by the ghost of former president Joaquín Balaguer, a despotic political figure whose socioeconomic policies and political persecutions motivated the large exodus of Dominican migrants to the US. Although he has lived in New York City almost his entire adult life, Nino reinforces the elitist, racist, and authoritarian qualities of Dominican nationalism by performing a hyper-masculine role parenting his American-born sons. Nino cannot fully embody a hegemonic male identity, however, since his first love was Jaston, a Haitian-Dominican man. Confronting his past suggests that Nino may abandon the role of dictator in his home to repair his relationship with his children.

In *Ashes of Light*, we learn that Nino has died, and his son with Luz, Julio César, returns to New York City to attend his funeral. Luz's implicit knowledge of Julio César's homosexuality creates much of the tension of the drama, though other facets of the mother-and-son relationship are also explored, such as the battle that Luz, an immigrant, and single mother, has waged to gain citizenship and support her American-born son. During the tense visit, Luz performs motherly, ostensibly loving behaviors that in reality support gender conformity and reveal the role of women in the cultural transmission of homophobia. Both *Ashes of Light* and *Barceló on the Rocks* are notable for featuring single-parent households and addressing the resistance to queer sexualities in Dominican culture with poignancy and humor. In his latest play, *Bloom* (2019), which awaits production at Instituto Arte Teatral Internacional (IATI) in New York City, Rodríguez uses a nonspecific setting in a darkly comic two-hander that features a nonbinary character, further developing the thematic thread of gender and sexual diversity in his plays.

Rodríguez has also helped claim a space for Dominican theatre in the US by adapting for the theatre English-language novels by celebrated Dominican American writers. Teatro Repertorio Español staged his Spanish-language adaptations of Julia Alvarez's novel *In the Name of Salomé* in 2017 and Junot Díaz's novel *The Brief Wondrous Life of Oscar Wao* in 2019. Rodríguez intended to reach audiences who may not be acquainted with the novels, and in rewriting the sprawling and complexly structured narratives for the stage, he stayed faithful to their language and themes while significantly condensing the plots. *In the Name of Salomé* is the story of poet and scholar Camila Henríquez Ureña discovering her own identity in her mission to keep alive the memory of her mother, Salomé, the Dominican Republic's most renowned nineteenth-century poet and co-founder of the nation's first institution of higher learning for women. Similar to *Barceló on the Rocks*, Rodríguez adds to his story a Haitian-Dominican character, a "pupil" or witness to Camila's evocations of the past to conscientize audiences about the current trajectory of racism that drives tensions between the two nations.

Rodríguez's adaptation of *The Brief Wondrous Life of Oscar Wao* is memorable for bringing Díaz's brilliantly drawn Dominican American character Oscar de León, a sexually inexperienced, dark-skinned, overweight, and science fiction-loving tragic hero to the three-dimensional world of the stage. Under Rodríguez's direction, Oscar's uniquely nerdy and Tolkien-inflected diction comes alive, and his fantasy worldview is supported by comic-book styled backdrops, Super Mario Brothers Nintendo sound effects, and science fiction musical motifs.

Rodríguez's work is linked to the legacies of realist Cuban and Puerto Rican dramas that carved a space in the US theatre landscape for exploring the Hispanic Caribbean diaspora. His original plays and adaptations represent the first sustained body of theatre works that examine the particularities of the Dominican culture and migration history. In 2017, in recognition of his impact as actor, director, and playwright on the New York City theatre scene, the Commissioner of Dominican Culture, the diasporic arm of the Dominican Ministry of Culture, dedicated its seventh annual International Theater Festival to Rodríguez. That same year, he was also honored with a Rising Star Award at the popular Dominican Day Parade. He has become an enduring figure in the theatre because his works entertain and forge a sense of community and identity, while at the same time they problematize notions of race, gender, and sexuality that have naturalized authoritarian patterns of political and social relation.

Camilla Stevens

Major works

Bloom (2019)
La breve y maravillosa vida de Oscar Wao [The Brief Wondrous Life of Oscar Wao] (2019)
En el nombre de Salomé [In the Name of Salomé] (2017)
Barceló on the Rocks/Barceló con hielo (2014)
Ashes of Light/La luz de un cigarillo (2011)

Published works

Ashes of Light/La luz de un cigarillo. South Gate, CA: NoPassport, 2018.
Barceló on the Rocks/Barceló con hielo. South Gate, CA: NoPassport, 2016.

Further reading

Stevens, Camilla. *Aquí and Allá: Transnational Dominican Theater and Performance*. Pittsburgh: University of Pittsburgh Press, 2019.

HUGO SALCEDO (CIUDAD GUZMÁN, JALISCO, MEXICO, 1964–)

Hugo Octavio Salcedo Larios is a playwright, poet, and short story writer. Salcedo is the author of more than fifty plays as well as a wide range of scholarly articles and essays. Many of his plays have been translated into English, French, German, and Korean and have been staged across Mexico, Latin America, and Europe as well as Asia and Africa. Salcedo's innovative use of language, complicated plot lines with twists and turns, and widespread use of interior monologues are central to his theatre. He explores topics as varied as the dialectics of love and hate through the prism of human relationships to inquire about migration issues in the US–Mexican border, often presenting them in tragic, mythical, and at times absurd ways. The language observed in his plays is colloquial but also poetic, classical, innovative, and risky.

Salcedo has been the recipient of many accolades. Among them, he received Punto de Partida [Starting Point] award by the National Autonomous University of Mexico for: *San Juan de Dios* [Saint John of God] (1986); *Dos a uno* [Two to One] (1987); and *El viaje de los cantores* [The Crossing] (1989). This last play was also awarded Spain's Tirso de Molina prize (the highest award given in dramaturgy in the Hispanic world) and the Best Author Award by the Mexican Critics Association and the Mexican Theatre Critics Award. In 2012 the University of Tennessee and the Centro Cultural Espacio 1900 honored him and dedicated their International Conference to the study of his dramaturgy. Hugo Salcedo's early plays and awards established him as a significant figure of the New Mexican Dramaturgy group of writers who began publishing and staging their plays at the turn of the twentieth century. Some of the most important writers of this movement are Estela Leñero, David Olguín, Jorge Celaya, Luis Mario Moncada, Ricardo Pérez Quitt, and Sabina Berman.

El viaje de los cantores, a one-act and ten-scene play, cemented him as one of the best playwrights of contemporary Mexico and the Spanish-speaking world. The play is partially based on an event that made headlines all over the world, where eighteen Mexican men suffocated to death in a hermetically sealed boxcar while trying to cross the border into the United States. The different scenes function like fragments of reality which are presented from many points of view. The US–Mexico border is seen through religious, mythical, psychological, philosophical, and socio-political themes. It appears as a geographical space full of opposing, mysterious, and conflictive qualities. The play is part of a trilogy centering on the border that includes *Arde el desierto con los vientos que vienen del sur* [The Desert is Burning with the Southern Winds] (1990), that explores the foundation of the city of Tijuana, which is reimagined as a mythical space that incorporates imagery of the desert and the Far West, and *Sinfonía en una botella* [Symphony in a Bottle] (1990), a play that shows the daily crossings in the San Ysidro–San Diego international border. Salcedo's trilogy presents the border as a geographical, historical, economical, and cultural point of departure to a better life.

In *Barbara Gandiaga: Crimen y condena en la misión de Santo Tomás* [Barbara Gandiaga: Crime and Punishment in the Mission of Saint Thomas] (1999), Salcedo continued focusing on historical events. The two-act play explores different stories told by witnesses to the murder of a Dominican friar, Eulaldo Surroca, perpetrated in 1803. Each version of the crime is supported by a different point of view consistent with the hegemonic perspective of the time, sentencing

Bárbara Gandiaga, his indian housekeeper, who had been sexually abused by him.

10 obras en un acto [10 One-Act Plays] (1996) is the first large compilation of his works. The collection includes a variety of plays that center on the themes of love between two people and the impossibility of communication (*Zona neutral* [Neutral Zone], *Endless Love*, *Descubiertos* [Exposed], and *Vuelve el pájaro a su nido* [The Bird Returns to its Nest]); social and political criticism (*Primero de mayo* [May First] and *Uno de octubre* [October First]); and plays that involve national myths (*La llorona* [The Weeping Woman]). The success of the collection allowed Salcedo to expand it into *21 obras en un acto* [21 One-Act Plays] (2002). In this new collection the plays continue to be poignantly Mexican while others are more global, focusing on violations of human rights.

Salcedo's dramaturgy portrays mythical and border heroes. *Bulevar* [Boulevard] (1995) rewrites the popular myth of the origin of a legendary five-and-dime store in downtown Tijuana. In the play the characters have similarities to the Greco-Roman figures whose names they bear. Their complicated lives of political intrigues, revenge, and unreciprocated love affairs come together for a brief moment in this Tijuana store. *Selena: La reina del Tex-Mex* [Selena: The Queen of Tex-Mex] (1999) explores the impact on the border communities of the death of the famous and mythical Tex-Mex singer Selena Quintanilla-Perez who is performed as a drag queen. Through a series of vignettes, the characters are continually obligated to cross geographical, political, and cultural borders to unite in another dimension and create a new country. Salcedo's dramaturgy also delves into biblical themes. *La estrella del norte* [The Northern Star] (published in 1999) is a border Christmas "Pastorela" play set in Tijuana. *Onania* (2010) and *Seis metros, dos mil quinientos kilos y un chorro de espuma* [Six Meters, Two Thousand Five Hundred Kilos and a Jet of Foam] (2010) are contemporary thrillers that revisit the biblical stories of Onan and Jonah, respectively.

We Women (2011) also explores stories from the Bible and Greek myths interspersed with contemporary stories of extreme violence. The play displays degrading, brutal, and abusive situations across different periods of time and geographies. Themes of religious and political persecutions appear through vignettes that provide a constant violent history on women's bodies. Other plays written by Salcedo focus on hate crimes against the LGBTQ+ community. In *La ley del ranchero* [The Law of the Cowboy] (2003) and *Adriana no es Adriana* [Adriana is not Adriana] (2020) the protagonists are the perpetrators of murders against a gay man and a transgender sexual worker. In both plays the killers will not be punished for these unresolved homicides.

Not content with just observing the violence in a country where criminal organizations control and bring fear to his homeland, Salcedo wrote *Música de balas* [Music to the Sound of Bullets] (2012). The play earned him the National Dramaturgy Prize awarded jointly by the Universidad Autónoma Metropolitana and the Universidad de Guadalajara in 2011. In *Música* scenes are numbered by the official counts of fatalities provided by the Mexican authorities at the time of the writing of the play. In *Noche estrellada sobre el campo de pepinos* [Starry Night Over the Cucumber Field] (2011) changes in urbanization, criminality, and unrest in cities along the US–Mexican border announce future violence and aggression. Finally, *El edificio* [The Building] (2020) delves into the corruption by police and local politicians while revisiting past themes of violence and social unrest.

Hugo Salcedo's dramaturgy continues to be at the forefront of contemporary Mexican and Latin American theatre. For over thirty years he has written a theatre that is very complex and combines popular language with poetic imagery. Even if his plays denounce violence, corruption and degradation, his characters always find ways of reflecting life and humanity. His theatre, though at times pessimistic and even schizophrenic as a consequence of contemporary financial, political, and ecological chaos, points to dim rays of light.

Iani Moreno

Major works

Adriana no es Adriana [Adriana is not Adriana] (2020)
We women (2019)
Música de balas [Music to the Sound of Bullets] (2012)
Onania (2010)
La ley del ranchero [The Law of the Cowboy] (2006)
Selena: La reina del Tex-Mex [Selena: The Queen of Tex-Mex] (1998)
Arde el desierto con los vientos que vienen del sur [The Desert is Burning with the Southern Winds] (1990)
El viaje de los cantores [The Crossing] (1990)
Sinfonía en una botella [Symphony in a Bottle] (1990)
San Juan de Dios [Saint John of God] (1986)

Published works

Música de balas. Mexico City: Universidad Autónoma Metropolitana, 2012.

Noche estrellada sobre el campo de pepinos; Nosotras que los queremos tanto. Tijuana, B.C.: Consejo Nacional para la Cultura y las Artes, 2011.
21 obras en un acto. Toluca, México: Consejo Nacional para la Cultura y las Artes, 2002.
10 obras en un acto. Tijuana, B.C.: CAEN, 1996.
El viaje de los cantores y otras obras de teatro: El viaje de los cantores, Arde el desierto con los vientos que vienen del sur, Sinfonía en una botella. Mexico City, Mexico: Consejo Nacional para la Cultura y las Artes, 1990.

Further reading

Alcántara Mejía, José Ramón, "Márgenes de textualidad y teatralidad en *El viaje de los cantores* de Hugo Salcedo," *Revista de Literatura Mexicana Contemporánea*, 10.22 (2004): 119–126.
Baker, Christina, "Sounds of a Modern Nation: From Nacocorridos to Hugo Salcedo's *Música de balas*," *Symposium*, 71.4 (2017): 179–194.
Beardsell, Peter, "Crossing the Border in Three Plays by Hugo Salcedo," *Latin American Theatre Review*, 29 (Spring 1996): 71–84.
Melendez, Priscilla, "The Body and the Law in the Mexico/U.S. Borderlands: Violence and Violations in *El viaje de los cantores* by Hugo Salcedo and *Backyard* by Sabina Berman," *Modern Drama*, 54.1 (Spring 2011): 24–44.
Moreno, Iani del Rosario, *Theatre of the Borderlands: Conflict, Violence, and Healing*. Lanham: Lexington Books, 2017.
Solis, Alejandro and Hugo Salcedo, eds., *Travesía Dramática: Análisis contextual de la obra de Hugo Salcedo*. Toluca, Mexico: Universidad del Estado de México, 2019.
Vargas, Margarita, "*El viaje de los cantores* como la dramatización de 'La dialéctica de la soledad'," *Latin American Theatre Review*, 44 (Spring 2011): 5–15.

LUIS RAFAEL SÁNCHEZ (HUMACAO, PUERTO RICO, 1936–)

Luis Rafael Sánchez is a Puerto Rican playwright, essayist, and novelist. A person of African descent, Sánchez was born in Humacao, Puerto Rico where he spent the early years of his life. Sánchez is lauded for connecting Puerto Rican literature to the New Theatre Movement and the Latin American Boom. Throughout his career, Sánchez has received numerous recognitions, including awards and fellowships from the prestigious Guggenheim Foundation, the Berlin Academy of Arts and Sciences, University of Guadalajara (Julio Cortázar Chair), and the Puerto Rican Foundation for the Humanities. He is professor emeritus of the University of Puerto Rico, Río Piedras and New York University.

As an author, Sánchez has always moved between drama and narrative prose, publishing his first book of short stories *En cuerpo de camisa* [In Clothed Flesh] (1957) before his first plays. His particular way of genre blending is likely indebted to the way theatre informs his prose and prose informs his theatre. In 1955, he traveled to Mexico as a student and was recognized with an acting award from the National Institute of Mexican Youth. The next year he began studying at the University of Puerto Rico and joined a university theatre group, Teatro Rodante (Traveling Theatre). Before completing his bachelor's degree in 1960, Sánchez had already received high praise and recognition. He had staged his existentialist short play *La espera* [The Wait] (1958); received an award for best children's theatre play from the Academy of Performing Arts of Santo Domingo for *Cuento de la Cucarachita Viudita* [Story of the Little Cockroach Widow] (1959); and had been awarded a grant to study playwriting in New York. He finished his master's degree at the City University of New York in 1963, and eventually earned a Ph.D. from the Complutense University in Madrid, writing his dissertation on the work of Puerto Rican writer Emilio S. Belaval.

Of his many contributions to theatre, Sánchez should be known for "ricanizing" universal themes and traditional genres through transculturation and adaptation. Likewise, his singular approach of integrating Puerto Rican vernacular expression into his dramatic language, his chronicling of Puerto Rican life, and his use of intertextuality and neobaroque aesthetics universalize *puertorriqueñidad* (Puerto Rican-ness). Especially with respect to his neobaroque approach of double-voiced pastiche or parody of vernacular ways of being and expression, Sánchez's writing shows us how postmodernism can do the work of transculturation and vice versa. As Efraín Barradas argues, it is this style, which he dubs "barroqueño," that creates a much-needed bridge between Puerto Rico and Latin American culture in general.[1]

Many of Sanchez's works for the stage adapt European forms through Puerto Rican themes, imaginaries, and affect. In *Farsa del amor compradito* [Farce of Love That's Just a Little Bit Paid For] (1959), Sánchez presents a unique take on Italian *commedia dell'arte*. The play utilizes many of the conventions of *commedia*, including a classic love-triangle scenario, improvisation, and literary interpolations, while introducing new Puerto Rican variations of stock characters alongside classic ones. Yet even a *commedia* staple like Colombina expresses her signature coquettish banter in Puerto Rican terms of affection. Upset with being tricked into marrying Arlequín, Colombina employs the audience to intervene in an alternative ending. The play ends with the hybrid stock characters literally transplanting themselves into a Puerto Rican context through improvised repartee with their public.

The *Passion According to Antígona Pérez* (1968) adapts Sophocles's tragedy to an ambiguous Latin American country. *Antígona* also borrows from saint plays or passion plays, comparing the protagonist's unjust persecution to Christ and Christian martyrs. Sánchez's text refers to the play as the chronicle of Antígona, introducing the clash of political narratives through the use of eight *periaktoi* that reveal newspaper headlines and political graffiti. This backdrop along with the sparse modernist platforms of the set estrange the action of the play which unfolds in the cell of Antígona, a political prisoner charged with an unauthorized burial. As a revolutionary, she has been an accomplice to the attempted assassination of the ruler, Creon Molina. A chorus of journalists representing the propaganda of the state-controlled press continuously defame Antígona while distorting her narrative. *Antígona* is sometimes discussed as introducing Brechtian aesthetics to the Puerto Rican stage. Despite suffering persecution, isolation, and execution, Antígona's resolve and resistance evokes the spirit of left-wing, decolonial movements throughout the mid twentieth century. The play suggests a fidelity to the "independentista" movement of Puerto Rico in particular.

Both *A Miracle for Maggie* (1965) and *Quíntuples* [Quintuplets] (1985) exemplify the postmodern sensibilities of Sánchez's dramaturgy, sensibilities which grow out of his neobaroque aesthetic and masterful approach to multiple genres of drama and narrative prose. *A Miracle for Maggie* is an adaptation of a Spanish *auto sacramental* or morality play with an existentialist spin querying the relationship between truth and reality. A mysterious man, El Hombre, draws Maggie, a prostitute, into proselytizing and persuades her to falsely proclaim that she has been reborn as the new Magdalena. When followers come to believe in Maggie's miracle, El Hombre underscores the postmodern critique of the play by convincing Maggie to continue the charade. Although Maggie is conflicted about lying, in the end, she internalizes her miracle and becomes la Magdalena. The text blends elements of theatre of cruelty—the ritualistic first act where El Hombre enraptures Maggie—with theatre of the absurd, understood through its themes and existentialist perspective. Maggie's transformation in the world of the play highlights the ways Sánchez's theatre anticipated theories of performativity and self-making in its critique of capital "T" Truth, something characteristic of theatre of the absurd.

Quíntuples pushes beyond the thematic level in its engagement with performance theory, scripting an audience-performance relationship that calls representational practices more broadly into question. The play consists of six monologues written to be performed by two actors who portray the Morrison quintuplets—three sisters (Dafne, Bianca, Carlota) and two brothers (Baby and Mandrake)—and their father, Papá Morrison. The Puerto Rican characters have an air of celebrity and speak to the audience as if they are addressing attendees at a conference on family issues. *Quíntuples* gives us yet another perspective on Sánchez dexterity in creating transculturation through postmodernism. Telling their family story, the Morrisons present themselves through a range of references, popular and traditional, from Elizabeth Taylor and Bianca Jagger to flamenco dancers and mobster movies.

According to Barradas, two actors performing alternating monologues structures a myriad of binaries throughout the play: male vs. female, extroverted vs. introverted, past vs. future, diegesis vs. mimesis. He brings our attention to the concept of *"fabular"* (to make up/storytelling)—a keyword from the end of the play when the two actors drop their characters and approach the audience. *Fabular* muddles another dichotomy at the core of Sánchez's work—prosaic vs. theatrical. As Barradas asserts, Sánchez's text shows us that dualities do not need to suggest opposition, rather they can be fluid, interchangeable, and transformative given the circumstances.[2] In many ways, undoing binaries in *Quíntuples* parallels a larger achievement of Sánchez's *oeuvre* to transgress dichotomies isolating Puerto Rico from the contemporary globalized world or Puerto Rican vernacular culture from "high art."

Within his work we find an unmatched commitment to Puerto Rico, its history, culture, affects, and imaginaries. And from that grounding, Sánchez innovated a multitude of approaches, traditional and contemporary, including theatre of the absurd, epic theatre, theatre of cruelty, postmodernism, and the Caribbean neobaroque. At the same time, the seamlessness of each individual work is irreducible to any of these frames of critical inquiry or categories of dramatic criticism. Whether it is by way of conscious transculturation or a more fluid style of *fabular*, Sánchez's work defies rigid compartmentalization, while interpreting the multifaceted critiques of Western modernity endemic to the late twentieth century through a Puerto Rican center.

Eric Mayer-García

Notes

1 Efraín Barradas, *Para devorarte otra vez: Nuevos acercamientos a la obra de Luis Rafael Sánchez* (Santo Domingo: Ediciones Cielonaranja, 2017), 17–19.
2 Ibid., 105–106.

Major works

Quíntuples [Quintuplets] (1985)
La pasión según Antígona Pérez [The Passion According to Antígona Pérez] (1968)
Casi el alma: Auto de fe en tres actos [A Miracle for Maggie] (1964)
La hiel nuestra de cada día [Our Daily Bitterness] (1961)
Los ángeles se han fatigado [The Angeles Are Tired] (1960)
Farsa del amor compradito [Farce of Love That's Just a Little Bit Paid For] (1960)
Cuento de la Cucarachita Viudita [Story of the Little Cockroach Widow] (1959)

Published works

Quíntuples. Hanover, NH: Ediciones del Norte, 1985.
Casi el alma: Auto de fe en tres actos [A Miracle for Maggie]. Río Piedras, PR: Editorial Cultural, 1974.
La pasión según Antígona Pérez: Crónica americana en dos actos. Hato Rey, PR: Ediciones Lugar, 1964.
Sol 13, Interior: Suite de obras en un acto y dos actos respectivamente: La hiel nuestra de cada día; Los ángeles se han fatigado in Teatro puertorriqueño: Cuarto festival. San Juan, PR: Instituto de Cultura Puertorriqueña, 1962.
Teatro: Los ángeles se han fatigado; Farsa del amor compradito. San Juan, PR: Ediciones Lugar, 1960.

Further reading

Barradas, Efraín. 1981. *Para leer en Puertorriqueño: Acercamiento de la obra de Luis Rafael Sánchez*. Río Piedras: Editorial Cultural, 1981.
Hernández Vargas, Nélida and Daisy Caraballo Abréu. *Luis Rafael Sánchez: Crítica y bibliografía*. Río Piedras: Editorial de la Universidad de Puerto Rico, 1985.
Mejías López, William, ed. *A lomo de tigre: Homenaje a Luis Rafael Sánchez*. Río Piedras: Editorial de la Universidad de Puerto Rico, 2015.
Waldman, Gloria F. *Luis Rafael Sánchez: Pasión teatral*. San Juan: Instituto Cultural Puertorriqueña, 1988.

OCTAVIO SOLIS (EL PASO, TEXAS, 1958–)

Born and raised in the bordertown of El Paso, Octavio Solis writes lyrical plays that engage his characters' inner conflicts through imagistic dialogue. Solis has written over twenty-five plays and directed several of his own works. Along with the Oregon Shakespeare Festival, Solis has worked extensively with Dallas Theater Center, the Magic Theatre, Intersection for the Arts, Thick Description in San Francisco, South Coast Repertory Theatre, and San Diego Repertory Theatre in southern California. Solis's plays confront intractable emotions and place the confrontations center stage; both characters and audiences are provocatively exposed to the darker side of the American Dream and of Latinx family life. They rarely require extensive sets; he prefers to convey theatricality through the actor and language. Many of his characters are good storytellers, suggesting the importance of a narrative capacity in everyone. He uses poetry and song to invoke the visuals and specificity of his settings.

The land of his birthplace and the places which he has made his home are enmeshed in his stories as characters. Born to Mexican parents and raised in El Paso and wary of labels, Solis shifts his embrace of categories, stating, "the Latino stuff is just labels, but the border is real … It is the repository of so many stories."[1] After El Paso, Solis lived in San Francisco for years and eventually settled in Medford, Oregon, where he currently lives. In each location, Solis connects with the community and collaborates with local theatres, and it is life on the border, or the experience of in-betweenness, that appears in a number of his plays. In 2010, Caridad Svich's NoPassport Press printed a collection entitled *The River Plays*, consisting of *Dreamlandia*, *El Otro*, and *Bethlehem*, all about US–Mexico borderlands.

Solis began as an actor in Dallas in the 1980s, and he later wrote and directed his own work. His writing contains echoes of the lyricism of Shakespeare and the imagistic writing of Mexican novelist Carlos Fuentes. Theatrically, he studied with Paul Baker, a Texas theatremaker known for his character-driven stagings, and later with Luis Valdez and El Teatro Campesino, on developing his early play *Prospect* (1989) for their 1993 production. The play was produced by the Latino Chicago Theatre Company later that year and it toured to the Edinburgh Theatre Festival in 1994. Solis's range of influences manifest in his breadth of work across a variety of sources and spaces. *The Ballad of Pancho and Lucy* (2005) is a Latinx version of the *Bonnie and Clyde* story, and *Hole in the Sky* (2018) was commissioned as a site-specific piece about water and drought, staged outdoors on a horse ranch in southern California.

Two early plays, both set in El Paso, create mythic stories through the specificity of Latinx images. *Santos & Santos* (1993) is based on a real story of a Lebanese family that came to El Paso through Mexico. Solis evokes a story from one snapshot and "only discovers by the end of the play where the central image will be located."[2] The play centers the images of *lotería* cards, drawing on such symbols as *el corazón* (the heart) and the figure of La Malinche (the Aztec woman famed for her role in the Mexican conquest) to signify character traits and plot foreshadowing. Along with these visual images, Solis brackets poetic subtext in his script, creating a theatrical writing style that is the equivalent of film montage. Similarly, *El Paso Blue* (1994) is a modern-day version of the Oedipus myth, and Latinx culture is imbued through music entirely in Spanish, combining country and blues styles. Playing on a familiar tale, Solis invokes culture through the Spanish language and musicality.

One connection across Solis's *oeuvre* is his poetic language, written in a mixture of English and Spanish. In many of his plays, his "characters feel just as alienated in Mexico as they do in the US, and so they find solace and inclusion in a language that moves from English to Spanish to a patois that exists only on the borderlands."[3] *Lydia* (2008) is considered Solis's hallmark play, and it is also his most poetic. The story centers on a Chicanx family that hires an undocumented Mexican housekeeper to care for the daughter who has suffered physical and mental harm due to a car accident. Her dialogue consists of sounds and syllables, not words, and it is the other characters who translate their meaning for the audience. The play also includes an incestuous homosexual relationship, atypical in theatre and especially Latinx dramas of the time, and the repercussions of political, sexual, and psychological trauma on a family.

A thematic through-line of his work are his characters whose flawed attempts toward the American Dream led them to travel emotionally and physically toward this goal. With resonances of playwrights such as Sam Shepard and Tennessee Williams, *Prospect* (1993) takes up its characters' desire for acceptance in US American culture that brushes against the possibility of full assimilation, and with novelist John Steinbeck's group of short stories rearranged for the stage, *The Pastures of Heaven* (2010), to address generational changes and desires in families and workers of California's Salinas Valley. Continuing in this vein, his recent play, *Mother Road* (2019), focuses on the Mexican and Chicanx descendants of the fictitious Joad family from *The Grapes of Wrath* as they travel a reverse migration from California to Oklahoma. Solis paints characters with poignant human flaws, from a Christmastime tale about a young girl in *La Posada Magica* [The Magic Inn] (1996) to the in-depth exploration of suicide and grief in *Gibraltar* (2005). Likewise, in *Se Llama Cristina* [Her Name is Cristina] (2013), the two characters remain in one room and move psychologically and emotionally through drugs, time, and locale. Solis acknowledges that none of his characters are model citizens. The honesty from which his characters speak is a reflection of Solis's personal exploration with truth and positionality.

Adaptation has always been part of Solis's work from the start, but with a Latinx theme. His first play, *Man of the Flesh* (1988), is an adaptation of José Zorilla's version of *Don Juan Tenorio* published in Mexico in 1844. He developed the play when studying under María Irene Fornés in her six-month workshop lab at International Arts Relations (INTAR). After *Man of the Flesh*, Solis later adapted other Spanish Golden Age stories, such as Calderón de la Barca's *Life is a Dream* to *Dreamlandia* (2000), set on the border in the present day. The Oregon Shakespeare Festival (OSF) commissioned Solis to adapt the first book of Cervantes's *Don Quixote* (2009), resulting in a large-cast, Elizabethan-style show that included twenty-five puppets. He later re-envisioned the story as *Quixote Nuevo* (2018), moving away from Cervantes's novel to contemporary bordertown theatre, with the fantasy elements transposed to Day of the Dead folklore and contemporary politics of immigration and deportation explicitly addressed.

In recent years, Solis has expanded beyond playwriting and directing to translation, voiceover work, and non-dramatic writing. He translated Shakespeare's little-known *Edward III* into contemporary English for the OSF's *Play on!* initiative (2015–2018) and worked as a consultant for the Disney film, *Coco* (2017), in which he also voiced the character of the Arrival Agent. In 2018, San Francisco's City Lights Books published *Retablos: Stories from a Life Lived Along the Border*, Solis's first foray into non-dramatic literature. Unlike his prior works that contain veiled autobiographical elements, Solis embraced an exposed semi-autobiographical mode by writing a series of fifty short memory-stories based on his childhood in El Paso.

Solis has received numerous writing awards, including the Distinguished Achievement in the American Theater Award from the William Inge Center for the Arts in 2019, a United States Artists Fellowship in 2011, and the National Latino Playwriting Award in 2002. He received an NEA Playwriting Fellowship, a McKnight Fellowship, and, in 2020, became a member of the Texas Institute of Letters. Through constant evolution in his creative form, Octavio Solis depicts Latinx life and language and redefines life on the border.

Carla Della Gatta

Notes

1 Teresa Marrero, "Q&A: Octavio Solis," *TheatreJones*, 21 (May 2013). Accessed December 1, 2020, http://theaterjones.com/ntx/features/20130521082921/2013-05-21/QA-Octavio-Solis

2 Nirmala Nataraj, "Octavio Solis Hits the National Stage," *Theatre Bay Area*, March 2009.
3 Octavio Solis, "American Enough," *PowellsBooksBlog*, September 26, 2019. Accessed December 1, 2020, www.powells.com/post/original-essays/american-enough

Major works

Retablos (2018)
Quixote Nuevo (2018)
Se Llama Cristina (2013)
Lydia (2008)
Gibraltar (2005)
Dreamlandia (2000)
El Paso Blue (1994)
Santos & Santos (1993)
Prospect (1993)
Man of the Flesh (1988)

Published works

The River Plays: Dreamlandia, Bethlehem, El Otro. South Gate, CA: NoPassport Press, 2010.
Lydia, in *Three Plays from the Colorado New Play Summit*. Denver: The Publishing House and Denver Center Theatre Company, 2007.

Further reading

Berson, Micha. "Octavio Solis's Journey to 'Mother Road.'" *American Theatre* 36.7 (September 2019): 38–41.
Rossini, Jon D. "Sitting Geography: Octavio Solis and the Circulation of Performance." In *Performance, Politics and Activism*, edited by Peter Lichtenfels and John Rouse, 207–219. London: Palgrave Macmillan, 2013.
Solis, Octavio. "Willful Invisibility: Translating William Shakespeare's *The Reign of King Edward III*." In *Shakespeare and Latinidad*, edited by Trevor Boffone and Carla Della Gatta, 202–216. Edinburgh: Edinburgh University Press, 2021.
Ybarra, Patricia A. *Latinx Theater in the Times of Neoliberalism*. Evanston: Northwestern University Press, 2017.

RAFAEL SPREGELBURD (BUENOS AIRES, ARGENTINA, 1970–)

Rafael Spregelburd is one of Argentina's most prolific and multifaceted artists. Playwright, theatre and film director, actor, translator, theatre theorist, and essayist, his work has intrigued and inspired Argentine and international spectators and artists since the early 1990s. Spregelburd's theatre crosses rich interdisciplinary boundaries, venturing into linguistics, science, history, and the visual arts. Mentored by theatre directors Mauricio Kartun and Ricardo Bartis, Spregelburd emerged as one of the leading playwrights, directors, and actors of Argentina's post-1983 dictatorship period. He began his career as a member of the Caraja-ji theatre group. In 1995 he co-founded, with Andrea Garrote, El Patrón Vásquez theatre company. Spregelburd has written, directed, and acted in more than forty plays, staged in Europe, Latin America, and the US. He is author of some sixty publications—original plays, translations, essays on theatre—and his plays have been translated into seventeen languages.

An intellectual and cross-disciplinary thinker, Spregelburd's theatrical vision and unique style eschew easy categorization. Osvaldo Pellettieri calls Spregelburd's work postmodern, classifying it as "theatre of disintegration" due to its fragmented structure, abstract language, pessimism, absurd-theatre tendencies, and "dissolution of character as a psychological entity."[1] Pellettieri distinguishes it from the social realist trends of the end of the twentieth century and from "theatre of resistance." Jorge Dubatti expands this definition, positing Spregelburd's work as "neo-modern," "post-postmodern," or "anti-postmodern."[2] Spregelburd's theatre is hybrid, experimental, intertextual, self-conscious, and self-referential. Even though he is an accomplished director and actor, who plays the lead role in most of his works, Spregelburd is more focused on the narrative dimensions of theatre than on performance. Paola Hernández sees Spregelburd and his generation as a turning point toward new twenty-first-century aesthetics, which both recycle and refresh past forms—theatre of the absurd and neo-vanguard techniques—and reject and "liberate themselves from the ancestral weight of realist theatre, which searched for a connection with the audience or some kind of link to social reality."[3]

Language, not reality, is the focus of Spregelburd's canon. Words, codes, books, linguistic structures, diversity of languages, the misuse of language, communication problems, and the ways in which language describes and circumscribes reality all come under Spregelburd's artistic microscope. Also fascinated by chaos theory, Spregelburd's plays deconstruct language and life, highlighting coincidences, chance, and entropy. Spregelburd sees his style as neo-baroque for the linguistic games it constructs, the inter-, intra-, and extra-textual references it integrates and the multiple twists and plots it intertwines.[4]

Spregelburd's earliest plays scrutinize language in diverse ways. *Destino de dos cosas o tres* [Destiny of Two Things or Three] (written

1990; staged 1993) posits and dismantles an invented language to tell a love story; *Cucha de almas* [Spoon of Souls] (1992) transgresses linguistic rules and linear narrative structures, interweaving five stories to parody and question traditional Argentine theatre forms; *Remanente de invierno* [Remainder of Winter] (written 1992; staged 1995) highlights the language of mass media and the violent ways in which it infiltrates the most intimate spaces of society.

Spregelburd's later works never lose their preoccupation with language, its function or deconstruction, but they expand definitions of language to interweave metaphysics, intertextuality, and chaos theory. Multiple, competing references, which go beyond obvious connections between one text and another, add to the complexity of Spregelburd's theatre. Each piece thematically and structurally embeds a plethora of verbal, visual, and cultural clues, transplanting and layering stories that don't seem to have anything to do with each other but are linked by the words, objects, and threads. For example, *Raspando la cruz* [Scraping the Cross] (1997) weaves word plays with references to German cinema, Umberto Eco, and Nietzsche to reflect on and dissect World War II narratives. *Cuadro de asfixia* [Suffocation Box] (1996) repurposes Ray Bradbury's *Fahrenheit 451* and features Dostoevsky, Kafka, and Argentina's José Hernández as characters to explore and unsettle the boundaries of memory and amnesia—so relevant in post-dictatorship Argentina. *Fractal: una especulación científica* [Fractal: A Scientific Speculation] (2000) is a theatrical experiment about chaos theory; the fourteen actors manipulate notions of entropy, the butterfly effect, the tsunami, and fractal geometry to collectively represent a back-and-forth journey between Argentina and Paraguay.

In *Heptalogía de Hieronymus Bosch* [Heptalogy of Hieronymus Bosch], Spregelburd demonstrates his expansive intertextual repertoire, his artistic brilliance, and the ways in which he might challenge spectatorship. The seven plays which form this series—written over more than a decade—are each independent productions with their own styles and themes; nonetheless, they are united through their relationship to Bosch's fifteenth-century painting, the *Tabletop of the Seven Deadly Sins*. His plays *Inappetence* (1997), *Extravagance* (2000), *Modesty* (2000), *Stupidity* (2004), *Panic* (2003), *Paranoia* (2007), and *Stubborness* (2009) reproduce, modernize, and interrogate the themes (the sins of one's time), the structure (repetitions of "contemporary" images of sins), and the aesthetic function (art's pull on receptors) of Bosch's painting to activate spectators' engagement with art, scrutinize the underpinnings of language, and cast new light on existential questions about personal and global crises. Spregelburd's characters are self-absorbed individuals trapped within themselves in a confusing, highly interconnected world. Like all of Spregelburd's works, the *Heptalogy* pieces interweave numerous stories and coincidences or present the same story from multiple perspectives. They are sometimes exaggeratedly long—*Stupidity*'s Chilean production lasted three hours and forty minutes—and often actors play numerous roles. In true Spregelburd-style, language is the key to decoding each; however, like his characters, just when spectators think they have found *the* key to understanding the play, they realize that it is *a* key that opens *a* door, but it may be the wrong key to the wrong door, and, furthermore, the key does not belong to them (as literally happens in *Panic*). Whether characters seek *The Book of the Dead*, a vanishing artwork, or an elusive dictionary of the invented language Katak, their search unleashes deep-rooted questions but never leads to answers.

In spite of its adherence to "text(s)," Spregelburd's theatre transgresses literary boundaries. *Bizarra* (2003)—a 500-page "theatre-novel," which parodies a telenovela, integrates multiple genres, cross-linguistic and cross-cultural references, and boasts over one hundred characters—is "trans-theatrical" and "like a party."[5] Another of Spregelburd's masterpieces, *Spam* "A Spoken Opera" (2014) takes the premise of internet junk mail to create a highly structured, hybrid (incorporating music, opera, even Caravaggio's painting), multimedia, and parodic exploration of art forms—including theatre—and spectators' viewing and digital habits. Even in Spregelburd's theatre based on historical events—such as works like *Stateless* (2011), *Acassuso* (2008), and *An Argentinian Moment* (2002)—representation, the absurdity of language, and the limits of fiction become the central focus. His cross-disciplinary references also inspire phenomenal *mises-en-scène*. The set design of most Spegelburd plays is brilliant and dynamic. His original combinations of the live and the virtual and his creative use of unconventional objects (like toilets), hotel room windows, and rotating, multi-platform stages engage audiences and have gained him national and international accolades too numerous to list.

Beyond their intellectual roots and intricate linguistic and structural games, Spregelburd's plays are accessible and attractive to audiences because they are also very funny. Spregelburd's humor is sophisticated but appealing. The author adeptly intercalates words, gestures, coincidences, and seemingly useless repetitions to construct a sarcastic and ironic form of humor, which keeps both Argentine and international audiences laughing even when they don't fully understand what they are laughing about.

Rafael Spregelburd's creativity embodies an all-encompassing originality that borders on genius. For these reasons, his plays have garnered some of Argentina's and the international theatre scene's most prestigious awards for almost every dimension of them at some point in his career: dramaturgy; best director; set design; costume design; lighting; best actor. A lauded artist in residence for several German theatres and the Chapter Arts Centre in Wales, he has been commissioned by the British Council and the Royal Court Theatre in London and invited as Director of the *Ecole des Maîtres* in Italy, Portugal, France, and Belgium. He has collaborated with dozens of international artists as director, actor, translator, and in published editions. Spregelburd's total immersion into all aspects of theatre and its production adds unique dimensions to spectators' and readers' notions of theatre and performance as artistic genres. His ideas, humor, and innovation are infectious, stimulating, and entertaining. Their affective and intellectual impact resonates with spectators long after the curtain has closed.

Gail A. Bulman

Notes

1 Osvaldo Pellettieri, "Modernidad y posmodernidad en el teatro argentino actual," in *El teatro y su crítica*, ed. Osvaldo Pellettieri (Buenos Aires: Galerna, 1998), 159–160.
2 Jorge Dubatti, "Hacia una relectura post-postmoderna del teatro argentino: notas sobre Rafael Spregelburd," in *El teatro sabe: La relación escena/conocimiento en once ensayos de teatro comparado* (Buenos Aires: Atuel, 2005), 249–253.
3 Paola Hernández, "Escenas desintegradas: Federico León y Rafael Spregelburd," *Telóndefondo: Revista de teoría y crítica teatral número* 11 (2010): 3–4, http://revistascientificas.filo.uba.ar/index.php/telondefondo/issue/view/294
4 Personal interview 2021.
5 Rafael Spregelburd, "A modo de epílogo: Conversación entre Rafael Spregelburd y Javier Daulte," in *Bizarra: una saga argentina* (Buenos Aires: Editorial Entropía, 2008), 517–518.

Major works

Spam (2014)
Apátrida [Stateless] (2010)
Todo [Everything] (2009)
La terquedad [Stubborness] (2007)
La paranoia [Paranoia] (2007)
Bizarra (2003)
El pánico [Panic] (2003)

Un momento argentino [An Argentinian Moment] (2002)
La escala humana [The Human Ladder] (2000)
Cuadro de asfixia [Suffocation Box] (1996)

Published works

Santa Cecilia de Borja en Zaragoza. Panorama teatral/Nuevo teatro argentino. Compiled by Jorge Dubatti. Buenos Aires: Editorial Interzona, 2014.
Todo. Apátrida. Envidia. Buenos Aires: Suplemento Escritores del Diario Perfil, 2011.
La terquedad. Buenos Aires: Atuel, 2009.
La inapetencia; La extravagancia; La modestia. Buenos Aires: Suplemento Escritores del Diario Perfil, 2009.
Bizarra. Buenos Aires: Editorial Entropía, 2008.
Heptalogía de Hieronymus Bosch I: La inapetencia; La extravagancia; La modestia. Buenos Aires: Adriana Hidalgo Editores, 2000.
Teatro incompleto I: Destino de dos cosas o de tres, Cucha de almas, Remanente de invierno, La tiniebla, Entretanto las grandes urbes. Buenos Aires: Edición del autor, 1996.

Further reading

Bulman, Gail. *Staging Words, Performing Worlds: Intertextuality and Nation in Contemporary Latin American Theatre*. Lewisburg, PA: Bucknell University Press, 2007.
Coce, María Victoria. "El Katak de Rafael Spregelburd y el triunfo del habla sin lengua." *Telóndefondo: Revista de teoría y crítica teatral* 29 (2019): 23–32.
Graham-Jones, Jean. "Anticipated Failure, or Translating Rafael Spregelburd's Plays into English." *Symposium: A Quarterly Journal in Modern Literatures* 68.3 (Fall 2014): 135–146.
Lencina, Victoria Julia. "¿El Estado es ficción? Absurdo, liminalidad y anacronismos en *Apátrida, doscientos años y unos meses* de Rafael Spregelburd." *Telóndefondo: Revista de teoría y crítica teatral* 27 (2018): 49–56.
Rodríguez Carranza, Luz. "Fábulas morales: *Todo*, de Rafael Spregelburd." In *Imágenes y realismos en América Latina*, edited by Miguel Caballero Vázquez and Luz Rodríguez Carranza, 119–130. Leiden, Netherlands: Almenara Press, 2014.
Spregelburd, Rafael and Jean Graham-Jones. "Life, of Course." *Theatre Journal* 59.3 (October 2007): 373–377.

CARIDAD SVICH (PHILADELPHIA, PENNSYLVANIA, 1963–)

Born in Philadelphia to Cuban-Argentine-Spanish-Croatian parents, playwright Caridad Svich's work is transnational and transcultural in scope, complicating notions of what Latinx identity can encompass.

Svich has written over eighty full-length plays and thirty-five translations. Her plays draw on diaspora, family legacies of migration, displacement, dislocation, and re-location to tackle notions of wanderlust, dispossession, biculturalism, bilingualism, and construction of identity, themes that run rampant through her prolific *oeuvre*. Poetry, musicality, and a fluid sense of space and time are central to Svich's writing and, oftentimes, are the playwright's entry point into the storytelling. Her theatre is imbued by her ethnic and cultural backgrounds which are fundamental to her writing. She embraces "hybridity and a syncretic way of seeing the world" in her work.[1] Her theatre is saturated with ancestral memories that are retold by family members.

Svich is closely tied with María Irene Fornés. While pursuing her MFA in Playwriting at the University of California, San Diego (UCSD), Svich read Fornés's *Sarita*, immediately feeling a connection with Fornés's style of writing, most notably form and content. Later, she spent four consecutive years in the Hispanic Playwrights-in-Residence program at International Arts Relations (INTAR) led by Fornés (1988–1992). During this time, Svich wrote four full-length plays, including *Any Place but Here* which received a New York City production in 1995 under the direction of Fornés at Theater for the New City.

Svich's work defies labels and genre. She sees herself as a writer first and foremost: "no borders, no party lines, just my imagination and what I can produce."[2] Her plays are not always necessarily about Latinxs. For instance, *Any Place but Here* uses realistic dialogue and a traditional plot structure to tell the story of two working-class couples in New Jersey; the play does not explicitly call for Latinx actors nor does it comment on Latinidad. The one-man show *The Booth Variations* (2004) (co-written with Todd Cerveris) is as much a multimedia performance as it is a play. The show focuses on Edwin Booth who is trying to overcome troublesome relationships with his alcoholic father and infamous brother. Svich expands on many of these themes in *Archipelago* (2016), a two-hander that questions the mystery of love, specifically asking what draws people together and what pushes them apart. While these plays can be performed with Latinx casts, nothing about the worlds of these plays is explicitly Latinx.

The same is true of Svich's later works commenting on climate change. These plays—*The Way of Water* (2012), *Red Bike* (2018), and *Trouble in Kind* (2018), for example—are experimental in format, save for *The Way of Water*, and can be staged in radically different ways. Branching off conversations about climate change and our responsibility to address the human impact on global warming, *Red Bike* questions what possibilities the future holds in the United States. The titular red bike, then, becomes a metaphor for the ways that bikes held endless possibilities and helped imagine a world bigger than the one immediately surrounding us. As with the majority of Svich's body of work, notions of (un)belonging and (dis)location drive the play forward.

Other plays, such as *Prodigal Kiss* (1999), explicitly tackle and disrupt Latinx identity. This play dramatizes the crises of displacement, in particular how being displaced disrupts one's understanding of identity and what one's place is in the new environment. The play, at its root, is about immigration, however not from a specific Latin American country, although the central character of Marcela is from Cuba. The other characters arrive in the United States from various cities called Santiago in different Latin American countries, and in one instance, from Spain. Once they arrive in the United States, they don't instantly become US Americans. Rather, they become some exoticized "Latin Other" who must negotiate their various identities throughout the play. *Prodigal Kiss* underscores how transculturation is never a simple experience; rather, it is tied to notions of trauma, the politics of identity, belonging, and (dis)location.

Svich's best known and most-produced works are *Twelve Ophelias (a play with broken songs)* (2008) and *Iphigenia Crash Land Falls on the Neon Shell That Was Once Her Heart (a rave fable)* (2004) in addition to notable adaptions such as *The House of the Spirits* (2008) and *In the Time of the Butterflies* (2011). *Twelve Ophelias* re-imagines *Hamlet*'s Ophelia in a neo-Elizabethan Appalachia; in this new world, Ophelia forges a new path for herself, reclaiming the agency that is taken from her in Shakespeare's play. Arguably, Svich's other major work is *Iphigenia Crash Land Falls*, which transposes the Greek tragedy into an underworld of sex, drugs, and trance music. The play uses video and live streaming images to tell the story of Iphigenia, now the daughter of a celebrity politician. In this new world, she gets involved with Achilles, now a transgender glam rock star, as she desperately tries to avoid her fate.

Svich's career is best understood as one focused on collaboration and community. Through her various translation, editing, and advocacy projects, she has forged inclusive spaces for Latinx and typically marginalized theatre-makers. Her edited and co-edited collections, such as *Out of the Fringe: Contemporary Latina/Latino Theatre and Performance* (1999), are field-defining collections that have addressed serious gaps in US transnational theatre. Moreover, Svich is the founder of NoPassport, a theatre alliance and press. She has also published over 100 books with NoPassport Press.

In 2012, Caridad Svich won the OBIE Award for Lifetime Achievement, making her one of only a handful of Latinx recipients of the prestigious award, joining María Irene Fornés and Repertorio Español. Svich's growing body of work continues to expand notions of what a Latinx play can be and, by extension, what heights a Latinx playwright can reach. As her work demonstrates, she adds complexity to identity, dislocation, belonging, and ancestral memories as they materialize onstage.

Trevor Boffone

Notes

1. Emilio Rodriguez, "This Thing of Hers: Caridad Svich Reflects on Her Body of Work," *HowlRound*, July 28, 2016. Accessed November 11, 2020, https://howlround.com/thing-hers
2. Caridad Svich, "Home, Desire, Memory: There Are No Borders Here (A Latina Playwright Comes of Age in America)," in *Puro Teatro: A Latina Anthology*, edited by Alberto Sandoval-Sánchez and Nancy Saporta Sternbach (Tucson: University of Arizona Press, 2000): 322.

Major works

Red Bike (2018)
Archipelago (2016)
Guapa (2012)
The House of the Spirits (2009)
Twelve Ophelias (a play with broken songs) (2008)
The Tropic of X (2007)
Iphigenia Crash Land Falls on the Neon Shell That Was Once Her Heart (a rave fable) (2004)
Prodigal Kiss (1999)
Alchemy of Desire/Dead-Man's Blues (1994)
Any Place but Here (1992)

Published works

Iphigenia Crash Land Falls on The Neon Shell That Was Once Her Heart. New York: Broadway Play Publishing, 2019.
The Hour of All Things and Other Plays. Chicago: University of Chicago Press, 2018.
JARMAN (All This Maddening Beauty) and Other Plays. Chicago: University of Chicago Press, 2016.
The Way of Water. New York City: NoPassport Press, 2013.

Further reading

Chirico, Miriam. "Hellenic Women Revisited: The Aesthetics of Mythic Revision in the Plays of Karen Hartman, Sarah Ruhl and Caridad Svich." In *Dramatic Revisions of Myths, Fairy Tales and Legends: Essays on Recent Plays*, edited by Verna A. Foster, 15–33. New York: McFarland, 2012.

Ford, Katherine. "Performing the in-between: Caridad Svich's *Iphigenia (A Rave Fable)*." *GESTOS: Revista de teoría y práctica del teatro hispánicos* 48 (2009): 89–110.

Ghavari, Lance. "Exploiting Race Technologies in Caridad Svich's *Iphigenia*." *Theatre Topics* 18.2 (2008): 223–242.

Nigro, Kirsten. "Riffing on Euripides (and Other Things): Caridad Svich's *Iphigenia Crash Land Falls on the Neon Shell That Was Once Her Heart (a Rave Fable)*." *Symposium: A Quarterly Journal in Modern Literatures* 74.1 (2020): 47–59.

Svich, Caridad. "Visions of Migrations: Internal Diasporas." *Performance Research: A Journal of Performing Arts* 6.1 (2001): 12–23.

TEATRO DE LOS ANDES (YOTALA, BOLIVIA, 1991–)

Teatro de los Andes came to life when Argentine actor, playwright, and director César Brie arrived in Bolivia in 1991 after living in Europe for sixteen years, where he participated in theatre groups such as Eugenio Barba's Odin Teatret. With Argentine actor Naira González, and Italian promoter Giampaolo Nalli (1944–2017), Brie founded the group in Yotala, near Sucre, building a self-sufficient community, with the objective of establishing an autonomous entity. Soon after, the Italians María Teresa Dal Pero (1966–2021) and Filippo Plancher, the Spaniard Emilio Martínez and the Bolivians Lucas Achirico and Gonzalo Callejas joined them. Immersed in the dramaturgical dimension of laboratory training, they started a theatrical adventure that would bring lasting national and international acclaim through plays where the Bolivian context reiteratively would come to the surface through innovative stagings. It should be noted that although Brie directed and penned most of the plays during the first stage of the group, the other members contributed to the final product using the so-called collective creation method. From their first pieces, *Colón* [Columbus] (1992), inspired mainly by Francesco Altan's cartoon character Christopher Columbus, and *Ubú en Bolivia* (1994), a free version of Alfred Jarry's (1872–1907) farce *Ubu roi* (1896), they implemented transnationalism and symbolic syncretism, as manifested, for instance, in the constant use of ritualistic artifacts from different ethnic groups that live in the country along with their particular music (one of the signature elements of their craft), problematizing any simplistic or stereotyped reading of Bolivian reality.

With the widely toured *Las abarcas del tiempo* [The Sandals of Time] (1995), in which the group pays tribute to the mining sector, their reputation was considerably cemented. The storyline follows Jacinto who gets married and in order "to build his home" goes to work in the mines, dying soon of tuberculosis only to continue his tireless wandering in the underworld. This is a fine thread that unravels around the living as well as the dead, markedly the historical and legendary characters whose stories and experiences contribute to an intertextual tapestry becoming the fundamental nucleus of the work. Among the visited real-life persons are the Indian Tomás Katari (1740–1781), who walked from Macha to the Spanish Court in Buenos Aires to demand justice; Juan Joselillo, the first Bolivian ethnologist, who died in misery in 1963; and the Italian Jesuit priest Luis Espinel (1932–1980), who was tortured and killed by paramilitary forces.

Their next major plays came at the beginning of the new millennium when Brie composed a "Political Trilogy": *The Iliad* (2000); *En un sol amarillo: Memorias de un temblor* [Under a Yellow Sun: Memories of an Earthquake] (2004); and *Otra vez Marcelo* [Once Again Marcelo] (2005). The plays reflect the worst years of the authoritarian dictatorships (1964–1982) that have ravaged the country. *The Illiad* is a meditation on violence and the use of force. Although the play's main theme was based on the King of Troy Priam's search for the body of his son Hector, from the epic poem attributed to Homer (c.800–c.701 BC), the piece was elevated to a national paradigm depicting the thousands of disappeared political victims of the military regimes. Other complementing sources came from *The Oresteia* by Aeschylus and *The Trojan Women* by Euripides, along with a letter written by Argentine author Rodolfo Walsh (1927–1977), who disappeared during his country's military repression. Besides placing the audience on both sides of the stage, the director resorted to a wide range of cultural references in the characterization of the *dramatis personae* using models from comic books, puppet shows, and even Japanese samurai warriors, among others.

In *En un sol amarillo* violence is again depicted, but this time inflicted by nature in one of the worst catastrophes in the history of the country; the earthquake that struck Aiquile, Cochabamba, on May 22, 1998. Divided into two acts, the first part of the play represents the seism based on the direct testimony of the victims. The second part exposes the shady actions of those who misappropriated the post-disaster foreign aid which included the fraudulent reconstruction of houses, some with no roofs or bathrooms. Amid the denunciations, Brie adds touches of humor for which he is well-known such as the inscription on a suspended table which reads: "The worst thing about God is that he lives in the clouds above."[1] By using ropes perched from the ceiling to which part of the props (furniture, frames, doors) were hung, the re-enactment of the cataclysmic movement was evoked by making the objects fly around with a sudden and violent thrust.

Otra vez Marcelo is based on the life of the Bolivian political leader Marcelo Quiroga Santa Cruz (1931–1980), founder of the Socialist Party in 1971, who was assassinated by orders of General Luis García Meza who took power in 1980. Marcelo and his wife Cristina share the stage and although his integrity and firmness of character come through, her loyal support and resignation are also underlined. The action sways back and forth from direct political documents (some of Quiroga's speeches and writings are included) to the poetic re-enactment of the great love they shared for their country and for democracy.

There were other topics explored by the group as expressed in *120 Kilos de Jazz* (2006) and *¿Te duele?* [Does it Hurt You?] (2007). The former, an adaptation of Brie's short story "The Jam Session of Méndez," depicts an enriched bourgeoisie whose condescending behavior and covert racism against anyone who is indigenous, or of mixed race, is extended to any object manufactured in the country. This attitude seems to have been aggravated by the imposition of neoliberalism, which rapidly swept the country from the 1990s on, and the lure of a US lifestyle. The latter play is about domestic violence focusing on how a happily wedded couple ends up living as if they were restricted to a boxing ring where two opponents have the task of destroying each other.

Brie ends his cycle of plays as director of Teatro de los Andes with *The Odyssey* (2008). He goes back to Greek mythology and its foundational stories, but this time it is Odysseus's ten-year trip back from the Trojan War to his kingdom of Ithaca which triggers his review of salient issues such as the precarious situation that some Latin American immigrants undergo when trying to make a decent living, especially in first-world countries. Another tacit topic was the return of the disillusioned migrants to their native land embroiled in civil conflicts and social unrest as Bolivia was experiencing during the onerous years of 2007–2008. The staging, surrounding the proscenium with ruffling bamboo canes, added to the symbolism expressed in the flaunting of basic elements such as water, sand, dust, and blood offered to the gods.

After Brie's departure, Nalli took the direction of the group assisted by long-standing members Achirico, Callejas, and Brazilian-born Alice

Guimarães. A transition period begins in 2010 during which other playwrights and directors have been invited to work with the group. Bolivian Diego Aramburo was recruited to give a workshop based on *Hamlet*, by Shakespeare, which became the play *Hamlet de los Andes* [Hamlet from the Andes] (2012). Reducing the characters to three and a musician, Aramburo concentrates first on the loss of the father, extending the metaphor to the situation the group was facing. Then, following Hamlet's constant wanderings throughout the Kingdom of Denmark, by association he examines the abysmal differences between the urban and the rural, meaning the Andean marginalized communities. The staging was based on the monochromic contrast of chiaroscuro, accentuated by black veiled curtains hung around the scenario, whose somber monotony was efficaciously interrupted by festive musical rhythms.

The last two productions that reached notoriety are *Mar* [Sea] (2014) and *Un buen morir* [A Good Death] (2018). Both deal with loss and survival. *Mar*, with final text by Argentine-born playwright Arístides Vargas, refers to the defeat that Bolivia suffered during the Pacific War with Chile (1879–1883), in which the country lost access to the sea, a wound that has still not been healed in the collective imaginary of its people. The plot is based on three siblings—Juana, Miguel, and Segundo—who try to carry out their mother's dying wish, to be taken, tied to a door, to the sea to rest there eternally. The mother thus becomes the metaphor of the homeland, whose heavy oppressive weight has been placed on the shoulders of her children. *Un buen morir*, a collective creation with texts by poet Alex Aillón Valverde and directed by Chilean Elías Cohen, is an intimate portrait of a mature couple facing sickness and death. The piece is a clear rumination of the vacuum left by Nalli's demise after a long sickness in 2017, by the performers Callejas and Guimarães who assumed the direction of the group.

Teatro de los Andes continues to accomplish what from the beginning was clear to them: to create theatre that would represent a physical action in the territory of Bolivia, above any illustration of an aesthetic dimension or a chosen topic. Their constant efforts to continue training and experimenting with a variety of forms have enabled them to generate historical-political oriented plays that reflect the vicissitudes of a reality which is sometimes quite difficult to discern, coming from a country called by some the "South American Tibet" for its remoteness.

Beatriz J. Rizk

Note

1 César Brie, *Teatro I* (*La ilíada*, *Las abarcas del tiempo*, *En un sol amarillo*, *Otra vez Marcelo*) (Buenos Aires: Atuel, 2014), 16.

Major works

Mar [Sea] (2014)
Hamlet de los Andes [Hamlet from the Andes] (2012)
¿Te duele? [Does it Hurt You?] (2007)
Otra vez Marcelo [Once Again Marcelo] (2005)
En un sol amarillo: Memorias de un temblor [Under a Yellow Sun: Memories of an Earthquake] (2004)
The Iliad (2000)
Las abarcas del tiempo [The Sandals of Time] (1995)
Ubú en Bolivia (1994)
Colón [Columbus] (1992)

Published works

Brie, César. *Teatro I* (*La ilíada*, *Las abarcas del tiempo*, *En un sol amarillo*, *Otra vez Marcelo*). Buenos Aires: Atuel, 2014.
Brie, César. *Teatro II* (*La odisea*, *¿Te duele?*, *Sólo los giles mueren de amor*, *El mar en el bolsillo*, *El grito de Alcorta*). Buenos Aires: Atuel, 2014.

Further reading

Aimaretti, María Gabriela. "Senderos, huellas y testimonios de un itinerario histórico: El grupo Teatro de los Andes y César Brie." *Telón de Fondo* 19 (2014): 40–80.
Atienza, Alicia María, "La Odisea de César Brie: Ulises en tiempos de la globalización. De ayer a hoy: influencias clásicas en la literatura," *Coimbra* (2012): 49–59.
Bournot, Magdalena. "Documentar la diversidad: el teatro de César Brie en Bolivia," *Iberoamericana* 18.67 (2018): 85–97.
D'Amico, Giulia. *La formazione delle'attore. Una finestra sul fare, insegnare ed assere del Teatro de los Andes*. Genova: Zona, 2017.
El Tonto del Pueblo, Revista de artes escénicas. Issues 1–5 (1995–2001). Published by Teatro de los Andes, Bolivia.
Marchiori, Fernando, ed. *César Brie e Il Teatro de los Andes*. Milano: Ubulibri, 2003.

EL TEATRO CAMPESINO (DELANO, CALIFORNIA, 1965–) AND LUIS VALDEZ (DELANO, CALIFORNIA, 1940–)

It is impossible to discuss the contributions and importance of Luis Miguel Valdez without also talking about the theatre troupe he founded in 1965, El Teatro Campesino (the Farmworkers Theatre), which moved to San Juan Bautista in 1971. The individual and the Teatro are interchangeable in their influence and impact on the American theatre as well as in the Mexican American and Latinx communities in the United States. Valdez and his troupe inspired and guided the development of a national Chicano Theatre Movement; opened the doors to Broadway and the mainstream regional theatres; and gave voices to Latinx theatre artists on stage, television, and film. Teatro Campesino is one of the longest-lasting theatres of its kind in the United States and its influence continues to inspire Latinx theatre artists across the country. No other individual or theatre company can claim such accomplishments.

Born in 1940 into a farm working family, Valdez had experienced the hardships and struggles of the people who plant and harvest the produce that feeds the nation. Valdez's early schooling was constantly interrupted, his family following the crops from farm-to-farm. Still, he earned a scholarship to San Jose State College, where his first full-length play, *The Shrunken Head of Pancho Villa*, was produced in 1964. The following year he worked with the San Francisco Mime Troupe, learning the efficacy of street theatre to educate audiences about any number of socio-political issues. Inspired by the simple but effective techniques of the Mime Troupe as well as the Mexican *carpas* (touring tent shows), he returned to his birthplace, Delano, California. There, he created what would become an international symbol of the farm workers' struggles, exposing audiences worldwide to the importance of supporting the farm workers' union being founded by the late Cesar Chavez and Dolores Huerta.

Working with people who had never seen theatre of any kind, Valdez guided the striking farm workers to improvise short satirical sketches which he termed "*actos*." The goal was to perform these actos at the edges of the fields, singing strike songs and satirizing the growers and their henchmen in order to dissuade non-union members from crossing the picket line. During this early period the Teatro's aesthetic could be described as "*rasquache*," a Mexican colloquialism that can denote something "funky," or "unsophisticated." The actos were simple but not simplistic. By 1967 the Teatro began to tour beyond the fields to other venues including union halls, colleges, high schools, and community centers, generating funds for the Union. They would go on to inspire other theatre troupes, culminating in a national network of Teatros inspired by Valdez and the Teatro's *actos*.

In 1971 Valdez and the Teatro published the *actos* in the first anthology of its kind, giving incipient Teatro members, mostly students, permission to produce them royalty-free. During this historical moment, Chicanxs were just beginning to gain entrance to colleges and universities on federal grants and the Teatro Campesino's performances gave these students a sense of pride and purpose, watching performers that looked and spoke like them. When students performed either the Campesino's *actos* or their own, their feelings of displacement were uplifted. With little or no training in theatre, these students could easily perform the *actos* by adapting them to their lived experiences.

While Valdez was guiding and directing the collective members of the Teatro in a performance style based on the *"rasquache"* aesthetic, he was also exploring the Chicanxs' roots in the Pre-Columbian cultures of the Mayans and the Aztecs. Valdez was basing his philosophy on the Maya-Quiche origin myth, *El Popol Vuh*, as well as on the influences of Mexican anthropologist, Domingo Martínez Parédez and ritual Conchero dancer and Aztec elder, Andrés Segura. Valdez hoped that other Chicanxs would study the Mayan view of life in order to understand their role(s) in the cosmos, their place in the greater scheme of things. In an effort to explain the power and energy of the indigenous spirit, Valdez wrote a poem, *"Pensamiento serpentino"* ("Serpentine Thought") in which he states:

> *El indio baila* [The indian dances]
> he dances his way to truth
> in a way intellectuals will
> never understand.[1]

For Valdez, the indigenous American dance evokes and affirms a belief in unseen powers that come from the cosmos. In this poem he was simply stating what is not palpable to the casual observer, but which is, to the indigenous dancer, Truth. This investigation of indigenous beliefs led to a new theatrical form he termed *"mitos,"* or myths. He wrote that the *acto* is the Chicano "through the eyes of man," while the *mito* is the Chicano "through the eyes of God."[2] Valdez's first exploration of the contrast between these two styles is titled *Dark Root of a Scream* (1967). This *mito* exposes the fact that thousands of Chicanos were being drafted into what many considered an immoral war in Vietnam. This play is a *mito* because it contrasts the fallen hero, Quetzalcóatl Gonzales with the actual Toltec/Aztec mythical figure of the same name, known as the Feathered Serpent. In contrast, *Soldado Razo* [Buck Private] (1971) is an *acto* about real people rather than mythical beings. Still, in a typical *acto* convention the narrator is portrayed as an allegorical figure, in this case La Muerte (Death) who (in a nod to Brecht) leaves no mystery for the audience by telling them from the beginning that Johnny is going to die.

Another essential aspect of the Valdezian/Campesino aesthetic is music; always at the core of the Teatro's creations as sung narrative, as well as instrumentally underscoring the mood and tone of a production. In 1971 Valdez and the Teatro developed another unique genre using music as its base: the *corridos* which are dramatizations of well-known Mexican ballads. Initially, the Teatro's first *corridos* were explorations of the intersections between music, narrative, and the moving body. In performance a *corrido* begins with a guitarist off to the side, singing the lyrics while the "characters" in the song move in stylized, dance-like movements, acting-out the narrative as the guitarist sings. In given moments, the actor/dancers verbalize the lyrics, speaking to one another in character.

These brief, early *corridos* developed into a full-length *corrido* titled *La carpa de los Rasquachis* [The Tent of the Underdogs] (1974–1976) about the life and death of a fictitious character named Jesús Pelado Rasquachi. It is an epic *corrido* which follows a Cantinflas-like Mexican character from crossing the border into the US and the subsequent indignities to which he is exposed until his ultimate death. The play brought together a Valdezian/Campesino style that could be defined as raucous, lively street theatre with deep socio-political and spiritual roots. The style combined elements of the *acto*, *mito*, and *corrido*, with an almost constant musical background as a handful of actors revealed the action in multiple roles with minimal costume, prop, or set changes. This was the apogee of Valdez's and the Teatro's "poor theatre," purposely based on the early twentieth-century Mexican touring tent shows.

Along with the *actos*, *corridos*, and *mitos*, Valdez began to write what he termed his *historias* or history plays. In 1978 he directed the world premiere of his first and best-known *historia*, *Zoot Suit*. Produced by the Center Theatre Group of Los Angeles, this play with music marked a turning-point in Valdez's trajectory: a fully professional production with a large multicultural cast, complete with dances and songs. This play reveals the historic injustices of the infamous Sleepy Lagoon Murder Trial and the Zoot Suit Riots that actually happened in the early 1940s in Los Angeles, California. While the Los Angeles production was filling the theatre, Valdez directed another production of the play on Broadway in 1979. Although that production lasted only one month, *Zoot Suit* kept running in Los Angeles for almost a year. It opened the doors to professional mainstream regional theatres across the country as non-Latinx producers sought to cash-in on the "Hispanic market."

In 1982 Valdez adapted *Zoot Suit* to the screen and because the motion picture was filmed as it was staged in the theatre, it gives the viewer a very good idea of the live production style. Because of the film, millions of people around the globe have witnessed this important document of Mexican/Chicanxs' history. Confirming the play's lasting relevance, Valdez directed a revival of the play in 2017 with the original producers in Los Angeles to great critical and audience acclaim. In 2010 he directed a Spanish translation of this play for the prestigious *Compañía Nacional de Teatro* (The National Theatre Company) to great success. The production toured to Bogotá, Colombia as well.

Valdez wrote and directed his second *historia*, *Bandido: Tales of Passion and Revolution*, first produced by the Teatro, in 1981. In this play Valdez revisits and revises a historical and mythical figure by dramatizing the life and death of Tiburcio Vazquez, the last man to be legally, publicly executed in California when he was hanged in 1875. Thus, he revives a historical figure who is a part of the Chicanxs' early presence in California. During the 1980s Valdez was balancing his theatrical career with his film work, a move that inspired his comedy, *I Don't Have to Show You No Stinking Badges*, which was produced by the Los Angeles Theatre Center in 1986. While Valdez had tackled stereotypical representations of Mexicans and Chicanxs throughout his playwriting career, this new play addressed a community with which he had now become all too familiar: Hollywood. This work is unique in the development of Chicanx dramaturgy as the first professionally produced play to deal with middle-class Chicanxs rather than the usual working poor and working-class characters and situations that concerned most Chicanx playwrights of the time.

By the waning years of the twentieth century Valdez continued to explore his Yaqui indigenous roots through another *historia* titled *Mummified Deer*, produced by the San Diego Repertory Theater in California in 2000, under his direction. The central figure is a fictional eighty-four-year-old Yaqui woman, Mama Chu, who has been carrying a fetus in her womb for sixty years. In true Valdezian fashion the action of the play goes back-and-forth in time and place, with Mama Chu's hospital bed as the central image. The action moves fluidly through time, a time that is measured not in minutes or hours but in heartbeats, a very important element of his neo-Mayan philosophy.

Throughout his theatrical career and in conjunction with members of the Teatro, Valdez was developing a very unique vision of theatrical theory and practice that he published as *Theatre of the Sphere: The Vibrant Being* (2021). In his Preface to Valdez's book Michael Chemers writes: "this book is as valuable to the student and practitioner of theatre as Peter Brook's *The Empty Space*, Augusto Boal's *Theatre of the Oppressed*, and Jerzy Grotowski's *Towards a Poor Theatre*."[3] Chemers also states that the book "provides the conceptual framework for Valdez's acting theory and practice, situating it in Mayan mathematics and metaphysics."

The Teatro Campesino has been Valdez's theatrical, spiritual, and creative laboratory since its inception, working with artists from all parts of the world. As the Teatro evolved it instinctively became a *familia* of people dedicated to the goals and ambitions of the troupe. Families were formed, children were born, and countless hundreds of people who have either been a part of the Teatro or who were inspired by its works over the years have gone on to start their own teatros. The Teatro Campesino is now under the leadership of a new generation that includes some of the children of the founders, producing workshops and their repertory of Spanish religious folk plays every Christmas in the San Juan Bautista mission. Most Latinx theatre scholars and artists, including actors, directors, playwrights, designers, and producers, owe their creative lives to Luis Valdez and El Teatro Campesino.

Jorge A. Huerta

Notes

1 Luis Valdez, *Early Works: Actos, Bernabe and Pensamiento Serpentino* (Houston: Arte Público Press, 1990), 177.
2 Ibid., 11.
3 Michael M. Chemers, "Introduction," in *Theatre of the Sphere: The Vibrant Being*, ed. Michael M. Chemers (London: Routledge, 2021): xiv.

Major works

Adiós, Mamá Carlota (2019)
Valley of the Heart (2018)
Mummified Deer (2000)
Bandido! (1981)
Zoot Suit (1978)

Soldado razo (acto) (1971)
Dark Root of a Scream (mito) (1967)
Los vendidos (acto) (1967)
Las dos caras del patroncito (acto) (1965)
The Shrunken Head of Pancho Villa (1964)

Published works

Mummified Deer. *Mummified Deer and Other Plays*. Houston: Arte Público Press, 2005.
Mundo Mata. Houston: Arte Público Press, 2005.
Zoot Suit and Other Plays. Houston: Arte Público Press, 1992.
Early Actos. Houston: Arte Público Press, 1990.
The Shrunken Head of Pancho Villa. In Jorge Huerta, *Necessary Theater: Six Plays About the Chicano Experience*. Houston: Arte Público Press, 1989.
Dark Root of a Scream. Faderman, Lilian and Salinas, Omar (eds). *From the Barrio*. San Francisco: Canfield Press, 1973.

Further reading

Broyles-Gonzalez, Yolanda. *El Teatro Campesino: Theater in the Chicano Movement*. Austin: University of Texas Press,1994.
Elam, Jr., Harry. *Taking it to the Streets: The Social Protest Theater of Luis Valdez and Amiri Baraka*. University of Michigan Press, 1997.
Huerta, Jorge. *Chicano Theater: Themes and Forms*. Tempe: Bilingual Press, 1982.
Huerta, Jorge. *Chicano Drama: Performance, Society and Myth*. Cambridge: Cambridge University Press, 2000.
Huerta, Jorge. "El Teatro Campesino: The Next Generation," *TheatreForum* (Fall 2001): 91–97.
Lucas, Ashley. "Prisoners on the Great White Way: *Short Eyes* and *Zoot Suit* as the First US Latino Plays on Broadway," *Latin American Theatre Review* (Fall 2009): 121–135.
Rossini, Jon D. *Contemporary Latina/o Theater: Wrighting Ethnicity*. Carbondale: Southern Illinois University Press, 2008.
Yarbro-Bejarano, Yvonne and Tomás Ybarra-Frausto. "*Zoot Suit* y el movimiento Chicano," *Plural* (April 1980): 49–56.

TEATRO LA CANDELARIA (BOGOTÁ, COLOMBIA, 1966–) AND SANTIAGO GARCÍA (1928–2020)

In a small, cobbled street in the most colonial neighborhood of Bogotá, one can find the Teatro La Candelaria, a Colombian icon of Latin American theatre. Directed by "El Maestro" Santiago García (1928–2020) from its inception until his death, more than 150 theatre professionals have been members of La Candelaria, forming a team of experimentation and creativity. Members like Patricia Ariza,

Nohra Ayala, Fernando Peñuela, César Badillo, and Santiago García have adopted a number of different roles, including directing, acting, and writing. La Candelaria is not only a place to train artists; it is also a bastion of dramatic experimentation. Together with the Experimental Theatre of Cali (TEC), La Candelaria is one of the founding centers of collective creation in Latin America, a movement that experienced a boom in the 1970s and is still popular today.

The beginning of La Candelaria parallels the transformation of theatre in Colombia. The arrival of the Japanese director Seki Sano (1905–1966) to Colombia in 1955 caused renewed interested in European trends, especially the Stanislavski method. Among the people that attended the workshops offered by Sano was the architect Santiago García, who would ultimately dedicate his life to theatre. After Sano's departure, Santiago García founded Teatro El Búho (1958–c. 1961) alongside Fausto Cabrera and Mónica Silva; this served as an important antecedent to La Candelaria and enabled García to start his career as a theatre director. Eventually, García left to hone his studies, visiting the Actors Studio in New York, Charles University in Prague, and the Berliner Ensemble. Especially important for García was Bertolt Brecht, with his ideas about the theatre's capacity to change the social reality and the promotion of theorical knowledge and self-reflection among his actors. These concepts were the beginning of the collective creation process of La Candelaria.

When García returned to the country, he became a founding member of "La Casa de la Cultura" (1966–1969), considered to be the first stage of La Candelaria. This institution was conceived to promote many art forms, but theatre was intended to financially support the enterprise. Many of the productions staged during this phase were by international playwrights (Peter Weiss, William Shakespeare, Witold Gombrowicz, Luigi Pirandello, Anton Chekhov). These early works exhibited many of the characteristics that Teatro La Candelaria maintained during its history: a centrality of the image, concrete dialogue, and exploration of the current issues in the country through plots based in a different time/space.

The second phase (1969–1971) began when the group found its headquarters in the historic Bogotá neighborhood of La Candelaria, from which they acquired their name and where they reside today. Though they continued to work on a "universal repertoire," they gave their artistic endeavors a distinctly Colombian/Latin American identity. In plays such as *La Orestiada* (1970) García aimed to nationalize the play through a collective search of images and other scenic elements in order to bring the Greek tragedy into a contemporary Colombian context. During these years, ideas intersecting theatre, praxis, politics, and aesthetics were central to debates about the creation of an authentic Latin American theatre. Different troupes found collective creation the best mechanism to achieve this goal. Especially during the 1970s and 1980s, amidst a revolutionary Latin America controlled by dictatorships, battling guerrillas, and with many artists favoring the political left, there was a desire to stage works that made all these injustices evident.

From this political reality, La Candelaria opened their third moment for the ensemble: Collective Creation (1972–1981). This moment focused on productions devised by the entire troupe under the guidance of García, a process that became their primary practice of producing original plays. By using collective creation, La Candelaria shifted power from director to actor. The actor became the central creator. They not only breathed life into the characters by giving their lines a voice, gestures, and personality, but they were also in charge of all the necessary steps to develop a new play: investigation (official and unofficial sources), improvisation about the conflicting forces of the situation, structuring of the play and final commissions for music, costumes, scenography, and dramaturgy. Although the final decisions continued to fall on the director, the director went from being able to unilaterally implement their vision, to an organizer of the group. Collective creation challenges the traditional hierarchy of the theatre through collaboration among all members and makes group negotiation its way of being.

The first work of collective creation, *Nosotros los Comunes* [We the People] (1972) was about the Colombian Comunero Rebellion (1780–1781). With minimal staging, it allowed the work to be presented in non-traditional spaces and opened opportunities for new audiences. In this play, the group raised the community as the protagonist rather than a single hero, something that would become their signature trait. This work reached such international acclaim that La Candelaria was personally invited to perform by Chilean president Salvador Allende. This success cemented their position as an essential referent in regard to collective creation.

For their next collective production, they travelled to the Llanos region in Colombia. There, they dialogued with historian Arturo Alape and researched oral traditions, including guerrilla songs from the region. The final result was *Guadalupe Años Sin Cuenta* [Guadalupe Fifty Years without Count] (1975), a play that follows the life of a guerrilla commander, Guadalupe Salcedo (1924–1957). The work sheds light on a dark Colombian reality: the state's extrajudicial murder of guerrilla fighters who had signed peace agreements with the government. The goal was, according to García, to allow the public to "see" the Colombian social conflicts from a new perspective. This reality has not lost its relevance almost fifty years after, granting the theme an unusual contemporary feel. It has been performed in Mexico, Cuba, Angola, and the United States. In Colombia alone, it exceeded a thousand performances over a period of thirteen years.

The fourth and final stage started around 1981, when García wrote *El Diálogo del Rebusque* [The Dialogue of the Search for Livelihood], which was based on texts by Francisco Quevedo. This started a period where La Candelaria devised plays written by just one of the members. Marina Lamus affirms that the group "felt the need to experiment, so that the collective method did not become a dogmatic pattern that worked like a boomerang."[1] Thus, single-author creations were also the result of the work of "what was gained in collective creation." This flexibility allowed many actors to become playwrights.

La Candelaria have performed more than fifty different plays in Colombia and done innumerable national and international tours, demonstrating their ability to stay relevant by creating original works with intelligence, humor, incisive images, and sharp dialogues. Their plays make clear the capacity of the group to foresee problems that would become endemic in Colombia, such as state-sanctioned violence and the breach of peace accords (*Guadalupe*, 1975) and the impact of drug trafficking and the ascension of drug dealers (*Lucky Strike*, 1980 and *The Roadhouse*, 1988). In the last decade, they have continued renewing their dramaturgy, as plays like *Nayra* (2012) or *Soma Mnemósine* (2013) make evident with the dislocation of the dialogue as the main axis and the use of the fragmented images that bestow a centrality to the visual. It is an effort that is maintained by their belief in the benefits of working together, despite the complications it can bring.

Collective creation allows the group to continue their labor even after the most visible leader of the group, Santiago García, died in 2020. La Candelaria keeps working with a mixture of collective and single-author plays based on solid research and the work of professionals that care about the image, aesthetics, and historical lessons of a country still immersed in a violent conflict. But their legacy stretches beyond the limits of the group. As past company members moved on to their own projects in both theatre and television, they carried with them the techniques and knowledge gained through their years with the group. La Candelaria's bequest is still present not only in groups such as Umbral Teatro or Petra Teatro, but also in many projects of community-based theatre that utilize collective creation, which is La Candelaria's greatest legacy.

Laissa M. Rodríguez Moreno

Note

1 Marina Lamus, "Del texto colectivo al individual," *Boletín Cultural y Bibliográfico*, vol. 40, no. 64 (2003), 106.

Major works

Camilo (2015)
Si el río hablara [If the River Would Talk] (2013)
A título personal (2008)
Antígona (2006)
Nayra. The Memory (2004)
En la raya [On the Verge] (1993)
The Roadhouse (1987)
Lucky Strike (1980)
Guadalupe años sin cuenta [Guadalupe Fifty Years without Count] (1975)
Nosotros los comunes [We the People] (1972)

Further reading

Aldana Cedeño, Janneth. *El Teatro de Santiago García*. Bogotá: Editorial Pontificia Universidad Javeriana, 2018.
Arcila, Gonzalo. *La Imagen Teatral en La Candelaria: Lógica y Génesis de su Proceso de Trabajo*. Bogotá: Ediciones Teatro La Candelaria, 1992.
Duque, Fernando and Prada, Jorge. *Santiago García: El Teatro como Coraje*. Bogotá: Investigación Teatral Editores; Ministerio de Cultura, 2004.
Floirán Navas, Carmen and Pecha Quimbay, Patricia. *El Teatro La Candelaria y el movimiento Teatral en Bogotá 1950–1991*. Bogotá: Alcaldía Mayor de Bogotá, 2013.
García, Santiago. *Teoría y Práctica del Teatro*. Volumes 1, 2, 3. Bogotá: Ediciones La Candelaria, 1994, 2002, 2006.
Llano Restrepo, Adriana. *Candelaria Adentro*. Bogotá: Ediciones Teatro La Candelaria, 2008.

TEATRO DE CIERTOS HABITANTES (MEXICO CITY, MEXICO, 1997–) AND CLAUDIO VALDÉS KURI (MEXICO CITY, MEXICO, 1965–)

Mexican theatre director and playwright Claudio Valdés Kuri is best known for creating theatrical pieces through intensive laboratory processes leading up to unique, interdisciplinary performances that defy traditional theatrical conventions by incorporating music, dance, film, and visual arts in surprising ways. He graduated from the Cinematographic Training Center, Mexico's premier film school. In addition, Valdés Kuri was an actor in the Austrian company Carpa Theater (1996–1999) and founded the prominent early music vocal ensemble Ars Nova (1984–2001), dedicated to the rescue and performance of Mexican Baroque music. Some of the most important institutions that have commissioned and coproduced his work include: the Edinburgh International Festival, Theater der Welt (Germany), Wiener Festwochen (Austria), Kunsten Festival des Arts (Belgium), Writers Theatre (US), Festival Internacional Cervantino (Mexico), and the National Institute of Fine Arts (Mexico), among others.

In 1997, he founded Teatro de Ciertos Habitantes (Certain Inhabitants' Theatre), a company in which he put into practice his interdisciplinary vocation as an actor, musician, and cinematographer. Teatro de Ciertos Habitantes has become one of the most recognized companies from Latin America for their innovative and avant-garde stagings. Their productions are not numerous after more than twenty years of success, but what matters to the company and the director is that they produce plays of great quality in small quantities. Their reputation has allowed them to thrive in international theatrical circuits and become an obligatory reference for any critic of Latin American contemporary theatre.

The company's poetics require continuous renovation and brings together various registers that entail the sensibility of multidisciplinary artists in order to tackle the various expressions of their art: these range from the use of musical instruments, dance, and opera singing to martial arts or Sufi dances. Valdés Kuri's aim has always been to explore the human condition through theatrical work, so the exploration and rehearsal processes include a rigorous scenic, visual, musical, and corporal investigation that has been at the core of his work. The entire rehearsal and laboratory process can last more than a year and includes intense daily work with the actors and the creative team dedicated to specific inquiries and artistic investigations. These could range from understanding the world of the Tarot to learning to play musical instruments or delving into the history of the *castrati*. Thus, the exploration stage is a laboratory process through which the actors explore themes that Valdés Kuri finds relevant to the production, but do not deal with the play itself. During the beginning of the exploration phase, actors often are not even aware of which play they will be performing.

Valdés Kuri's first production with Teatro de Ciertos Habitantes was Jean Anouilh's *Becket or The Honour of God* (1998). This play was a defining moment in the Mexican theatre scene, primarily because of its innovative staging. In this adaptation of Anouilh's play, five actors play multiple roles (the original requires more than thirty actors) on a stone stairway inside a convent as the only stage. The staging required the actors to make very precise movements set to live music. Originally, the company planned on twenty presentations, but the play was such an enormous success that the season extended to 100 sold-out performances and a national tour. Yet, it was their second play, *De monstruos y prodigios, la historia de los castrati* [Of Monsters and Prodigies, the History of the Castrati] that led the company towards rising international recognition. The play, written by Jorge Kuri and Valdés Kuri, premiered in Spain in 2000 and continued with a long and successful string of performances that lasted until 2011. The story spans several centuries, from the seventeenth century to the present, and focuses on the Italian *castrati* whose voices were considered a true phenomenon of human nature. The performance itself was created as a didactic concert of sorts since the text is written as a scientific treatise. It is told by a few main characters that add their own performative subtexts to the play, as they alter the text through their playful gestures and the incorporation of elements unrelated to the main purpose of the scientific treatise (music, dance, mime, and the art of classical equestrian). Like *Becket*, this play thrives on an economy of scenic resources, with an empty stage where actors dramatize an academic lecture.

Their production of *The Gray Automobile* (2003) is of even simpler format with respect to the previous ones in which Valdés Kuri unites cinema with theatre and music, in this case the 1919 film by Enrique Rosas of the same title. The performance builds upon the *benshi* tradition, a silent film narrative in which an actor next to the screen plays all the voices of the characters. In Japan, there was usually only one *benshi*. Valdés Kuri added a Japanese *benshi*, a Mexican *benshi*, and a pianist. The work is a reflection on sound, which moves from language to the extreme of noises. Other important works have been *¿Dónde estaré esta noche?* [Where Will I Be Tonight?] (2004), authored by Maricarmen Gutierrez and Valdés Kuri, a collaboration done with Teatro de los Andes's actress María Teresa dal Pero in which she portrays Joan of Arc. This play invited the audience to listen to their inner voices regardless of external stimuli. *El Gallo* (2009), an opera for actors composed by Paul Barker for the company in an invented language, is nourished by the interpretation of a multi-tasking interpreter that can be a singer, actor, and dancer. The performance expresses the inner longings and fears faced by the interpreters as they embark on the creative challenges of staging an artistic production. The need to promote this type of multidisciplinary actor increases with the staging of the Spanish Golden Age auto sacramental *Life is a Dream* (2014) by Pedro Calderón de la Barca, where actors had to perform as well as sing, dance, and play instruments while saying a text in verse and moving in geometrical patterns.

Valdés Kuri understands his theatrical aesthetic as "Baroque austerity," in the sense that his performances occurs on an empty space, even if they have large-scale elements. For example, in *De monstruos y prodigios* he used several tons of sand to cover the stage, but the actors were still in an empty space; or in his staging of Arthur Honegger's symphonic oratory *Joan of Arc at the Stake* (2018), where an entire concert hall is invaded with one tall ladder as the only scenic element. Nevertheless, the empty space is filled with the baroque in terms of interpretation and levels of discourse. His productions are characterized by a great deal of simultaneity, with multiple events occurring concurrently onstage. Another characteristic is that generally all the actors have the same level of stage presence without protagonists. His work has been presented throughout more than 200 venues in the five continents, from the most sophisticated stages in major cities to the most remote populations in rural areas. Thus, Valdés Kuri has opened new routes for Mexican and Latin American theatre abroad and models for creation/production in the country. In addition, he founded ArtBoretum, Center for the Creation, Education, and Collaboration in the Performing Arts in 2018 with the goal of sharing knowledge and experience and supporting the laboratory processes of the company and other artists. Throughout it all, he continues the type of work that characterizes him to date: an interdisciplinary theatre that aims to communicate a human experience in search of an expanded consciousness.

Analola Santana

Major works

Joan of Arc at the Stake (2018)
Life is a Dream (2013)
El gallo (2009)
¿Dónde estaré esta noche? [Where Will I Be Tonight?] (2004)
El automobil gris [The Gray Automobile] (2002)
De monstruos y prodigios, la historia de los castrati [Of Monsters and Prodigies, the History of the Castrati] (2000)
Becket or The Honour of God (1998)

Further reading

Perales, Rosalina. "El mundo al revés: Inversión y carnavalización de la historia." *Discursos teatrales en los albores del siglo XXI.* Eds. Juan Villegas, Alicia del Campo, and Mario Rojas. Irvine: Gestos, 2001. 173–185.

Rizk, Beatriz. "El teatro ante la globalización." *Artes La Revista* 11.8 (2012): 35–49.

Valdés Kuri, Claudio. "Breaking the North/South Paradigm." *Theatre and Cartographies of Power: Repositioning the Latina/o Americas.* Eds. Jimmy Noriega and Analola Santana. Carbondale: Southern Illinois University Press, 2018. 227–230.

Valdés Kuri, Claudio and Analola Santana. "Between Pen and Sweat: An Account of an Experience between a Director and a Dramaturg." *Theatre Topics* 26.1 (March 2016): 131–140.

Zien, Katherine. "Troubling Multiculturalisms: Staging Trans/National Identities in Teatro de Ciertos Habitantes's *El Gallo.*" *Theatre Survey* 55.3 (2014): 343–361.

TEATRO LA FRAGUA (EL PROGRESO, HONDURAS, 1979–)

Founded in 1979 by US-born Jesuit priest Jack Warner and based in El Progreso, Yoro, Teatro La Fragua (TLF) has been creating theatre for over four decades. La Fragua serves community needs, honors Honduran culture, and brings education and theatre to multi-generational audiences. The company's repertoire includes original works devised from Central American indigenous stories and Honduran history, Western classics adapted to Honduran contexts, re-mountings of scripts created by renowned hemispheric political theatres (such as Teatro Campesino and Teatro Experimental de Cali), children's theatre, and ecclesiastic performances. TLF's diverse work is inextricable from its mission: "to awaken the creativity of the people through art in order to find solutions to present day problems."[1] TLF is a vital resource for its local communities. Through tours and collaborations around the world, the company has also built a national and international profile.

Warner first visited Latin America in the mid-1970s, after finishing his education as a Jesuit priest. Upon completing his MFA at the Goodman School of Theatre in Chicago, Warner relocated to Honduras with the express intent of forming a theatre. While Warner sees La Fragua as carrying on aspects of Jesuit theatre traditions, his theatre training in the poor theatre aesthetics and physical rigor of Jerzy Grotowski also contours the work of the company. La Fragua presented their first performance in July 1979 in Olanchito. They used a small adobe house as a makeshift theatre for an audience of eighty. In 1980, the company relocated to El Progreso and moved into a large, long-neglected building. Through decades of making theatre, TLF has grown into a home base that now includes a 300-seat theatre, multiple studio spaces, and dedicated rehearsal rooms. The company hosts an annual, summer festival of theatre (La Temporada de Expresión Artística); a residency for new Honduran theatre companies (Muestra Cultural en Escena); a dance school for children; theatre training for emerging actors and artists; and multi-disciplinary performances, from improv comedy to music concerts. La Fragua regularly tours theatre performances to rural and urban communities of their region. Simultaneously, their hemispheric and global production schedule has grown, as well. In the 1990s and early 2000s, La Fragua presented work throughout the Americas and Europe, and the company was featured in the award-winning documentary ¡Theatre! And the Spirit of Change in Honduras.

The company's productions are bare-bones endeavors. Performers are the storytellers, supported by elemental props, costumes, and sets. Set pieces might consist of a painted cardboard sun, mountains, or a moon. A character change may be represented solely by the donning of a hat or a large name tag.[2] These aesthetics call Bertolt Brecht to mind. Warner is well aware that Brecht (like Grotowski) has been a major influence throughout Latin America, but he is careful to distinguish La Fragua from explicitly political theatre. Brecht's practices, according to Warner, are too directly confrontational for La Fragua. Though the group engages with the contemporary struggles of its communities, they do so indirectly, situating specific issues within allegorical or archetypal circumstances. The delicate dance of serving the community while simultaneously surviving national and local social and governmental precarity has been key to the company's longevity. In terms of La Fragua's Jesuit foundations, Warner often expresses his belief that theatre and religion share the same goals. "Art and religion," Warner holds, "spring from the same roots—our need to be in touch with something beyond us"; the priest and the director are "working toward the same thing: to make people realize themselves."[3]

In La Fragua's production work, Honduran artists and audiences see their values, cultures, and circumstances represented and celebrated. The group mines Honduran history to create original works while also regularly adapting extant material to Honduran contexts. The company performs new and adapted work in El Progreso and on tour, with the goal of cultivating cultural pride. Among the most popular and successful endeavors of the company are its ecclesiastic performances.

These, too, are adapted to include Honduran aesthetic, geographical, cultural, and historical details. La Fragua's annual *Navidad Nuestra* [Our Christmas] (1984), for example, remains grounded in the structure of medieval religious performance, *pastorelas*, and the Christian story of the birth of Jesus, but has been infused with Honduran details and sensibilities. When María and José visit her cousin, the house is described by the actors as a "a typical Honduran village" replete with a yard surrounded by animals. The comic shepherds' jokes and antics are tailored to Honduran references. Keeping with poor theatre aesthetics, an actor serves as the donkey María rides, and José mimes holding a baby Jesus.

Warner, the central visionary of La Fragua, stewards the company with a core group of fellow artists. A number of these artists, such as Edy Baharona, who has increasingly taken on leadership responsibilities, have been with the group from its first production. Members of the company are paid living wages and complete a regular work week with hours dedicated to training, performing, and teaching. La Fragua welcomes company members of all ages, from all backgrounds and professions. The company always hails its communities into a collaborative relationship, intoning at every performance: "Earth, air, water and fire; we are all Teatro La Fragua."

In the aftermath of the devastation of Hurricane Mitch (1988), La Fragua created "Emergency Theatre," workshops through which displaced Hondurans could "express and process their experience."[4] From these workshops grew the "cuentos infantiles," children's theatre performances that are both educational and therapeutic. Later, in 1996, La Fragua collaborated with striking workers at the Tacamiche banana camp to tour a double bill: an original work created and performed with the workers and a La Fragua adaptation of *Fuente Ovejuna* (Lope de Vega). Throughout the 1990s, the group developed a trilogy of plays dedicated to Central American history. Warner describes the trilogy as an intervention into an educational system that fails to adequately address local and regional history.

The company's work with adaptation, translation, and multi-disciplinary exploration has been vast. In the early 1990s, La Fragua explored hemispheric experiences of longing and freedom through dance, video, and drama with US based artist Anita González (*Dreams and Reality*, 1993), who trained and worked with the company in residence in El Progreso. TLF's collaborations with US playwright Carlos Morton have connected Honduran history to hemispheric history. *Romero de las Américas* (1999, Honduras; North America tour 2001) tells the story of the assassination of social justice activist Archbishop Oscar Romero of El Salvador. TLF's 2006 production of *Los Fatherless*, Morton's play about youth gangs at the US–Mexico border, situated border violence as hemispheric violence, with resonances across both central and North America.[5] In the midst of international tours and collaborations, La Fragua has maintained its commitment to local communities, staging their annual productions, such as *Nuestra Navidad*, regardless of their international schedule. During the COVID-19 pandemic, the company continued to support community through regular broadcasts of radio adaptations of work by Ruben Darío, José Martí, and others.

La Fragua translates to "the forge," and the company indeed figures itself as such: a site through which Hondurans might tend their past, care for their present, and imagine and enact a future. "We put on plays," the company states, "because it is our way of saying: we are alive. Honduras counts and no matter if you are poor or illiterate, we all have a voice."[6] La Fragua's deep and abiding connection to its communities is evidenced by their work, growth, and sustained presence in El Progreso and beyond.

Lisa Jackson-Schebetta

Notes

1 "About Us," *Teatro La Fragua*, accessed March 2, 2021, www.teatrolafragua.org/INDICE.HTM
2 These aesthetics are showcased in the 1991 film *¡Teatro!: Theatre and the Spirit of Change in Honduras*, which includes clips of a La Fragua production of *Two Faces of the Boss* by Luis Valdez and el Teatro Campesino.
3 *¡Teatro!: Theatre and the Spirit of Change in Honduras*. Warner often returns to and repeats these ideas in multiple publications.
4 Deb Cohen, "Teatro La Fragua: The Impact of 25 Years," *Latin American Theatre Review* (Fall 2005): 135.
5 Both of these plays were written by Morton and adapted by Morton for TLF.
6 *¡Teatro!: Theatre and the Spirit of Change in Honduras*.

Major works

Radio teatro (2020)
Los Fatherless (in collaboration with Carlos Morton) (2006)
Réquiem por el Padre de Las Casas [Requiem for Father Las Casas] (2001)
Romero de las Américas (in collaboration with Carlos Morton) [Romero of the Americas] (1999)
Tacamiche and *Fuente Ovejuna* (1996)
Sueño nuevo (in collaboration with Anita González) [Dreams and Reality] (1993)
El origen del maíz [The Origin of Corn] (1988)

El asesinato de Jesús [The Murder of Jesus] (1984–present)
Navidad nuestra [Our Christmas] (1984–present)
Misión de la isla Vacabeza [Mission to the Vacabeza Island] (1982, remounted in 2019)

Further reading

Castro, Carlos M. "Teatro en Honduras: La década en cuatro escenas y un intermedio." *Latin American Theatre Review* (Fall 2000): 133–142.
Fleming, John. "Honduras's Teatro La Fragua: The Many Faces of Political Theatre." *TDR* 174 (Summer 2002): 47–65.
Inczauskis, David J. *La Fragua: El teatro jesuita de Centroamerica*. San Salvador, El Salvador: UCA Editores, 2019.
Warner, Jack. *Teatro in Times of Plague*. Teatro La Fragua (2020). www.teatrolafragua.org/ayuda/NL60.html
Yates, Pamela, Ruth Shapiro, and Edward Burke, dirs. *¡Teatro!: Theatre and the Spirit of Change in Honduras*. New York: Burke/Shapiro Productions, 1991. Film.

TEATRO EL GALPÓN (MONTEVIDEO, URUGUAY, 1949–)

Emerging in the post-war years, Teatro El Galpón opened its doors on September 2, 1949, in a country that was experiencing a cultural and artistic period that continues to have lasting impacts. Since 1949, this institution has functioned as a cultural center and school for artists and practitioners to gather, create productions, train, and invite the public to enjoy socially, politically, and aesthetically engaged theatre. Uruguay's agricultural and livestock production during World War II resulted in a period of economic prosperity. This economic boom combined with the liberal reforms put in place earlier in the twentieth century by President José Battle y Ordóñez helped make Uruguay one of the most egalitarian and advanced countries in South America in the immediate post-war years. Uruguay was often referred to as the "Switzerland of the Americas" because of its political stability, high literacy rates, progressive social laws, and wealth attributed to secret banking laws. Artistic and cultural movements flourished in this atmosphere. Uruguay was investing in the arts, and the arts could be seen by some as offering potential spaces to educate citizens. Although Uruguay already had a tradition of supporting official theatre through La Casa de Arte since 1928, the 1940s saw transformations that resulted in the contemporary theatre landscape that is present today and includes state-supported venues.

At the same time, writers and artists who formed part of the Generation of '45 began bringing Modernist elements and focused a critical eye toward traditional pillars of society and urban life as they published in newspapers, journals and editorial houses. In addition to the infrastructure being built through universities and state-supported theatres, other practitioners were continuing to nurture the independent theatre scene that had given rise to the impetus for building those institutional venues. Often, these independent directors, actors, and artists found themselves at odds with traditional works staged in official theatres and the elitist structures that supported them. In response, many of the independent theatres organized to form the Uruguayan Federation of Independent Theatres (FUTI) in 1947. One of the most significant promoters of the independent theatre movement was director Atahualpa del Cioppo, whose troupe La Isla joined forces with some of the members from the Teatro del Pueblo del Uruguay (founded in 1937 by Manuel Domínguez Santamaría) to create Teatro El Galpón. César Campodónico, who had become a member of Teatro del Pueblo in 1948, joined del Cioppo in co-founding El Galpón. The group took its name from the shed they rented as a place to rehearse and stage their performances. Their first staging was in 1950, with *Las de Barranco* [Those from the Ravine] by Gregorio Laferrere, a comedy about the widow of a military officer left to raise three daughters with few economic resources, and who will do anything to survive. Eventually they would open a real theatre space in 1951, named the Sala Mercedes, which was later demolished.

In 1957, del Cioppo directed Bertolt Brecht's *Threepenny Opera* in Uruguay for the first time, and he would also stage works by internationally acclaimed dramatists such as Anton Chekhov, Arthur Miller, Henrik Ibsen, Luigi Pirandello, and Roberto Arlt along with those by prominent national authors such as Mario Benedetti. Del Cioppo was instrumental in bringing European vanguardist theatre to Latin America, and his productions often featured aesthetics from Brechtian epic theatre, as well as an emphasis on psychological and emotional realism as seen in Stanislavski's methods for acting. Del Cioppo's work reflected his indefatigable advocacy for high-quality independent theatre that often promoted historical and leftist themes. El Galpón also fulfilled the mission of bringing theatre to children. In 1952, it founded the Escuela Titiriterosa for puppetry arts, which flourished under the direction of Rosita Baffico.

El Galpón continued to grow in the 1960s, expanding to acquire the Grand Palace movie theatre, which it transformed into a theatre space. However, by 1973 the independent theatre scene was beginning to feel the pressure from the military dictatorship. Juan M. Bordaberry's coup in 1973 and his dissolution of the democratically elected legislative branches of government plunged Uruguay into a dictatorship that lasted until 1985. El Galpón persevered despite threats and other state violence until 1976, when it was closed by the government and its assets were seized. Two plays in particular were responsible for provoking the government's ire, *Libertad, Libertad* [Liberty, Liberty] (1968) written by Flavio Rangel and Millôr Fernandes and originally directed in Rio de Janeiro by Augusto Boal. The play centered on the theme of freedom and was considered to be a subversive and Communist text by the Uruguayan government. The play itself is a collage of intertextual materials taken from other well-known plays, musical pieces, political speeches and essays, negro hymns, revolutionary war songs, and other pieces from all over the world. These scenes incorporate dialogue and lyrics along with actor testimonies that deal with themes of resistance and revolution. The Uruguayan version was performed on May Day in various cities around the country as well as at Frente Amplio union committee meetings (the Frente Amplio is considered a leftist political party). Participation in the theatre piece resulted in imprisonment and torture for some of its actors.

The other play, *La Reja* [The Grille] (1972), written by Andrés Castillo, and directed by Rosita Baffico, was about women prisoners detained in a center located in the former School of Nursing in Montevideo, and it was a direct affront to Jorge Pacheco Areco's establishment of Emergency Security Powers, which eventually allowed for the suspension of constitutional and individual liberties by the government. The military and the police confiscated El Galpón's version of the play and suspended production in 1976, when they stormed the theatre. Many of El Galpón's members fled to Mexico to avoid persecution, where they were granted asylum. El Galpón resided in Mexico between 1976 and 1984, and del Cioppo and co-founder César Campodónico continued to stage productions.

In 1979, they established El Galpón's Mexican headquarters, where they hosted writers, performance troupes, films, concerts, and many other cultural activities, in addition to staging their own performances. Benedetti's *Pedro y el capitán* [Pedro and the Captain] (1979) was one of the group's most popular plays during this time, as it denounced the use of torture during the dictatorship. El Galpón toured throughout Mexico and traveled abroad in the Americas and Europe. Another important play from the group's time in exile was *Artigas General del Pueblo* [Artigas, the People's General] (1981), written by Milton Schinca and Rubén Yañez, and co-directed by del Cioppo and Campodónico.

This play showed Uruguay's national founder in stark contrast to the military government in place at the time. Artigas created the national army to liberate the people of Uruguay, and El Galpón wanted to use the historical figure to demonstrate how the current army was incarcerating students, workers, and its own members through repressive means that subverted Artigas's original drive for freedom. During their time in exile, the group performed over 2,500 times, with 250 of those performances outside of Mexico. In addition to plays already mentioned, the group performed texts by Brecht, Aristophanes, Alfred Jarry, and Molière. During this time the troupe also created collective theatre pieces and innovated with plays such as *Puro cuento* [Tall Tales] (1981), which was based on a collage of excerpts taken from short stories by Latin American writers in which they relied on audience participation and improvisation during the performance. Another branch of the group also continued to perform puppet theatre during this time in Mexico.

As the dictatorship was nearing its end, del Cioppo returned to Uruguay in September 1984, and the rest of the cast followed in October of that same year. They were reunited with members who had stayed behind and worked to combat censorship and other repression by the government. Although El Galpón was officially re-instituted under the democratically elected government of Julio María Sanguinetti in 1985, during the dictatorship the Sala Mercedes was demolished and most of the group's assets and archives were sold off, lost, or dispersed. The group re-opened in the Sala 18 with *Artigas, General del Pueblo*. El Galpón performed this play throughout its years in exile as an opposition to dictatorship, so it was an apt new beginning as they re-established their presence in Montevideo. Recently the Brazilian theatre company Ponto de Partida performed their musical *Voy a Volver* [I am Going to Return] in 2018 in Uruguay at El Galpón, where they tell the story of El Galpón's exile in Mexico. Ponto de Partida interviewed many of El Galpón's members who spent time in exile, collected historical documents and information in Montevideo, and incorporated the words of authors like Eduardo Galeano and Mario Benedetti, who were exiled and fought against the dictatorships. The piece is not a typical musical, although it includes many songs from Latin America and Brazil, and the only objects used on stage were large trunks symbolizing the plight of those who are exiled and refugeed, and other conditions of displacement.

The Teatro Galpón has continued to be a leader in promoting theatre arts, music, and publishing, by expanding access for Uruguayans through community partnerships. These partnerships reveal El Galpón's long-standing commitment to fostering an infrastructure that supports independent cultural development and removes barriers to access for the public to enjoy these activities. In 1997, El Galpón entered into a unique partnership with the Teatro Circular de Montevideo and launched the Socio Espectacular. For a monthly payment, spectators have free access to performances at El Galpón, the Teatro Circular, the Comedia Nacional, screenings at movie theatres, a monthly collection of books organized by the Editorial Banda Oriental, sporting events and musical programs at the Orquestra Filarmónica. El Galpón's legacy is twofold. The theatre is the longest continuously running theatre in South America, having produced hundreds of plays, and it now participates in a national network of united theatre practitioners that has increased visibility and support for art and culture in diverse fields. El Galpón also counts a legacy of international influence through its eight years of exile in Mexico, as well as its robust history of international tours.

Sarah M. Misemer

Major works

La travesía involuntaria [The Involuntary Crossing] (2020)
Nosotros los héroes [We the Heroes] (2003)
Un cielo de diamantes [A Diamond Sky] (1996)
Artigas, General del pueblo [Artigas, the People's General] (1981)
Pedro y el capitán [Pedro and the Captain] (1979)
La reja [The Grille] (1972)
Libertad, Libertad [Liberty, Liberty] (1968)
La tregua [The Truce] (1963)
The Caucasian Chalk Circle (1959)
Las brujas de Salem [The Crucible] (1955)

Further reading

Campodónico, César. *El vestuario se apolliló*. Montevideo: Ediciones Banda Oriental, 1999.
Mirza, Roger. *La Escena bajo vigilancia: teatro, dictadura y resistencia: un microsistema teatral emergente bajo la dictadura*. Montevideo: Ediciones Banda Oriental, 2007.
Pignatorio Calero, Jorge. *La aventura del teatro independiente uruguayo*. Montevideo: Cal y Canto, 1997.
Reherman, Carlos. *Vanguardias retrasadas en el teatro uruguayo: el rol actualizador de Teatro Uno*. 2014, www.colibri.udelar.edu.uy/jspui/bitstream/ 20.500.12008/9273/1/Rehermann%2C%20Carlos.pdf
Ulive, Ugo. *Memorias de teatro y cine*. Montevideo: Ediciones Trilce, 2007.
Yañez, Rubén. "Los ocho años de exilio de El Galpón." *Revista Conjunto* 79 (1986): 10–14.

TEATRO LÍNEA DE SOMBRA (MONTERREY, MEXICO, 1993–)

Founded in Monterrey, but based in Mexico City since 1994, Teatro Línea de Sombra (TLS) has become one of the most innovative Latin American theatre groups that fuses theatre, documentary research, human rights work, and education. Composed of a diverse group of actors, visual and digital artists, musicians, sociologists, director Jorge Vargas, and other members (Alicia Laguna, Eduardo Bernal, Zuadd Atala, and Raúl Mendoza, among others) study, research, and document historical events to create theatrical stories. The group engages with social justice, be it through the exploration of themes in their performances, for example migration, femicides, and forced disappearances, or directly through their involvement with migrant shelters in border towns (building a chapel, providing a bread oven, among other contributions). Their aesthetics and methodology combine research materials, such as documents, archives, newspaper stories, biographies, while also providing an intertextuality through fragments from novels, short stories, and poetry. Thus, their plays are born from a laboratory, through collective work, that make their research become a visual aspect in almost all their work. Long tables, documentary objects (letters, photographs, recordings), music, digital cameras all become central in their performances.

While the group has been in existence since the early 1990s, their laboratory technique and documentary modes did not become apparent until 2009, with *Amarillo*. Until then, they were known for staging traditional plays by other playwrights. *Amarillo* became a turning point in their career and its success has made TLS one of the most renowned companies in Latin America. The play has now been performed at national and international festivals. As a result, the piece has also gained recognition for its production quality and longevity, keeping in mind that the play is still being staged with the original cast. Centered on documentary evidence gathered from fragments of films provided by the Documentary Center for Voices Against the Silence, an open and free platform to access documentary film about human rights atrocities in Latin America, TLS begins the performance by introducing audiences to their laboratory stage. The voices and images from the films are projected onto the back wall of the stage, while members of the troupe prepare their working tables at the sides of the stage by arranging photographs, cameras, clothing, and other documentary props.

Amarillo is a play that shows a migrant's journey from somewhere in Mexico or Central America to Amarillo, Texas. The perils of the border-crossing journey are recorded through a multimedia performance via a documentary technique that brings to the stage real documents (such as letters and photographs from migrants) and privileges issues of cultural identity, human suffering, and human rights. In *Amarillo*, an Everyman is the only interpreter with a certain protagonist function, while a throat-singing rancher wanders around, and four other women exchange roles as stage scenographers, camerawomen, dancers, and letter readers. In a desert that is sometimes enchanting and at other times deadly, it also becomes an allegorical space in nature. Onstage, actors employ sandbags that hang from the ceiling, while the water from jugs is illuminated in an attractive, dreamy, aquatic blue, shimmering and reflecting on the floor. Throughout the play, these natural elements mark nature's persistent threat, pushing the multisensorial forward by hearing water, seeing the sand spilling out of the bags, and imagining the ocean close by, even in a desert.

Since 2013, TLS, with the support of SERTULL, a socially and humanly committed institution, has worked with other human rights organizations and has taken *Amarillo* to border towns through the company's own project "*Amarillo* on the Migrant Route," which seeks to bring awareness and community building to hundreds of migrants who are about to cross the border. Some of TLS's work can be seen in their interventions with groups such as Casa del Migrante la 72, Grupo de Mujeres Las Patronas, Casa del Migrante de Ixtepec, among other cultural and social agencies in the south, center, and north of Mexico. To this day, TLS is committed to working with different migrant shelters to help them with basic needs as well as information. One of TLS's main purposes is to study issues of human rights and migration, as well as to explore topics of femicides and extermination. Whereas other important playwrights and theatre collectives have staged similar topics on border issues (for instance, Mexican playwright Hugo Salcedo or Lagartijas tiradas al sol), TLS critically examines intersections between the value of conducting research through residencies and their artistic process of creation.

Other important plays, such as *Baños Roma* [Roman Baths] (2013) explores the current ghostly state of the border town of Ciudad Juárez, a center of unresolved femicides and drug traffickers. TLS was first attracted to a 2009 newspaper story written for Mexican daily newspaper *La Jornada*. It discussed Cuban Mexican boxer José Angel "Mantequilla" Nápoles's life, now deceased, his gym for teenagers named Baños Roma, and what it was like to live in the gruesome state of Ciudad Juárez. Captivated by his life story and by the fact that one of their actors was a former boxer, TLS decided to travel to this border city to conduct research. Featuring live music, three working tables, boxing bags, five actors, and one live musician, *Baños Roma* explores the theatricality and performativity in telling this retired boxer's story, stating from the beginning that "when a story is retold, it is already altered." As a group they spent six weeks researching and documenting stories in Ciudad Juárez, as well as spending hours interviewing "Mantequilla" Nápoles. In a similar fashion as they did with *Amarillo*, TLS's research for this play involved a social aspect: rebuilding the gym that was in almost complete ruins. While the play focuses on boxing and the life of "Mantequilla" Nápoles, Ciudad Juárez and its femicides take a gruesome centrality, making *Baños Roma* a visually attractive play that confronts the audience with the tacit violence that this city has dealt with since femicides became a major issue in 1993.

The group's commitment to a variety of issues involving human rights has also taken them to create large-scale installations like *Artículo 13* [Article 13] (2012) that took place in France and a site-specific performance, *El puro lugar* [Nothing But the Place] (2016–2017) in Xalapa, Veracruz. Joining forces with the French theatre collective Campaigne Carabosse, they created *Artículo 13*, an artistic and testimonial documentary memorial in honor of the thousands of anonymous migrants who have disappeared all over the world. Spectators are invited to walk through the open-air large installation taking part in lighting candles and congregating as a community. *El puro lugar* is an in situ, urban documentary installation that allows for one hundred spectators divided into groups of ten and distributed over four days around the town of San Bruno of Xalapa, Veracruz, a city filled with a violent history. The work is a compilation of six installations, performed in different spaces, that bridge multiple times to focus on the atrocities and violence that have taken place in Xalapa in three separate periods: a textile factory where workers were killed, presumably for having Marxist ideals in 1924; twelve actors in Oscar Liera's play, *Cúcara y Mácara*, who were violently attacked by a right-wing group due to the play's controversial nature in regard to religion in 1981; and finally the small dorm where eight students from the University of Veracruz were attacked and beaten by the police in 2015 for being considered radicals. A coproduction between TLS and the Actors Organization of the University of Veracruz (ORTEUV), this work incorporates geographical and historical fieldwork undertaken by director Jorge Vargas, Alejandro Flores Valencia, and Luis Mario Moncada regarding three different instances of historical violence in Xalapa, Veracruz, the largest city on the Gulf of Mexico.

Teatro Línea de Sombra's ongoing work with human rights and their commitment to pedagogy is also part of their project Transversales, a yearly festival/educational encounter of international artists that has been active since 1998 to today. This cultural project, supported by the Ministry of Culture, has welcomed a network of artists, scholars, and students to come together to be part of a theatrical/educational encounter that includes workshops, presentations, and performances in Mexico City. Together with their artistic sophistication, and constant work with and about social justice, TLS is a true example of how documentary practices have been key in recent Latin American theatre, and this group is one of the best at connecting them.

Paola S. Hernández

Major works

Danzantes del alba [Dancers of the Dawn] (2020)
Filo de caballo(s) (2018)
El puro lugar [The Main Place] (2016–2017)
Durango 66 (2015)
Pequeños territorios [Small Territories] (2014)
Baños Roma (2013)
Artículo 13 (2012)
Amarillo (2009)

Further reading

Delgadillo, Theresa. "Artists in the Americas Confront the Fracturing Effects of Violence." Mujeres Talk (blog), Ohio State University Libraries, April 19, 2016.https://library.osu.edu/blogs/mujerestalk/2016/04/19/artists-in-the-americas-confront-the-fracturing-effects-of-violence/

Hernández, Paola S. *Staging Lives in Latin American Theater: Bodies, Objects, Archives*. Evanston: Northwestern University Press, 2021.

Lamadrid Guerrero, Geraldine. "Informe sobre El puro lugar: Recuento y preguntas." *Revista Conjunto*, 183 (2017): 2–13.

Parrini, Rodrigo. "Figuras del límite: Documentos, etnografía y teatro." *Investigación Teatral: Revista de artes escénicas*, 9:13 (2018). https://investigacionteatral.uv.mx/index.php/investigacionteatral/article/view/2553

Prieto Stambaugh, Antonio. "El puro lugar de la violencia: docuficción escénica en la ciudad de Xalapa, Veracruz." *LATR*, 52.1 (Fall 2018): 125–148.

Truett, Joshua L. "Spectacles of Disappearance: Migration, Man, and Machine." *LATR*, 52.1 (Fall 2018): 207–214.

TEATRO MALAYERBA (QUITO, ECUADOR, 1979–) AND ARÍSTIDES VARGAS (CÓRDOBA, ARGENTINA/QUITO, ECUADOR, 1954–)

Arístides Vargas is an internationally recognized and influential playwright and director of Latin American theatre. He has won countless awards, including the LUKAS Award at the CASA Festival, London (2014); the Critics Award, *LA Weekly* (2011); El Gallo Lifetime Achievement Award from Havana, Cuba (2012); and the World's Theater Award from the Rojas Cultural Center (UBA), Buenos Aires (2015). As a playwright, actor, director, and teacher, he has made his mark on generations across various continents. He was born in Córdoba, Argentina, but due to the unjust persecution of the military dictatorship (1976–1983), he was forced to emigrate to Ecuador in 1975. There, he founded the Malayerba theatre group in 1979 alongside other exiles, Charo Francés (formerly of Grupo TEI, Madrid) and Susana Pautasso (Libre Teatro Libre [LTL] from Córdoba, Argentina). Malayerba gave a new impulse to Ecuadorian theatre. They approached theatre-making as an artistic, ethical, and technical endeavor through which they could engage in meaningful, creative experiences to assume and confront current socio-political processes. They expanded their mission through the Malayerba Laboratory (1982–), which has become an important theatre school for acting and writing for many theatre artists from Latin America.

As a teacher, Vargas became an international figure, which resulted in collaborative work with different groups, always centering on the value of political and social content in their productions. For instance, in 2000, he collaborated with Spanish playwright José Sanchíz Sinisterra in the dramaturgical project *La cruzada de los niños de la calle* [Children of the Street Crusade]. The play was inspired by the real episode of the 1212 children's crusade to the Holy Land to comment on the terrible conditions faced by children who live on the streets today. Another collaboration was with Teatro de Los Andes (Bolivia), for whom he wrote and directed *El mar* [The Sea] (2015), the story of three brothers who go on a journey to the ocean to fulfill their mother's last wish, a direct commentary on the War of the Pacific (1879–1884) between Bolivia-Peru and Chile, in which Bolivia lost its access to the ocean. The play lingers on the ongoing question about whether the restitution of the ocean can bring back those lost in the war.

In 1982 he debuted as a director with *Mujeres* [Women] by Darío Fo and Franca Rama, which anticipates the agency female characters will have in his plays. This paved the way for combining writing and directing in *Francisco de Cariamanga* [Francisco from Cariamanga] (1991), inspired by G. Buchner's play *Woyzeck*. The play centers on the war between Ecuador and Peru (1941) as a way of highlighting the access to land denied to the indigenous communities. From then on, his plays focus primarily on notions of displacement, memory, and marginalization as is the case in some of his better-known works: *Jardín de Pulpos* [The Garden of Octopuses] (1992); *La edad de la ciruela* [The Age of the Plum] (1995); and *Pluma y la tempestad* [Feather and The Tempest] (1995). In 1997 he wrote, directed, and performed in *Nuestra Señora de las Nubes* [Our Lady of the Clouds], a play that delves into magic realism through a short, episodic structure, to tell the various stories of a town through the fragmented memories of two characters who keep running into each other. This is one of his most successful works and has been translated into several languages.

Vargas proposes a poetics that raises fundamental philosophical questions through writing and staging techniques with multiple and original dramaturgical and scenic resources. With surreal interweaving, his texts generate dreamlike sequences that reveal the end of the century's unsteady political climate in Latin America. The most outstanding characteristic of his writing is his work with memory and history. His characters dream and remember, and the dramatic action is built upon the dynamics of the past, present, and sometimes a future that is also a memory. For instance, in *Nuestra señora de las nubes*, Óscar and Bruna, the two central characters, rely on the memory of the town they are from to understand their place in the world, an absurdist aesthetic that centers on the human condition. In *La muchacha de los libros usados* [The Girl with the Used Books] (2003), the story of a girl who escapes rape to end up run over by a bus leads the protagonist to look back at her own life to understand the control and repression that people have in their lives. Finally, in *El jardín de los pulpos* José has lost his memory and dialogues with Antonia about the importance of memory recovery. In Vargas's theatre, even if it hurts, it is necessary to remember, because it is the only possibility not only to recover the past but to live a future.

His *oeuvre* displays a superior sensitivity expressed in a rich and singular language that marks Vargas's dramaturgy and makes it unmistakable. His writing has the condensing power of poetry, underlining the double meaning of words and remarking their double referentiality, bringing up ridiculous and unexpected situations and images. Vargas's artistic *oeuvre*, then, constitutes a poetics that includes a lot of humor but is also grounded in bitterness and a sense of poetry, which allows for the belief in a world that can be changed. Humor is felt through the presence of the absurd, highlighting actions or statements emerging out of context. He uses unexpected combinations and surprising endings. With his always present and subtle absurdity, Vargas's theatrical discourse results in a simultaneously dense and light texture that produces Brechtian distance. Among his linguistic resources are, for example, an emphasis on alliteration, contradictions, and antagonisms, and the use of repetition to emphasize situations.

A constant concern in Vargas's theatricality is the status he affords women. By providing them with a voice and agency, he makes evident his political position in favor of women and those less favored in society. He characterizes women as subjects filled with potential, and his female characters are custodians of memory and the engine of dramatic action. His marginal characters include women, prostitutes, immigrants, political persecuted subjects, and opponents of the current political system. His theatrical techniques for producing this denouncement come from humor, linguistic turns, the creation of mysterious and strongly suggestive environments with surreal overtones. Visually, this is made apparent through the use of a precise contrast between light and shadow, providing a dream-like space. For the actors, this translates to a plethora of rhythms in both speech and body movement, making for a very exaggerated presence for the actor, referencing an avant-garde aesthetic to remove all references to direct reality. Music is also a fundamental part of Vargas's performances, accompanied by chords that transport the viewer to unexpected places.

Many of the elements mentioned above are present in *La razón blindada* [Armored Reason] (2005), a play based on the classic novel *El Quijote* by Miguel de Cervantes, Franz Kafka's *The Truth about Sancho Panza*, and testimonies by "Chicho" Vargas and other political prisoners held in the 1970s at the Rawson Prison during Argentina's dictatorship. The play takes place in a prison in which two political prisoners meet to tell the story of Don Quixote and Sancho Panza every Sunday. This is Vargas's most-awarded work and also his most characteristic: full of linguistic games, intelligent and deep humor, and meta-theatricality that allows the prisoners to dream and to imagine other worlds.

Vargas's dramaturgy brings to the scene a new modality of political theatre that, far from proposing a bold political pamphlet, brings to the stage the main issues of our times: gender discrimination, immigration, persecution, and marginalization. His theatre involves processes of discursive meaning that uncover symptoms indicating the state of the world; communication is achieved mainly at the pragmatic level of discourse. For the most part, the spectator decodes what is on the stage with contextual knowledge and the ability to establish a connection between his/her reality and the scene. Vargas's theatrical resources produce presences, absences, or silences and leave the viewer immersed in realities that are not easily recognized or acknowledged within our own social and political contexts.

Lola Proaño Gómez

Major works

Instrucciones para abrazar el aire [Instructions for Embracing the Air] (2012)
De un suave color blanco [Of a Soft, White Color] (2009)
La razón blindada [Armored Reason] (2005)
La muchacha de los libros usados [The Girl with the Used Books] (2003)
Nuestra señora de las nubes [Our Lady of the Clouds] (1997)
Pluma y tempestad [Feather and The Tempest] (1995)
Jardín de pulpos [The Garden of Octopuses] (1992)

Published works

Arístides Vargas: Tres obras. La Habana: Colección Pasamanos, Fondo Editorial Casa de las Américas, 2020.
Instrucciones para abrazar el aire. In *Paso de Gato* 50, 2017.
Teatro I, Arístides Vargas. Edited by Marita Foix. Buenos Aires: EUDEBA, 2016.
Teatro Ausente. Buenos Aires: Instituto Nacional del Teatro, 2006.
Tres obras del mar: "Ana, el mago y el aprendiz", "Tres viejos mares" y "El zaguán de aluminio". Quito: Editorial el Conejo, 2003.

Further reading

Dávila-López, Grace. "El teatro de Arístides Vargas y el poder de la imaginación." *Gestos* 28 (November 2013): 109–114.
Dubatti, Jorge. "Nuestra Señora de las Nubes de Arístides Vargas: exilio, contario y estatus dramático múltiple de los recuerdos-relatos escenificados." *La revista del CCC* 16 (September/December 2012), www.centrocultural. coop/revista/articulo/364/
Lara, Eliseo. "La dramaturgia de Arístides Vargas." *Revista Archipiélago* 15.58 (2007), www.revistas.unam.mx/index.php/archipielago/issue/view/1628
Longan Phillips, S. "El desafío de la ideología y los Aparatos Ideológicos de Estado en Pluma y la tempestad de Arístides Vargas." *Revista Comunicación* 21.1 (2012): 33–41.
Meléndez, Priscilla. "Paisajes en movimiento: Desplazamiento y peregrinaje en *Nuestra señora de las nubes* de Arístides Vargas." *Revista Canadiense de Estudios Hispánicos* 39.3 (Primavera 2015): 653–671.
Proaño-Gómez, Lola. *Desarticulaciones teatrales del neoliberalismo. La escena latinoamericana, 1990–2007*. Buenos Aires: CELCIT, 2019, www.celcit.org. ar/publicaciones/teatro-teoria-y-practica/39/039/

TEATRO DA VERTIGEM (SÃO PAULO, 1992–)

Created in 1992, Teatro da Vertigem quickly became a powerhouse of radically experimental theatre in Brazil. Within nearly three decades, the company conceived and produced nineteen major theatrical projects, including operas, dramatic readings, and urban interventions. Having performed in various cities across Latin America and Europe, Teatro da Vertigem has been awarded the most prestigious prizes in theatre arts in Brazil and the Best Realization prize at the 2011 Prague Quadrennial.

From its origins as a study group interested in the interplay between Newtonian mechanics and the body's potential for expression, the company retained a collaborative *modus operandi* in each stage of the production and a full commitment to extensive research. According to director and founder Antonio Araújo, the fertile precariousness of rehearsals, their unfinished and unpredictable nature, embodies the essence of theatre. In that sense, Teatro da Vertigem builds on and radicalizes the ideas of some of its Brazilian antecessors, namely directors Antunes Filho, José Celso Martinez Correa, and Gerald Thomas. Discussion sessions, workshops, fieldwork, scouting trips, self-investigation, improvisation, collective sharing, and cross-cutting experimentation are some of the practices that embed the company's creative working process. Often, a dramatist is invited to collaborate, but rather than delivering a finished piece they are expected to get deeply involved in the group dynamics and embark on what Araújo calls a "dramaturgy in process," which balances individual authorship and collective contribution.[1]

The word *vertigem*, which means vertigo in English, captures well the unsettling and challenging aesthetics developed by Araújo and his associate artists. Since its debut, Teatro da Vertigem has adopted a site-specific approach and has staged in various non-conventional spaces—churches, hospitals, prisons, shopping malls, waterbodies, underground passages, stock exchange headquarters. Beyond a search for a certain ambience, this choice reflects the desire to critically engage with the symbolic, historical, and political meanings of each space. Thereby, it deconstructs the audience's knee-jerk perceptions of the city. Also, it requires a great deal of physical and emotional involvement from spectators, who, in most of the group's productions, are steered through an itinerant performance that they must follow from place to place but obviously do not control and cannot predict. A relentless, unfathomable chain of scenes gradually unveils different sections of buildings or territories and continuously shifts viewpoints, tones, and moods. Encircling the action and often in great proximity to the actors, spectators sometimes are invited to participate in the play.

Paraíso perdido [Paradise Lost], *O livro de Jó* [The Book of Job], and *Apocalipse 1,11* [Apocalypse 1:11] form what came to be known as the Biblical Trilogy (1992–2000). Inspired by religious and poetic texts, these first theatrical ventures examined the place of the sacred in contemporary times. They explored the clash between transcendental anxieties and the overwhelming constraints of earthly reality. Together, the three plays offer a fable of the fall, from Eden to Hell, with no clear prospect of redemption. Marked by extreme physicality, imposing use of voice, sounds, and lighting, and gruesome realism, the trilogy echoes Artaud's theatre of cruelty and Grotowski's poor theatre. The spiritual quest intertwines with traumatic events in Brazil's recent history, which generates the "allegorical hyper-realism" that became the company's hallmark.[2] For example, in *O livro de Jó*, Job's spiritual, moral, and corporal vulnerability are represented by the naked body of the actor bathed in blood. He spends part of the performance hanging from a *pau de arara*, a torture device frequently used during the military dictatorship in Brazil. The same two-edged type of symbolic reference is found in *Apocalipse 1,11*, whose title alludes to both the Last Judgement in the *Revelation of St. John* and the 1992 massacre at the Carandiru Penitentiary in São Paulo, where the military police crushed a rebellion by killing 111 inmates. In the play, the spectators are dragged into the corridors and cells of an unoccupied jail, where they witness a series of humiliating and sinister events that culminate in merciless trials infused with sexual tensions and unnerving vitriol. Authoritarian discourses and practices along with arbitrary verdicts draw an insightful parallel with state brutality and political violence in Brazil.

In the productions that followed, Teatro da Vertigem explored space in more volatile and anarchic ways by prompting spectators to venture outdoors into murky and dilapidated areas of the city. *BR-3* (2006) is a boat expedition through the smelly and filthy Tietê river, whose history is tightly connected to the enslavement of indigenous Brazilians, the enrichment of São Paulo's elite, unbridled capitalism, and environmental catastrophe. The polluted waters and their chaotic and rather uninviting surroundings set the stage for a complex inquiry into Brazil's national identity. *Bom Retiro 958 metros* [Bom Retiro 958 Meters] (2012) proposes a nocturnal stroll through the—at those late hours, rather ghostly and deserted—streets of Bom Retiro, a manufacturing and commercial neighborhood in São Paulo that has been home to several waves of immigrant workers. To a great extent, the performance is a porous, unstable piece of art. Passers-by, the homeless, buses and cars, the sound of horns, dwellers watching from apartment windows, streetlights, garbage bins, everything converges on the spectacle and begs for not only a renewed engagement with the urban space but also an unconventional attitude toward theatre itself. At a certain point, spectators enter a shopping mall and are ushered through a dense critique of consumerism, labor exploitation, and the "thingification of humans."[3]

In its most recent work, *Marcha à ré* [Reverse Gear] (2020), Teatro da Vertigem attuned the performance to the dire circumstances brought by the COVID-19 pandemic. Ever committed to unlocking the political power of public spaces while respecting the need for social distancing, the company organized a "funeral procession" of about 120 cars that slowly moved in reverse gear through one of the most important avenues in São Paulo. The parade, accompanied by the loud, rhythmic hissing of a ventilator, aimed to challenge the reactionary, abusive, and irresponsible politics of the current far-right Brazilian government. Firmly committed to a collaborative and interdisciplinary creative praxis, Teatro da Vertigem has produced groundbreaking site-specific performances. Physically intense, visually striking, and emotionally disquieting, they challenge the audience's relationship to places and spaces by interrogating their history and redefining their symbolic, moral, and political coordinates.

Carlos Cortez Minchillo

Notes

1 Sílvia Fernandes, *Teatro da Vertigem* (Rio de Janeiro: Cobogó, 2018), 15.
2 Sílvia Fernandes, "O Lugar da Vertigem," *Teatro da Vertigem: Trilogia Bíblica* (São Paulo: Publifolha, 2002), 35.
3 Diana Taylor, "Archiving the 'Thing': Teatro da Vertigem's Bom Retiro 958 metros," *The Drama Review* 59.2 (2015): 64.

Major works

Marcha à ré [Reverse Gear] (2020)
Dire ce qu'on ne pense pas dans des langues qu'on ne parle pas [Say What You Don't Mean, in a Language You Don't Speak] (2014)
Bom Retiro 958 metros [Bom Retiro 958 Meters] (2012)
A última palavra é a penúltima [The Last Word is the Next to Last] (2008)
Trilogia bíblica [Bible Trilogy] (1992–2000) (*Paraíso perdido* [Paradise Lost] (1992); *O livro de Jó* [The Book of Job] (1995); *Apocalipse 1,11* [Apocalypse 1:11] (2000)
BR-3 (2006)

Published works

Trilogía Bíblica. Rio de Janeiro: Publifolha, 2002.

Further reading

Araújo Silva, Antonio C. *A Gênese da Vertigem: o processo de criação de o paraísoperdido.* São Paulo: FAPESP, 2011.
Fernandes, Sílvia. *Teatro da Vertigem.* Rio de Janeiro: Cobogó, 2018.
Fernandes, Sílvia, and Roberto Audio. *Teatro da Vertigem: BR-3.* São Paulo: Perspectiva, 2006.
Moraes, Marcos. "Teatro da Vertigem (and the City of São Paulo)." *Afterall* 35 (2014): 48–59.
Nascimento, Claudia Tatinge. "Brazil's Teatro da Vertigem: Fall as Creation." *TheatreForum* 24 (2004): 34–44.
Nestrovski, Arthur, ed. *Teatro da Vertigem: Trilogia bíblica.* São Paulo: PubliFolha, 2002.
Stanton, William. "*Apocalipse 1,11* in São Paulo: Aesthetic Vertigo or Exploitation?" *The Drama Review* 46.4 (2002): 86–100.

VIVI TELLAS (BUENOS AIRES, ARGENTINA, 1955–)

With a vast production and a clearly traceable influence in her field, Vivi Tellas stands out as one of the leading artists in the Argentine stage. She defines herself mainly as a theatre director and curator, but she also holds an extensive career in other roles and disciplines, namely the visual arts and literature. Her work is characterized by a strong conceptual and experimental form, generally including unexpected and often cleverly humorous twists. Tellas was born in Buenos Aires, where she has lived most of her life. While finishing her initial education in visual arts and during the early years of her university studies in theatre direction, she began her public artistic career as an active participant of the 1980s Buenos Aires *underground* scene. During this period, she became known for her solo performances carried out in legendary spaces such as Café Einstein or the Parakultural, and for creating the all-girl musical-theatrical group Las Baybiscuit, famous for their unique playful numbers featured as part of the concerts of many emergent rock bands and singers (such as Patricio Rey y sus Redonditos de Ricota, Seru Girán, or Virus).

In the second half of the 1980s Tellas focused completely on her role as director, leaving aside (although never fully abandoning) her roles as actress and performance artist. Her main official project—and this is an important definition in her professional biography, since her work has very often been conceived as something bigger and more conceptually guided than just a singular play—was named Teatro Malo [Bad Theatre]. It involved the staging of a set of rare plays she came across. They seemed to have been presented at a contest decades ago by an amateur playwright under the name Orfeo Andrade and they were full of all sorts of errors (from spelling and grammatical mistakes to dramaturgical incongruities). Tellas welcomed the challenge of working with raw and imperfect materials based on the idea of using each play's main flaw as the constructive principle for its staging. This set the path for an important aspect of her personal poetics, in which error and the possibility of failure are seen as a powerful and exciting source of theatricality. The critical, metatheatrical reflections that framed the stagings of this "bad theatre" were aimed more at the theatre of the time than at Andrade's plays. This immediately positioned her as a bold, innovative artist whose conceptual approach to theatre direction was to be followed closely.

Throughout her career, Tellas has sought to inhabit the margins and push the boundaries of theatre by choosing unconventional locations, materials, and formats for her work. Yet, at the same time, she has an important presence in its central institutions by staging her work in the most renowned theatres, such as the Teatro San Martín—where she presented her widely remembered version of Lorca's *Bernarda Alba*—or the Teatro Colón, and by having formal institutional responsibilities. These two dimensions of her career have always complemented one another, as it is evidenced in her conception of the role of theatrical curator, which she developed from those institutional positions as a way to engage theatre makers in an avant-garde investigation of theatre's limits and new possibilities.

Her first curatorial project was Museos [Museums] (1994–2000), conducted at the Centro de Experimentación Teatral, a theatrical experimentation space Tellas founded at the Centro Cultural Ricardo Rojas of the University of Buenos Aires. In Museos, Tellas invited various theatre makers to explore the city's non-artistic museums (such as the Museum of Odontology or the Museum of the Eye) and to use them as triggers for new theatrical productions, thus inciting a reflection both on the city and its memory policies and on theatre itself. The result through its five editions was a diverse number of performances and installations, many of which left a long-lasting impression in the local scene.

After this experience, in 2001 Tellas was appointed as artistic director of the Teatro Sarmiento, one of Buenos Aires public theatres, which she also geared toward experimentation. There, she designed a new curatorial project she named Biodrama (2002–2008); often referred to as "Ciclo Biodrama." It was subtitled "Sobre la vida de las personas" [About People's Lives] and invited directors and playwrights to investigate the multiple possibilities for bringing a living person's life to the stage. In a global context of hyper-mediatization and a local context of socio-economic crisis (the 2001 economic collapse), Biodrama aimed to make a humanistic statement, while promoting the investigation of new approaches to biographical and documentary practices onstage as a way to question the conventional theatrical representation, also in crisis at the turn of the century. The project had an enormous repercussion, not only because of the fifteen original plays it produced, but because of the debates that emerged, mainly regarding the ethic and aesthetic implications of the different forms of documentary and biographical practices. Its guidelines were embraced by many other theatre makers as creative incentive, helping create a productive research framework that fueled the documentary experimentations of other practitioners, such as Mariano Pensotti, Beatriz Catani, and Lola Arias. Additionally, the name—or rather, the concept—*biodrama* itself had a rapid, widespread reception amongst practitioners and critics, probably due to its capacity to stress the theatrical focus of the biographical quest.

Meanwhile, just as Biodrama—as a curatorial series—was taking off, Tellas began to develop her own interpretation as a director of the same tasks she assigned to other artists as a curator. This led to the creation of a series she initially called Proyecto Archivos [Archives Project] (2003–2008) and presented as documentary theatre. In it, she asked non-professional performers to share their stories and personal *documents* (letters, photographs, clothes, etc.) while carrying out a sort of metatheatrical experiment. She focused her work on the *search for theatricality outside theatre* and one of her premises was that every person carries within themselves a theatrical ability: their life stories and material possessions (or archives) are imbued with the capacity for theatricality. To bring this to stage, Tellas designed a unique form of staging with many complex, intertwined layers of reality and fiction (both augmented and blurred at the same time). The first subjects of these personal, theatrical archives were Tellas's mother and aunt in *Mi mamá y mi tía* [My Mother and My Aunt] (2003), an original, intimate and fun production which set the base for all her bio-documentary plays to come. Some of the common characteristics of the six plays in Proyecto Archivos (and of the many other that followed) are: a small cast (two or three people connected by a profession or personal relationship); an alternation between testimonial monologues, purely performative scenes (like dancing, singing or playing games), and ludic recreations of biographical episodes; a spatial setting based on a few key elements (a table for the documents, a set of chairs, and a working clock showing the real time) and a final moment in which performers and audience share an informal meal onstage.

After 2008, once the Ciclo Biodrama came to an end, Tellas adopted the name for all her work, thus retroactively reframing Archivos and the initial curatorial series as its two foundational expressions. Over the past two decades, Biodrama has become the center of Tellas's creative work (leading to the staging of over a dozen original plays), as well as of her continuously growing teaching practice displayed in workshops, university classes, lectures, and advising of multiple *biodramatic* projects nationally and internationally. Therefore, whether it is due to the indirect influence of her work or by the direct guidance of her curatorial or teaching activity, Tellas has impacted the work of many contemporary Latin American theatre artists, whose work account for the vast productivity of the theatrical models she developed and encouraged others to explore.

Pamela Brownell

Major works

Biodrama/Proyecto Archivos: *Mi mamá y mi tía* [My Mother and My Aunt] (2003), *Tres filósofos con bigotes* [Three Philosophers with Moustaches] (2004), *Mujeres Guía* [Tour Guides] (2008), *Rabbi Rabino* (2011), *Las personas* [The People] (2014), and *Los amigos* [Friends] (2018), among others
El precio de un brazo derecho [The Price of a Right Arm] (2000)
Proyecto Museos [Museums] (1995–2000)
Teatro Malo [Bad Theatre] (1986–1990)

Published works

"*Maruja enamorada*" and "*Cozarinszy y su médico.*" In *Hablar desde el yo. Voces del teatro documental argentino*, by VV.AA. La Habana: Alarcos, 2018.
Biodrama | Proyecto Archivos: seis documentales escénicos, edited by Pamela Brownell and Paola Hernández. Córdoba: Papeles Teatrales/FFyH/UNC, 2017.
"*Cozarinsky y su médico.*" In *Antología de argumentos teatrales en Argentina 2003–2013, Vol. I: Formas de reconocimiento*, by VV.AA. Buenos Aires: Libretto, 2016.

Further reading

Brownell, Pamela. *Proyecto Biodrama. El teatro biográfico-documental de Vivi Tellas y lo real como utopía en la escena contemporánea*. Buenos Aires: Antítesis / Red Editorial, 2021.

Brownell, Pamela and Paola Hernández, "Introduction." In *Biodrama | Proyecto Archivos: seis documentales escénicos*, by Vivi Tellas. Córdoba: Papeles Teatrales/FFyH/UNC, 2017. [Includes essays by G. Montaldo, B. Werth, B. Trastoy, J. Graham-Jones, J. Ward, F. Baeza, F. Pinta, and J. Guerrero.]
Fuentes, Marcela. "Theater as Event: The Politics of Interruption in Vivi Tellas' Documentary Theater." In *Calling Out of Context*. Edited by Joachim Hamou, 15–31. Paris: Paraguay Press, 2017.
Hernández, Paola S. *Staging Lives in Latin American Theater: Bodies, Objects, Archives*. Evanston: Northwestern University Press, 2021.
Pauls, Alan. "Kidnapping Reality: An Interview with Vivi Tellas." In *Dramaturgy of the Real on the World Stage*, by Carol Martin, 246–252. Translated by Sarah Townsend. Basingstoke/New York: Palgrave Macmillan, 2010.
Sosa, Cecilia. "Cuéntame Tu Vida." *Radar. Página/12*, October 17, 2004. www.pagina12.com.ar/diario/suplementos/radar/9-1748-2004-10-17.html

TIMBRE 4 (BUENOS AIRES, ARGENTINA, 1999–) AND CLAUDIO TOLCACHIR (BUENOS AIRES, ARGENTINA, 1975–)

The Argentine playwright, director, actor, and educator Claudio Tolcachir has made an indelible mark on twenty-first-century theatre in Buenos Aires through plays that explore relationships in crisis. Although he gained early notoriety as an actor, Tolcachir is most widely known as the director of the Timbre 4 theatre company, which he founded in 1999, and which began performing in Tolcachir's own home at the height of the 2001 economic crisis. From its humble beginnings in an unmarked house, Timbre 4 has since become a mainstay of the city's independent theatre circuit. Meanwhile, Tolcachir's original plays, which have consistently drawn loyal audiences and maintained a tireless itinerary of festivals abroad, often enact social and economic turmoil from within intimate domestic spaces.

Tolcachir's significance for Argentine and Latin American theatre is anchored in the rapid ascent of Timbre 4, and the runaway success of his first original play, *The Omission of the Coleman Family* (2005). Like many theatre makers in Buenos Aires —a city that boasts hundreds of independent performance venues—Tolcachir's aesthetic is intimately linked to his theatre space. The name "Timbre 4" originated from the buzzer the public was instructed to ring to enter Tolcachir's home, a condominium unit in the Boedo neighborhood of Buenos Aires. Adding to the venue's mystique was the oft-repeated story of an unhappy neighbor who complained to the police that a prostitution house was operating in his building. At the time, the company was performing *Jamón del diablo* [Deviled Ham] (2002), a cabaret adaptation of *Trescientos milliones* [Three Hundred Million] (1932) by

Roberto Arlt. When the police showed up, Tolcachir was performing in drag, and greeted the officers wearing a red dress. Although the police quickly understood that the home was doubling as a theatre, not a brothel, the story was incorporated into Timbre 4 lore, a testament to its transgressive beginnings.

Timbre 4 is exemplary of the proliferation of non-traditional venues in Buenos Aires over the last few decades. With performances at state-run theatres declining steadily from 1990 into the 2000s, and commercial theatres suffering diminished spectatorship during the financial crisis of 2001–2002, many theatre makers turned to *autogestión* (self-management), drawing on a long-standing tradition of independent theatre in Argentina. Artists often bought or rented a space not only for rehearsals and performances, but also as a place to teach theatre classes for added revenue. Tolcachir himself trained in acting with one of the pioneers of this model, the director Alejandra Boero, who in 1990 founded the theatre and acting school *Andiamo 90* in a renovated warehouse. Tolcachir describes Timbre 4 as an explicit response to the 2001 economic crisis, which involved skyrocketing unemployment, widespread protests and looting, a historic sovereign loan default, and the abrupt resignation of the president. "[Timbre 4] was a refuge," Tolcachir remembers, "where we didn't have to be as aware of the catastrophe that surrounded us."[1]

Perhaps due to the initial doubling of his own home as a rehearsal and performance venue, Tolcachir's early plays are portraits of intimate relationships stretched to their limits. When developing his characters, he often begins from connections between people who, as he explains, share a "certain immaturity and an alarmist perspective on life, that feeling that you can't cope with reality."[2] *The Omission of the Coleman Family* (2005), for instance, follows three generations of an Argentine family whose economic destitution and personal dysfunction threaten to unravel their family ties. The matriarchal grandmother holds everyone together under one roof: a mother who can't cope with the weight of motherhood, and three of her children from different fathers. When the grandmother suffers a medical emergency, the fourth child, Verónica, shows up to finance the hospital bills, but she is not as eager to reacquaint with her estranged family. The context for this familial dysfunction is an increasingly impoverished middle class, facing both an absent state and the experience of fraying community ties.

Tolcachir wrote the play based on months of improvisation, in which he asked the actors to explore how their characters would simply survive together in his one-bedroom home. The sense of entrapment during the rehearsal process carries through to the first scene of the play, in which no one can find the energy to make breakfast. After arguing about who will make food, the mother exclaims, "we'll die and they'll find our bones, scattered all over the sofas."[3] In a clear homage to the morbid pessimism of the Argentine *grotesco criollo* tradition, characters envision the closure of future possibilities by imagining their bodies decomposing on the furniture.

The audience initially experienced this same domestic infrastructure. As spectators walked toward Tolcachir's home-theatre through a long passageway, typical of so-called "casa chorizo" buildings, the theatre critic Federico Irazábal remembers signs requesting that spectators keep quiet because "the neighbor at the end of the hall was sleeping."[4] Despite, or perhaps because of, this clandestine setting, the play quickly packed dozens of eager spectators into the small home, and boasted celebrity attendees including Francis Ford Coppola and Gael García Bernal. But although Timbre 4's domestic environs shaped not only the dramaturgy but also its underground appeal, the play soon transcended its location. In 2007, Tolcachir's company annexed a nearby abandoned chair factory and created a multi-space venue that helped raise the profile of the Boedo neighborhood, which began to gentrify alongside Timbre 4's success. During *The Omission of the Coleman Family*'s fifteen-year run, which included tours to dozens of countries, and performances in one of the larger theatres on the Broadway equivalent, Avenida Corrientes, the original cast (with a few exceptions) performed the play well over 2,000 times.

In his subsequent plays, *Third Wing* (2008), *Wind in a Violin* (2011), and *Emilia* (2013), and continuing with *Dynamo* (2015) and *Próximo* [Near] (2017), Tolcachir again presents scenarios in which characters make and remake kinship ties to survive with limited resources. *Third Wing*, for instance, is set in an office where three work colleagues—Héctor, Mónica, and Sandra—carry out everyday responsibilities. Superimposed onto this setting are domestic scenes between Manuel and Sofia, a couple trying to have a baby. The collapse of work and home creates a sense of urban claustrophobia in which physical closeness only fuels isolation. The two worlds finally collide when Manuel bursts into the office and reveals that he was having an affair with the office worker, Héctor, thereby retroactively making apparent the relationship between seemingly separate spheres. The more recent play, *Dynamo*, which Tolcachir wrote with frequent collaborators Lautaro Perotti and Melisa Hermida, takes more formal risks to explore the confines and solitude of domestic space. In the play, three women live inside a small trailer, while almost never becoming aware of one another's presence amid their own search for ways to communicate.

Although Tolcachir's original works have effectively brought the drama of family dysfunction into the twenty-first century, he has equally shaped contemporary Argentine theatre through his role as director of the Timbre 4 venue, which showcases original works by local playwrights and has built an economically viable model for alternative theatres. Moreover, Tolcachir has trained a new generation of theatre makers, many who have opened spaces of their own. Tolcachir's plays ask audiences to reflect on how theatre and family—in the broadest senses of each word—are mutually dependent and each offer relational possibilities for living through contemporary crises.

Anna White-Nockleby

Notes

1 Quoted in Alejandro Lingenti, "Entrevista: El Teatro de Claudio Tolcachir," *Los Inrockuptibles*, May 16, 2013, https://medium.com/los-inrockuptibles/entrevista-el-teatro-de-claudio-tolcachir-8aed8b4631ce.
2 Ibid.
3 Claudio Tolcachir, *Timbre 4: Two Plays*, trans. Jean Graham-Jones and Elisa Legón (New York: Martin Segal Theatre Center Publications, 2010), 7.
4 Federico Irazábal, *Teatro anaurático: espacio y representación después del fin del arte* (Córdoba, Argentina: A/E, Ediciones DocumentA/Escénicas, 2015), 192.

Major works

Próximo [Near] (2017)
Dynamo (2015)
Emilia (2013)
Wind in a Violin (2011)
Third Wing (2008)
The Coleman Family Omission (2005)

Published Works

Próximo. Madrid: Ediciones Antígona, 2019.
El viento en un violín y otros textos. Edited by Jorge Dubatti. Buenos Aires: Atuel, 2011.
La omisión de la familia Coleman. Buenos Aires: Teatro Timbre 4, 2010.
Timbre 4: Two Plays. Edited by Jean Graham-Jones. Translated by Jean Graham-Jones and Elisa Legón. New York: Martin E. Segal Theatre Center Publications, 2010.

Further reading

Cotilla Vaca, Marcelino. "Valores sociolingüísticos e interculturales en la recepción de *La omisión de la Familia Coleman* de Claudio Tolcachir." *Les Cahiers de l'ILCEA*, 22 (2015).
Graham-Jones, Jean. "Buenos Aires's Independent Theatre Scene." *Theatre Journal* 68.2 (2016): 249–260.
Graham-Jones, Jean. "Introduction: The Irresistible Rise of Claudio Tolcachir and Timbre 4." In *Timbre 4: Two Plays*, edited by Jean Graham-Jones. Translated by Jean Graham-Jones and Elisa Legón. New York: Martin ESegal Theatre Center Publications, 2010.
Irazábal, Federico. *Teatro anaurático: espacio y representación después del fin del arte*. Córdoba, Argentina: A/E, Ediciones DocumentA/Escénicas, 2015.
Jelen, Marcela. "El silencio representado: 'La omisión de la familia Coleman' de Claudio Tolcachir." *Telón de fondo. Revista de Teoría y Crítica Teatral* 3 (July 1, 2006): 1–4.
Yaccar, María Daniela. "El Último Sueño, El de La Sala Propia." *Página 12*, September 12, 2010. www.pagina12.com.ar/diario/suplementos/espectaculos/10-19244-2010-09-12.html

CÁNDIDO TIRADO (CAGUAS, PUERTO RICO/NEW YORK CITY, 1955–)

Cándido Tirado is a Puerto Rican born, Nuyorican bred playwright, television writer, theatrical director, and educational theatre pioneer. A self-described *jíbaro* until the age of eleven, Tirado has penned dozens of theatrical texts since the early 1980s. He is a prolific writer, director, and occasional performer of varied theatrical genres, including full-length and one-act plays, musicals, ten-minute plays, and monologues. In addition, Tirado serves as co-founder of Educational Plays Productions which tours New York City public schools and helps students create and interact with socially relevant theatre for youth. He pursued a bachelor's degree in Creative Writing at the City University of New York, eventually earning theatrical apprenticeships with distinguished icons: María Irene Fornés at International Art Relations (INTAR) Theatre; as a resident playwright and director with Miriam Colón's Puerto Rican Traveling Theater; and most profoundly, under the mentorship of Argentinian practitioner and theatrical theorist, Guillermo Gentilé—a fellow student in María Irene Fornés's Hispanic Playwrights in Residence Laboratory at INTAR.

As a member of Fornés's Hispanic Playwrights in Residence Laboratory and Miriam Colón's Puerto Rican Traveling Theater's Professional Playwright's Unit, Tirado established decades-long friendships with Latinx playwrights Migdalia Cruz, Edwin Sánchez, and Caridad Svich—though his most fruitful relationship remains his marriage to Latina iconic playwright, Carmen Rivera (*La Gringa*, 1996). In the mid-1980s, interest in Tirado's plays attracted commercial theatres, including the Goodman Theatre, Repertorio Español, the Adrienne Arscht Center, and the Sundance Theatre Institute. Tirado has earned four prestigious New York Foundation for the Arts fellowships and a Theatre Communications Group Best Play Award for *Fish Men* (2012), amongst other prestigious awards and accolades.

Tirado's trajectory as a playwright is characterized by the variety of his texts, which include historical biographies, musicals, and hip hop fables. One of his goals as a playwright is to make the audience aware of the problems facing humanity in this contemporary world. This means that his plays do not necessarily focus on Latinx characters, instead he writes them as metaphors representing facets of contemporary ailments. For example, *Momma's Boyz* (2000), is a play that centers on three uneducated young drug dealers and their self-destructive behavior, named Mimic, Shine, and Thug. Their names do not reflect ethnicity, rather the conditions found in the impoverished streets, where drugs and crime abund.

As a playwright, director, and producer Tirado has earned a reputation as a no-nonsense, theatrical powerhouse. He finds that playwriting allows for an intimacy that he cannot find in any other art form. His ability to adapt his dramaturgy to both commercial theatrical productions and absurdist aesthetics show his range as a playwright. *Fish Men* (2000), for instance, which centers on chess hustlers in pre-9/11 New York City, who are also victims of twentieth-century genocides in both Latin America and the Holocaust, is a comic drama that grapples with individuals overcoming their inner demons. The biographical *Celia: The Musical* (2007), about salsa icon Celia Cruz, alternates with his more absurdist fare, such as *When Nature Calls* (1993), which Tirado describes as "an absurd, scatological, anti-fascist, farce/black comedy" which he wrote to "keep up with [Pedro] Pietri and [Miguel] Piñero's toilet plays."[1] Tirado's praise of Latino playwriting masters, and their impact on his own socio-political ideologies, is contrasted with his belief that "although I like the absurd writers, they were white men of a certain time which informed them of how far down humanity can fall and all the pretenses fall alongside with it."[2] This reference to canonical absurdist writers still shows the remnants of colonizing thought in theatre today, which Tirado tries to overthrow throughout his work.

However, it is the mentorship of master playwright and theatrical pioneer Guillermo Gentilé, and the development of his own "Fantastic Realism" that has most impacted Tirado's development as a writer and theatrical practitioner. Gentilé considers this to be a revolutionary genre that uses the irrational as a metaphor to explore the inner desires and dreams of the characters onstage. For Tirado, this means using symbols and metaphors to "recognize those absurd moments in our lives that are hard to explain ... Gentilé gave me a vessel, a way of thinking about a play that had embedded a technique of approaching the work."[3] Gentilé's central belief that human beings are driven by their fantasies allowed Tirado entry to an exploration of dramatic characters as steeped in the "fantastic" world of their desires—not quite *aquí* ... not quite *allá*—or what Puerto Rican playwright Papo Marqués satirizes as a Puerto Rican Schizophrenia.

Tirado's plays have garnered him a reputation as one of the most prominent cultural founders of the Latinx theatrical movement. His early successes with the Puerto Rican Traveling Theater led to the publication of *Some People Have All the Luck* (1987) in John Antush's iconic *Nuestro New York: Anthology of Puerto Rican Theater* (1994). The play introduces Carlos, who is considering suicide on account of his broken dreams, and his relationship with a character seeking a spirit to incarnate to flee the present world. This publication is groundbreaking because it was the first time that Nuyorican playwrights were published as a collective, including Carmen Rivera with *La Gringa*, and José Rivera with *Marisol*. The anthology's use of "Puerto Rican" in the title suggested a different canon of dramatic texts—yet perfectly describing Tirado himself as an island/mainland transplant.

As a director, Tirado is commited to deconstructing commercial and academic theatre's imposition of "lumping," which he describes as the white American tendency to combine people from different backgrounds into one homogenous group that makes it easier to consume as a singular identity of otherness. Thus, Tirado's decades-long advice to other Latinx directors emphasizes the ability to self-produce work, in lieu of accepting economic funds from mainstream producers. In doing so, Latinx directors seize the monetary modes of production and can avoid being "lumped" in with groups who may write from differing histories, sociologies, and languages. The commercial (and academic) theatre's agreed upon, yet unethical practice of "lumping" becomes a disguise for neoliberal *pan-Latinidad*.

Tirado notes that his directing style is to make the work on stage look as natural as possible while at the same time framing each moment as a photograph. He is keenly aware that the audience has the ability to frame the action onstage, and thus he wants them to understand the play through scenic imagery. His ability to (re)construct the humanity in our everyday lives had led him to balance writing, producing, teaching, and serving as a mentor to Latinx artists regionally, nationally, and internationally. Over four decades, Tirado has mastered a sharp theatrical critique of neocolonial indoctrination as well as a denunciation of the tamer, yet just as destructive, limitations of post-millennial neoliberalism in commercial theatre, popular culture, and academic institutions of theatrical training and learning.

Jason Ramírez

Notes

1 Personal interview with Cándido Tirado.
2 Ibid.
3 Ibid.

Major works

La Canción (2016)
The Border Game (2013)
Fish Men (2012)
Celia: The Life and Music of Celia Cruz (with Carmen Rivera) (2007)
Momma's Boyz (2000)
Ilka: The Dream (1997)
Checking Out (1996)
When Nature Calls (1993)
Some People Have All the Luck (1987)
King Without a Castle (1986)

Published works

Fish Men in *The Chess Plays*, No Passport Press, 2021.
King Without a Castle in *The Chess Plays*, No Passport Press, 2021.
Momma's Boyz in *Nuestras Voces Anthology of Repertorio Español*, No Passport Press, 2012.
Ilka: The Dream in *Positive/Negative: Women of Color and HIV/AIDS*, Aunt Lute Publishing, 2002.
First Class in *Five Playwrights from New York*, Arte Publico Press, 1990.

Further reading

Gibson, Lesley. "A Conversation with Cándido Tirado," *On Stage*, 2012.
Goodman, Stephanie. "Celia: The Life and Music of Celia Cruz," *New York Times*, 2007.
Orozco, Gisela. "*Fish Men*: Pescadores y Pescados," *Chicago Tribune/Vivelo Hoy*, 2012.
Weiss, Hedy. "Momma's Boyz: A Vivid Portrait of Kids in a Troubled, Violent World," *Chicago Sun Times*, 2011.

GRUPO CULTURAL YUYACHKANI (LIMA, PERU, 1971–)

Grupo Cultural Yuyachkani (a Quechua word meaning I am thinking/ I am remembering) is one of the most significant theatre collectives in Latin America. The group was founded in 1971 and is now one of the longest running theatre collectives in the world, with almost all the original members of the group actively involved today. The group currently consists of director Miguel Rubio and collective members Teresa Ralli, Rebeca Ralli, Ana Correa, Debora Correa, Augusto Casafranca, and Julián Vargas. As is the case with some of the more renowned theatre collectives in Latin America, the group owns their own space, Casa Yuyachkani, located in Magdalena del Mar (an area of Lima next to the Pacific), a laboratory and rehearsal space where they hold their performances, house a library, hold their archives, and created a space dedicated for their collections of masks, costumes, and other popular cultural artifacts. Yuyachkani is known for their unique performances, often in support of social movements and protests, as well as their distinct aesthetic which incorporates a diverse range of Peruvian performance and ritual practices. In addition, their humanitarian work uses theatre as a tool for personal and collective healing. The group often creates their pieces based on ethnographic experiences—living with, protesting alongside, and interviewing members of the community who then become centered in their performances.

Yuyachkani works as a collective, which means that while Miguel Rubio is the designated director of the group, each performance is created collaboratively between all the members. Typically, either an individual member, or the group as a whole, will propose a topic they want to explore. Their work is very interdisciplinary, incorporating with equal or greater importance: spectacle, dance, movement, mask work, music, and ritual. The ceremonial aspect of their theatre incorporates a combination of popular culture, religious traditions, and indigenous aesthetics to the stories they present on the stage. Some of their performances incorporate an agit-prop aesthetic with larger-than-life props, stilt-work and the use of bullhorns, since their performances need to grab the attention of people going about their everyday lives in spaces such as city squares and marketplaces. This distinct style can be traced back to the group's origins.

From the beginning, Yuyachkani's activism was central to their repertoire and mission as a company. In the early 1970s, Yuyachkani's members were intricately involved in the movements for miners' rights as well as the Peasant Confederation of Peru (CPP), who focused on the rights of agrarian workers. Through first-hand encounters with these workers and activists, they created their first performance, *Puño de cobre* [Copper Fist] (1972). Nevertheless, the miners did not see their own customs and identities reflected in this first play. Taking this critique to heart, the group went on to create *Allpa Rayku* (1978), which combines the structure of the popular Andahuaylas festival while focusing on elements of the town's history. This time the group incorporated local masks, costumes, dance practices, and songs spoken in Quechua. This experience continues to influence the way in which the group creates works to this day.

Though Yuyachkani has worked with and been influenced by companies from around the world (such as Odin Teatret and The Berliner Ensemble), they continue to be rooted in local theatrical traditions and cultures of Peru, mainly by bringing in indigenous stories to the stage. In a country where indigenous peoples have been historically and routinely oppressed, this representation is a form of activism and resistance. An example of this cultural celebration is one of their most popular pieces, *Los músicos ambulantes* [The Traveling Musicians] (1983), a light-hearted musical piece centered on a group of animals who each come from distinct regions of Peru and play their traditional instruments and music. As is often the case with Peruvians, at first these animals believe they have nothing in common, but they eventually learn to work together (blending their musical languages and cultural customs) in order to succeed.

From 1980 to 2000 Peru experienced an internal conflict—a "war" between Peruvian terrorist groups the Shining Path, the Túpac Amaru Revolutionary Movement (MRTA) and Peruvian paramilitary groups, which resulted in the murder of an estimated 70,000 Peruvians. An overwhelming percentage of victims were indigenous/Quechua-speaking. The cultural divides between the rural and developed parts of the country played a large part in this internal conflict. Yuyachkani responded to this period with a number of performances that captured various elements of this time and its devastating impact on Peruvians as well as a number of street actions/protests that criticized key players in this devastating historical period. One of these performances was an adaptation of Sophocles' *Antigone*. *Antígona* (2000) was created by Teresa Ralli combining the original Greek tragedy with her own experience witnessing the violence of the country as well as interviews she conducted with women who had been impacted by the conflict. Ralli performs the piece, playing all characters, with only a chair, one costume, a mask, and a box of sand. This minimalist aesthetic was often utilized by the group at this time not only reflecting the deep mourning taking place, but also for practical reasons, so that their plays could easily travel and be performed throughout the country. In 2001 the Truth and Reconciliation Commission (TRC) was established to investigate the human right abuses that had devastated the country. Yuyachkani was invited to participate in the TRC's Public Testimonies with the belief that their connection to the indigenous communities and their ability to reflect local customs and languages could help bridge the cultural and linguistic divide between the commissioners (all of whom were from Lima and did not speak Quechua) and the survivors of the conflict. The night before the testimonies were to take place, Augusto Casafranca and Ana Correa performed their respective plays *Adiós Ayacucho* (1992) and *Rosa Cuchillo* (2002). Both performances represented the victims of the internal conflict and centered on the search of the bodies of the disappeared, ultimately lending their artistic voices for peace and justice. This work with the TRC earned the group the Peruvian Human Rights Award (2000).

After their experiences working with the TRC, the group began to create a theatre that could address and hopefully heal some of the deep national wounds that existed long before the internal conflict took place. In 2004 they developed *Sin título, técnica mixta* [Untitled, Mixed Media], which explored centuries of violence and warfare within and across Peruvian borders. Significantly, the play also addressed issues that had been omitted by the TRC's Final Report, including the forced sterilizations of indigenous women—which nearly twenty years later has finally gained large-scale public recognition in Peru. For this play, the theatre space was set up like a museum and the audience never sat down, constantly being pushed around the space creating more an experience of being an active witness, rather than a passive audience member to the show. The staging became a metaphor for the willingness (or lack thereof) of Peruvians to witness what had occurred during the conflict. In later years, Yuyachkani's work has moved away from addressing the violence directly and has shifted to focus more on historical figures and national nostalgia. In *El último ensayo* [The Last Rehearsal] (2008), they explore the life of Yma Sumac, a Peruvian singer from the Andes who became an international star. Or as seen in *Cartas de Chimbote* [Letters of Chimbote] (2015), a close study of Jose Maria Arguedas, a famed Peruvian novelist and anthropologist.

In addition to their performances, the group has several projects that utilize theatre for social change and personal healing, including workshops with women traumatized during the conflict. Yuyachkani has continued to work closely with human rights groups and national efforts to further the work of the TRC including involvement in the design and creation of the El Lugar de la Memoria, la Tolerancia y la Inclusión Social (LUM) (a museum in Lima dedicated to commemorating the years of violence and repression) and the "El ojo que llora" [The Eye That Cries] (a memorial to the victims of the conflict also located in Lima). The members of Yuyachkani have dedicated their lives to creating a theatre that represents the people and cultures of Peru both through the stories they tell and the way they tell them. As they mark their fiftieth anniversary in 2021, the future of Grupo Cultural Yuyachkani is unclear but, like memory itself, the group persists.

Katherine Jean Nigh

Major works

Discurso de promoción [Speech of Promotion] (2017)
Cartas de Chimbote [Letters of Chimbote] (2015)
Concierto olvido [The Forgotten Concert] (2010)
El último ensayo [The Last Rehearsal] (2008)
Hecho en el Perú [Made in Peru] (2001)
Antígona (2000)
Hasta cuando corazón [Until When Love?] (1994)
No me toquen ese valse [Don't Play me that Waltz] (1990)
Allpa Rayku [For the Land] (1978)
Puño de cobre [Copper Fist] (1972)

Further reading

A'ness, Francine. "Resisting Amnesia: Yuyachkani, Performance, and the Postwar Reconstruction of Peru." *Theatre Journal* (2004): 395–414.
Garza, Cynthia. "Colliding With Memory: Grupo Cultural Yuyachkani's *Sin Título Técnica Mixta*." In *Art from a Fractured Past: Memory and Truth-Telling in Post-Shining Path Peru*. Edited by Cynthia Milton (Durham, NC: Duke University Press, 2013).
Lambright, Anne. "A Nation Embodied: Woman in the Work of Yuyachkani." *Letras Femeninas* 35, no. 2 (2009): 133–152.
Lerner Febres, Salomón. "Memory of Violence and Drama in Peru: The Experience of the Truth Commission and Grupo Cultural Yuyachkani– Violence and Dehumanization." *International Journal of Transitional Justice* 14, no. 1 (2020): 232–241.
Nigh, Katherine Jean. "Forgetting to Remember: Performance and Conflict in a Post TRC Peru." *Journal of Dramatic Theory and Criticism* 27, no. 2 (2013): 145–157.

Persino, María Silvina. "Cuerpo y memoria en el Teatro de los Andes y Yuyachkani." *Gestos* 22 (2007): 87–103.

Taylor, Diana. "Staging Social Memory: Yuyachkani." In *The Color of Theatre: Race, Culture, and Contemporary Performance.* Edited by Roberto Uno and Lucy Mae San Pablo Burns (London and New York: Continuum Press, 2005): 39–59.

For Product Safety Concerns and Information please contact our EU representative GPSR@taylorandfrancis.com
Taylor & Francis Verlag GmbH, Kaufingerstraße 24, 80331 München, Germany